Event of Signature

SUNY series in Contemporary French Thought
―――――――
David Pettigrew and François Raffoul, editors

Event of Signature

*Jacques Derrida and
Repeating the Unrepeatable*

Michaela Fišerová

Published by State University of New York Press, Albany

© 2022 State University of New York

All rights reserved

Printed in the United States of America

No part of this book may be used or reproduced in any manner whatsoever without written permission. No part of this book may be stored in a retrieval system or transmitted in any form or by any means including electronic, electrostatic, magnetic tape, mechanical, photocopying, recording, or otherwise without the prior permission in writing of the publisher.

For information, contact State University of New York Press, Albany, NY
www.sunypress.edu

Library of Congress Cataloging-in-Publication Data

Name: Fišerová, Michaela, author.
Title: Event of signature : Jacques Derrida and repeating the unrepeatable / Michaela Fišerová.
Description: Albany : State University of New York Press, [2022] | Series: SUNY series in contemporary French thought | Includes bibliographical references and indexes.
Identifiers: LCCN 2022005587 | ISBN 9781438489735 (hardcover : alk. paper) | ISBN 9781438489742 (ebook) | ISBN 9781438489728 (pbk. : alk. paper)
Subjects: LCSH: Signatures (Writing)—Philosophy. | Signature (Law)—Philosophy.
Classification: LCC Z41 .F57 2022 | DDC 652/.101—dc23/eng/20220505
LC record available at https://lccn.loc.gov/2022005587

10 9 8 7 6 5 4 3 2 1

Contents

Acknowledgments	vii
Preface	ix
Introduction	1
Chapter I. Handwritten Signature's Interval Between Life and Law	7
What Can Be Expected of Handwritten Signature?	17
What Are Metaphysical and Discursive Expectations?	27
Chapter II. The Discursive Expectations of Handwritten Signature	37
Discourse of Graphology: The Transparent Expression	54
Discourse of Forensic Analysis: The Original Style	59
Chapter III. The Metaphysical Expectations of Handwritten Signature	67
"Natural" Resemblance	81
"Authentic" Tracing	85
"Identical" Repetition	90
Chapter IV. Deconstructing Handwritten Signature I	97
Aporia of Natural Resemblance	100
Spectral Resemblance	105
Chapter V. Deconstructing Handwritten Signature II	113
Aporia of Authentic Tracing	117
Disseminated Tracing	122

Chapter VI. Deconstructing Handwritten Signature III 131
    Aporia of Identical Repetition 135
    Iterated Repetition 145

Chapter VII. Event of Manual Signing: On Repeating of the Unrepeatable 155
    Event Trapped in Interpretation 161
    Event Trapped in Representation 169
    The Event of Iteration 179

Postscript 191

Notes 203

Bibliography 221

Name Index 233

Subject Index 237

Acknowledgments

The book is a revised version of a Czech monograph titled *Deconstruction of Signature*, published by Togga in Prague in 2016, translated by the author, and copyedited by Kate Sotejeff-Wilson in 2020.

Some aspects of the problems addressed here were partially discussed in the chapter "Hopes of Derrida's Reading? On Emergence of Peirce's Texts in the Poststructuralist Context" published by Brill in the edited volume *How to Make Our Signs Clear: C. S. Peirce and Semiotics* in 2017, and in the paper "Pragmatical Paradox of Signature" published in the journal *Signata* in 2018.

This monograph is the result of Metropolitan University Prague research project no. 74–01 "Political Sciences, Culture, Language" (2020) based on a grant from the Institutional Fund for the Long-term Strategic Development of Research Organizations.

Preface

This monograph focuses on the precarious status of the handwritten signature as a sign of civic identity. On the one hand, a handwritten signature legally introduces the relationship of identity between the signer's civic name and the shape of it traced in her handwriting. On the other hand, it can never achieve identity: because the trace is different each time, a handwritten signature makes identification of the signer impossible. Following the double strategy of Derrida's deconstruction, I propose to understand this double bind of our expectation of legal handwritten signature as a complex metaphysical aporia.

Before moving on, I wish to clarify my intention, which is not to simply present Derrida's own philosophical work. As the title suggests, this book's goal is not to bring an exegetic reading dedicated to Derrida's treatment of the concept of signature. If I intentionally use *addition* ("and") in the title, it is to suggest a *relation* to Derrida's work. A relation that is both inspiring and problematic for the innovative purpose here.

Let me explain the unusual philosophical strategy I propose. To understand legal handwritten signature philosophically, as an event expected to produce a legally reliable civic sign, I formulate a new philosophical problem and propose a double-sided research strategy, both inspired by Derrida's deconstruction. The philosophical problem to solve is the unreducible *gap* between the reliable, repeatable civic *sign* (which legal handwritten signature is expected to be, in positivist scientific discourses) and a singular, unrepeatable *trace* occasionally written by hand (which the handwritten signature also can be, in the perspective of Derrida's deconstruction). To understand this gap philosophically, I decided to start by distinguishing two kinds of scientific expectations: *discursive expectations*, which differ in every scientific knowledge on handwritten signature, and *metaphysical expectations*, which are shared by all of these discourses and which I find deconstructable.

Because I need to start my work by understanding the knowledge of graphological and forensic discourses on handwritten signature, I have to begin my research into scientific positivity by turning to the scientifically positive method of discursive analysis. Although it is methodologically incompatible with Derrida's deconstruction, this primary strategical step is crucial for my understanding of the common scientific prejudices regarding handwritten signature.

Once defined, I propose to turn from discursive analysis to another scientific analysis incompatible with Derrida's work, which is Peirce's semiotics of ontological realism. If I operate this second strategical step, it is because I want to clarify the metaphysical conditions of possibility for scientific understanding of handwritten signature as a recognizable, authentic, and legally reliable civic sign. It is precisely these metaphysical expectations (conditioning the common scientific knowledge) that will be finally deconstructed.

My last—and crucial—strategic turn is therefore based on quitting scientific methodologies for the philosophical benefits of deconstruction. Because Derrida is neither a positivist historian of media and discourses, nor a scientifically oriented semiotician, I suppose that his aporetical understanding of handwritten signature—as both singular trace and legal sign—is able to shake the presuppositions of discursive and semiotic knowledges. However, because deconstruction is no positivist method of analysis, it cannot be simply applied. I therefore conceive this final part of my work as a deconstructive dialogue based on my reading of Derrida. If this reading is not exegetic, it is because I do not intend to explain Derrida's conception of signature in all of its senses, but rather to follow his working strategy in order to shake the metaphysical expectations of legal handwritten signature alone. To shake means not to simply criticize them. It means to grasp them as aporias.

For the reasons mentioned above, the proposed research is thematically unique: it concentrates the attention of philosophers on what media scholars, historians, graphologists, forensic experts, and semioticians have to say about the handwritten signature—a legal sign that is prevalent in everyday social communication and that every citizen is obliged to use. A legal handwritten signature substitutes for its signer—but in what respect? What do experts expect from this handwritten trace? How does it represent the signer? Why does it have such legal importance? To answer these questions, considering the problem in terms of Derrida's deconstruction, I claim that although these expectations determine the range of possible interpretations and give legitimacy to the signature as a sign of civic identification, they will never be fulfilled. The legal handwritten signature remains a problematic entity, both sign and trace, which is determined by the aporia of the unsatisfiable legal obligation to repeat the unrepeatable in the event of signing.

The research presented here primarily contributes to the following areas of contemporary philosophical inquiry: metaphysics, because it reveals new connections between juridical science, psychology, and aesthetics; deconstruction, because it concentrates attention on the pragmatic possibilities and limits of Derrida's conception of writing; discursive analysis, because it focuses on rarely analyzed discourses and shows the limits of discursive analysis as such; semiotics and theory of interpretation, because it shows the advantages and disadvantages of Eco's thinking in comparison with deconstruction; legal and political thought, because it reveals interpretative questions and gaps in legal formulations that have not previously been considered; aesthetics, because it proposes understanding the signature as a deconstructed stylized self-portrait, formally close to calligraphy and calligram; media studies, because it rethinks McLuhan's conception of media as message and compares it with Derrida's deconstruction. This complex philosophical discussion could lead to calls for media and forensic legislation to be amended to include an exact definition of handwritten signature, and to reflection on the three aporetic expectations linked to the current legal conception of the handwritten signature.

The book offers an innovative conception of the handwritten signature as a specific sign of civic identity legitimated by current *legal mediation politics*, or the politics determining the legal setting of discursive expectations. In Derrida's view, legal mediation politics can be deconstructed. Because the book critically revises not only the metaphysical dimension of this politics but also the possibilities and limits of its deconstruction, it serves a dual function. First, it can enrich academic research and teaching on contemporary continental philosophy, especially in the fields of poststructuralism and deconstruction. Second, its interdisciplinary scope makes it suitable for scholars and students of media studies, juridical sciences, comparative literature, aesthetics, rhetoric, and semiotics.

Introduction

A handwritten signature is a sign of civic identification that has important psychological and juridical functions: signers sign contracts, invoices, letters, demands, petitions, charts, and attendance sheets. To obtain their handwritten signatures, employees are asked to show up at a certain office at a certain time. To collect autographs, devoted fans queue up for hours to meet their stars.

But signing does not mean just writing one's own name in one's own hand. Rather, it means trying to cite the signer's unique style of handwriting, which is supposed to be recognizable by others. At banks, each client is asked to register the first signature she gives—the specimen signature—as a sample of her handwriting style. Later on, she will be asked every time to sign again in a way that is supposed to be graphically compatible with her registered specimen signature. To keep her manual expressions as similar as possible across all her attempts to sign, she will be obliged to observe the limit of their acceptable resemblance.

In other words, a handwritten signature is not only a civic sign, but also a personal one. If someone signed in a very different way each time or did not sign at all, she would not get money in her bank, her agreements would not be valid, she would not be believed about her presence at work meetings, her invoices would not be reimbursed, and so forth. Moreover, without having the power of attorney signed by another person's own hand, she cannot sign on behalf of that other person. A handwritten signature is a strictly personal sign.

These reflections are prompted by something that happened to me during my doctoral studies in Paris several years ago. I was living on the Cité Internationale Universitaire de Paris campus, where I had rented a room. One time I wanted to pay my rent, which had to be done in cash.

Unfortunately, local cash dispensers refused to give me money because I had reached my daily limit. This was a new situation for me because I was used to withdrawing my money from cash dispensers. So I went to the bank to withdraw money at the counter. The bank officer asked me for my ID and checked whether there was enough money in my account. Then she asked me to manually sign the document certifying the withdrawal of money from my account. Immediately, a problem occurred. The clerk started to analyze my signature, and clearly did not find it satisfactory. She told me that it was not my signature and she could not give me any money. I asked her what she meant when she said that it was not my signature. After all, she had just seen me signing. She told me that I had signed, "but not with my own signature." Surprised, I asked for an explanation. From a brief exchange, it transpired that five years ago I had registered a specimen signature that did not sufficiently resemble the signature I had written that day. As a result, she was not allowed to give me money from my account. After I protested, the clerk gave me one more chance. She asked me to sign again one more time, emphasizing that my new attempt must "more exactly resemble" my specimen signature, a scanned copy of which she could see on the computer screen, but which was not visible to me. She wanted to test me. If I passed the test of exact resemblance, I would get money from my account. If not, I would not. Unfortunately, she was visibly even less satisfied with my second signature. This precarious situation made me unhappy because I needed the money so I could pay my rent on time. I asked her to call the branch manager. When he arrived, he came up with a solution to the problem: if I could not sign in a way that sufficiently resembled my registered specimen signature, I would have to register a new official specimen signature instead. But the branch manager warned me strictly that, in the future, I would have to reproduce my signature in a manner sufficiently similar to my newly registered specimen signature. Otherwise, the same situation would occur again. I quickly agreed to this proposed solution, because I realized that it would be useless to discuss with bank employees the fact that I did not know where exactly the limit of sufficient resemblance lies, or the fact that the newly registered specimen signature did not guarantee that the next time I would sign in a way that sufficiently resembles it. Finally, I left the bank with the money for my rent. One could say that it was a satisfactory outcome for both sides. But at the same time, I realized I had just agreed to a solution that did not solve the problem at all. Later on, I could not stop thinking about this incident.

Six years later, I decided to address the philosophical problem that it had been impossible to solve in the bank by investigating the handwritten signature as a medium that represents the civic identity of its signer in contemporary legal mediation politics.

To determine the prevailing scholarly conception of handwritten signature, I concentrate on shared discursive and metaphysical expectations of signature, which I understand as double a priori conditions of possibility for interpreting a handwritten signature. Mapping the discursive limits of scholarly interpretation of signature helps to explain why, in recent decades, graphology has been relegated to the status of esoteric quasi-science and replaced by more "scientific" forensic analysis. The analysis of these two discursive expectations of signature should reveal the reasons for the hierarchy between them. Inspired by Derrida's deconstruction, I propose to show that the limits of discursive and metaphysical expectations differ, because all discourses are metaphysically conditioned.

While my attempt to understand the metaphysical expectations of handwritten signatures is inspired by deconstruction, unlike Derrida, I emphasize how metaphysical expectations are determined by specific media. I regard the handwritten signature as a specific medium, which is determined by three unsatisfiable metaphysical obligations: the aporia of the naturalness of metaphorical identity; the aporia of the authenticity of the writing act; and the aporia of the identity of the composed style. By means of deconstruction, I seek to show that these complex aporias of handwritten signature are linked to the metaphysical dimension of current legal mediation politics. Despite the differences between investigations in graphology and forensic analysis, both disciplines deal with characteristics of the signer's psyche: both discourses expect the handwritten signature to be an authentic medium that naturally represents the signer's unique *soul*. If I systematically prefer the concept of soul to the concept of consciousness, it is because the concept of *soul* concerns both the conscious and the unconscious aspects of the mind. Here I follow Derrida's books *Psyché* and *On Touching*, but also my own work on graphology as *psych*ology and on *psycho*analysis as hauntology.

I start by outlining the philosophical strategy I use in my work. For this purpose, I examine the possibilities and limits of Derrida's deconstruction, primarily in relation to his understanding of meta-representation, or representation of representation, deferred meaning, unlimited text, writing that overlaps voice, and disseminated *supplementarity*. I initially attempted to understand deconstruction as a kind of critique or interpretation, but soon realized that it is neither of these things.

From the outset, I seek to give theoretical formulation to the problems that shape my philosophical approach to deconstruction. I note that Derrida's deconstruction does not allow for solving three methodological problems that affect every empirical analysis, including discursive analysis. First, it does not allow any historical, epistemological, or discursive analysis—all of which involve the metaphysically positive historicism that Derrida aims to deconstruct. Second, Derrida's deconstruction admits no positive definition, analysis, or method, so it cannot be used to achieve a positive semiotics. Derrida does not admit any limits of interpretation or context. He admits only a negative ontology of infinite spectrality, tracing, and grafting, which has no unique beginning or end. Derrida's deconstruction of logos produces his version of the ethical problem of the sublime (understood here as writing, *grammé*, which precedes and overlaps logos). In this respect, it is close to Lyotard's postmodern ethics of the sublime as the unrepresentable, the alterity.[1] Third, as everything is text in deconstruction, Derrida's thinking does not allow for particular media or technology, such as the written word and drawn image, to be characterized or analyzed. In these three ways, deconstruction is incompatible with discursive, semiotic, and media analysis. I suggest overcoming these incompatibilities by comparing Derrida's conception of representation with other philosophical approaches, primarily with the work of Foucault, Benjamin, Benveniste, Deleuze, Austin, Searle, Peirce, Eco, and Rousseau.

I also focus on how Derrida's deconstruction could be used to understand the results of discursive analysis of legal texts on signature and handwriting, especially textbooks from the legal field of forensic analysis and from the psychological domain of graphology. As I consider this application methodologically problematic, I supplement Derrida's own work with other philosophical conceptions of representation. Nevertheless, I realize that to make possible the impossible task of deconstruction, I need to deconstruct Derrida's deconstruction. Positive methods such as media, semiotic, or discursive analysis operate outside the marginal philosophical domain where deconstruction operates. I bring them in, using a positive discursive media semiotics to analyze contemporary mediation politics based on a reading of legal texts on handwriting and handwritten signature. This supplementation is necessary to show that discursive semiotics is not aware of its own totalitarian violence: it is not haunted by Derrida's ethical "ghost," a memento of the method as such.

Finally, I formulate a deconstructed media semiotics, inspired both by Derrida's deconstruction and Eco's semiotics of conventional realism. I understand the handwritten signature as a specific medium that produces aporetic signs. This allows me to shift from the ethically conscious melancholy of deconstruction toward a politically effective positivity of the signature sign.

Chapter I

Handwritten Signature's Interval Between Life and Law

What does it mean that a handwritten signature is supposed to be a civic and a personal sign at the same time? While this sign always refers to the same obvious thing—the signer's own civic name—the way it does so is not obvious. The civic name must be written not only by the signer's own hand but also in a way that is recognizable as the signer's nominal picture. In other words, handwriting generates not only words of names, but also pictures of names, which are not necessarily legible. By trying to read someone's handwriting, I face the unpredictable materiality of signs: through the (not always easily legible) visual aspect of the words, I access their (in principle easily legible) linguistic aspect. Illegible pictures of words here represent the legible words. It is therefore difficult to say who the audience of a handwritten text is. A spectator? A reader?

I find this philosophical problem especially interesting in relation to the practice of handwritten signing. I have observed that it is legitimate to believe that the graphic appearance of a handwritten signature is replaceable by the signer's civic name, which is replaceable by the signer herself. While the act of producing a handwritten signature converts a word into a picture of that word, an expert's interpretation of a signature performs the opposite translation: it changes the picture of a word into a word. Through their observation of a picture of a name, handwriting experts can discern the signer's psychological qualities and authenticity.

To elaborate on this problem, I suggest deconstructing the legal expectation that one can identify the signer by a handwritten signature. More precisely, I propose to question the belief that one can reach identity by means of translation. I claim no identity can be attaint by translation, not in the least this double translation between the civic name of the signer and the picture of the signer's civic name; between an officially registered, conventionally fixed legal attribute and a manually produced, constantly varying existential trace.

I claim it is only possible to identify the signer by a handwritten signature because of this legal expectation, which considers the processes of translation and identification as equal. This expectation sanctifies the metaphysical belief that there is a naturally produced identity between the convention of legal procedure and the event of manual signing.

To better understand this precarious belief, I suggest situating it in an aporetic interval between the expectable demands of law and the unexpectable events of life. On the one hand, a handwritten signature is an existential trace, which is supposed to have a particular personal shape. On the other hand, to be recognized by it, the signer is supposed to identically repeat her signature's shape using her own hand. But when the signer tries to repeat it by hand, the shape of the signature varies from case to case. This aporia renders identification of the signer precarious. While the law strives to achieve identity *by repetition of traces, life turns repetition into an iteration.*

Despite this aporia, handwritten signature is commonly believed to be both a true mirror of the signer's essential qualities and legal proof of the signer's authentic presence. We even expect the handwritten signature can confirm the signer's civic identity. Why? What does the law "force" us to believe in? Under what conditions are such expectations possible? What kind of knowledge do they found?

To answer these questions, I propose to show how legal practices of manual signing were implemented and how legitimate uses of the medium of handwritten signature changed as civic societies developed between the nineteenth and twenty-first centuries. As Dekeyser puts in "Authenticity in Bites and Bytes," the habit of using handwritten signature to identify the signer is relatively recent. In Ancient Rome and the Middle Ages, handwritten documentary evidence worked as a reference to the person linked with a given document. Nevertheless, signets and seals that usually accompanied handwritten inscriptions were considered to be more important and more reliable than handwritten inscriptions. As literacy grew in the late Middle Ages, documentary evidence was more frequently produced by the contracting parties themselves and not dictated to a scribe. As Dekeyser shows, as printing technology was implemented, handwritten documentary evidence gradually gained legal value. Contrary to the mechanical aspect of seals or stamps that can be used identically by many individuals representing the same institution, a handwritten signature is strictly personal: it can be done only by the person who signs by her own hand. In Western Europe, another discursive change occurred with new rules of legal argumentation formulated by the Napoleonic codes, which established the legal prevalence of written documents over scientific statements. According to Dekeyser, "Documentary evidence became mandatory for certain transactions and was the only form of evidence admissible in court" (Dekeyser 2006, 77). In the nineteenth and twentieth centuries, modern criminalists and historians started to take personal traces—such as fingerprints, photographs, and handwritten signatures—for the most reliable signs of civic identification. This "modern" approach to signatures can be understood as a legitimate belief that all kinds of imprints are ultimate proofs of a citizen's identity, because they are physical remains of the unique individual and her unique past presence and actions.

The goal of the two scientific disciplines of handwritten signature established in the nineteenth and twentieth centuries—graphology and forensic analysis—was to examine the signature as a psychologically interesting personal sign and a legally reliable civic sign. Being a personal trace, the signature was expected to certify both the nature of its signer's mind and the authenticity of her past presence. Moreover, the signature was supposed to be not only a result of both natural expression of the signer's soul and authentic trace of her physical presence, but also manually—not mechanically—repeatable. The degree of similarity was supposed to be sufficient to be recognized as identical. Put otherwise, graphological and forensic examination of a handwritten signature is fixed on the signer's unique soul and remaining material trace. Verification of a handwritten signature is a result of comparison of shapes of several handwritten signatures, where the supposed graphic qualities of the specimen signature should be recognized. A handwritten signature is analyzed as a picture made of handwriting, which is expected to naturally express the essential psychological qualities of its signer.

To better understand this reasoning in its complexity, I propose to examine the difference in expertise between the psychological graphology of the nineteenth century and the forensic analysis of handwriting of the twentieth century. As Beatrice Fraenkel indicates in *La signature. Genèse d'un signe*, toward the end of the eighteenth century, "Grohmann claimed that it is possible to determine physical appearance of the signer according to her handwriting; he even distinguished which ones of his correspondents had blue eyes!" (Fraenkel 1992, 211). Later in the nineteenth century, this ambition was accomplished by police officer Alphonse Berthillon, father of criminalistic dactyloscopy and inventor of the set of mugshots called *bertillonage*[1] that were celebrated as the most objective referential photographic portraits of citizens, whose physical appearance could be analyzed to reveal their psychological qualities. In his *Système de graphologie*, Jean-Hyppolite Michon established graphology as a new psychological discipline dealing with manual writing. According to Fraenkel, Michon was the first to describe an analogy between the characteristics of the signer and the characteristics of handwriting (Fraenkel 1992, 211).

Nevertheless, in the twentieth century, both anthropometry and graphology became pseudo-sciences, perceived as outdated remains of nineteenth-century positivism. Nowadays, the positivism that appeared as social Darwinism is considered to be ethically dangerous, as it led directly from anthropometry to discriminatory biopolitics and eugenics.

This interconnection of disciplinary insights is not random. Graphology and anthropometry share the discursive presupposition that every person's physical appearance expresses her psychological qualities: the physical shapes of an individual are supposed to refer naturally to her soul. Based on measurements and typologies of head, eyes, nose, mouth shapes, and so forth, it was supposed to be possible to determine the natural psychological disposition of measured individuals. The results of examination were used to prove the supposed criminal disposition of suspects.

Medical inventor Cesare Lombroso, founder of a positivist scientific school of penal law and forensic psychiatry, was influenced by social Darwinism, anthropometry, and eugenics. Lombroso based his research on observation, cataloging, and statistical comparison of physical differences, from which he produced race and gender typologies. He understood his own research into human physiognomy as an introduction to a new science, criminalist anthropology, which was supposed to be able to determine a patient's natural psychological predisposition just by interpreting the shapes of his or her head and face. Because he considered the physical traits of his patients to be expressions of their psychological qualities, he supposed that by analyzing these traits one could determine the so-called criminal type, characterized by citizens' inherited physiognomic predisposition to murder, alcoholism, or prostitution. Lombroso also noticed these physical symptoms in the shapes of the patients' handwriting. In *Criminal Man*, Lombroso draws on graphology to describe the handwriting of criminals by means of his diagnostic typology of human abnormalities. Lombroso attempted to distinguish various symptomatic signs of handwriting, which could indicate the signer's hidden tendencies. To recognize and predict signers' predisposition to various criminal activities, Lombroso observes criminals' handwriting styles and classifies them according to their criminal "specialization." He even recognizes two main styles[2] of criminal handwriting used by murderers[3] and thieves.[4]

To translate Darwin's idea into effective means for managing human inheritance, late nineteenth-century science needed to find a mechanism "according to which inheritance works: the key to, the truth of, life itself" (McCance 2019, 89). For this reason, the anthropometrical practice of correlating people's souls with their physical appearance quickly turned to eugenics, a "science which deals with all influences that improve the inborn qualities of a race; also with those that develop them to the utmost advantage" (Galton 1909, 35). The ethical threat of eugenics, consisting of racist shaping of people's "breeding"[5] confirmed by Nazism, uncovered the scientific failures of criminal anthropology and led to its categorization among totalitarian pseudo-sciences.[6]

Besides its kinship with anthropometry, graphology shares its basic ambition with psychology: it supposes that it is possible to uncover the psychological qualities of an individual by observing her ways of acting. This ambition leads to the presupposition that each action of an individual is an expression of her qualities, which form together her nature, soul, mind, and psyche. All actions of the given individual are expressions of her soul, which inevitably and repeatedly appear in her handwriting. If we projected this psychological ambition onto the area of handwriting analysis, we would get the ambition of graphology, which appropriated the psychological presupposition that manual writing expresses the signer's mind. Just like psychology, graphology supposes that individual human qualities can be recognized, sorted, listed, and cataloged. Particular shapes of manually written letters correspond to particular qualities of the signer: they refer to their origin, the unique soul of the given individual. In graphology, the collection of the signer's particularly shaped handwritten letters means the collection of her psychological qualities. The signer's style naturally expresses the signer's soul and leaves its authentic imprint on the legal document.

Up to this point, I have focused on discursive criteria for authentication, which were different in the nineteenth and twentieth centuries. They differ even more in the twenty-first century. With digitization, handwritten signatures are changing into electronic signatures, and this new regime of signing is initiating a complex transformation of the metaphysical expectation of mediation. In the twenty-first century, paper is no longer the medium of choice for recording and sharing legally important information. Dekeyser notes that its place has been taken by digital technology offering new possibilities of *tele-presence* and *tele-authenticity*: "As this technology is based on electronic pulses represented by zeros and ones, it does not accommodate handwriting very well. For legal systems that only recognize manual signatures, the writing was on the wall—an alternative had to be found to fulfil the functions of the signature, and, by extension, of handwriting" (Dekeyser 2006, 80).

Next, I try to demonstrate that this technological change initiates a complex semantic transformation. New politico-philosophical and legal-semiotic perspectives could be opened up by comparing media expectations of handwritten and electronic signatures, mostly in terms of risks to their authenticity and legal reliability. The main result of the transition from handwritten to electronic media is the disappearance of the manual or craft component of signing. To quote Dekeyser: "Digital signatures do not resemble handwritten signatures in any way. Where the handwritten signature is a graphic mark with a more or less stable form, the digital signature is unique for each file to which it is appended. The reason for this is that the digital signature is derived from the file to which it belongs by means of a series of complicated mathematical computations" (Dekeyser 2006, 80–81).

A computer cannot be programmed to deal with the founding metaphysical aporia of handwritten signature as an unrepeatable occasional trace of a unique personal style, because no aporia has a logical solution and one can never be certain what should and what should not be part of a signer's personal style. Inventors of the electronic signature carefully avoided this aporia. The new kind of signature they invented was no longer merely similar to the specimen signature but matched it exactly (in the language of computers, it was 1 or 0, original and unoriginal, true or false). It was not possible to give a logical answer to the basic question of when a handwritten signature was not similar enough or too similar to be handmade and might be suspected of being forged. As the whole similarity is not logically exact, no computer is able to decide which signature is authentic and which one is forged. Graphological and forensic analysis of handwriting is based on evaluation of resemblance. A machine cannot do this because there can be no logical answer to the basic question of when a handwritten signature is similar enough to correspond to the author's style of handwriting, or indeed is too similar. A specimen signature is not a representative logo or stamp of the signer's soul that could be mechanically copied and identically reproduced each time. Every signer's manual expression, which is to confirm the signer's identity, is unique, each time slightly different, never the same.

All of these difficulties of interpretation, inevitably associated with the translation of meaning between picture and text, are excluded from the electronic signature. To verify the electronic signature, one needs to reach the identity of the code—neither similarity of picture nor authenticity of traces can be sufficiently reliable in digital communication. Mathematics are not as precarious as the psychological examination searching for natural expression of the signer's soul in the picture of handwritten signature. Moreover, the digital medium overcomes the biometric expectation of authenticity of handwritten traces, which was characteristic for manual writing. In "Authenticity and Objectivity in Scientific Communication," Owen pointed out that "with regard to authenticity, it could be argued that where there is no common ground, every utterance and every experience is 'authentic.' But when everything is authentic, the whole concept loses its meaning" (Owen 2006, 68). Correlatively, in "Signature à l'âge de l'électronique," Fraenkel and Pontille claim that electronic signature is a medium of identification and authorization of the signer. It is neither a way to discover psychological qualities, nor a way to verify physical presence of the signer, as the handwritten signature was. Both of the previously important presuppositions no longer matter here. Verification is not done "from the viewpoint of the person who signs, it is not her writing act. It becomes mostly a tool of identification of a person, even if her own name is not cited. Signature became a true actant, charged by the primary task: to identify someone. From the signer's viewpoint this means that we have resigned to the situation where I act by signing. We moved to the situation where my signature acts instead of me" (Fraenkel and Pontille 2006, 106–7). New identification procedures produce significant mutual effects in the legal and scientific worlds, which understand the individual "as an element which is strange to their own system. Authenticated electronic signature absolutely escapes the competences of previous professionals, it becomes a matter of experts in cryptography" (Fraenkel and Pontille 2006, 106). The current hesitation about the handwritten signature's status as an authentic proof of the signer's civic identity may be explained by two different, but synergic, theoretical shifts in the second half of the twentieth century: one caused by changes in discursive settings, the other by digitization.

Let us start with the discursive change. Both graphological and forensic discourses of handwritten signatures focused on the signer and her handwritten trace. Notarial approval of a signature was, thus, the result of comparing signatures and recognizing the supposed graphic qualities in the specimen signature. By contrast, an electronic signature is based on the value of an arbitrary code, which is assigned by computer. As Mason claims in *Electronic Signatures in Law*, "the process of authentication is between software protocols, not between human beings, and it is not clear whether the authentication relates to the origin of the data or acts to verify the identity of a person or entity" (Mason 2012, 115). Thus, the discursive conditions of possibility under which new media authenticity can be constructed are quite clear. The new media semantics cannot be based on the double bind of traces because a computer cannot understand human aporias or magical thinking: it operates solely on mathematical logic. Therefore, there is a shift from the trace to the code when it comes to the legal effectiveness of signatures. According to Mason, "an electronic signature cannot be denied legal effectiveness or be held inadmissible because it is in electronic form" (Mason 2012, 112).

To understand this discursive turn to cryptography, I propose to examine the way that digital signing works as a medium. What are our metaphysical expectations of the medium of digital signature? By definition, writes Mason, an " 'electronic signature' means data in electronic form, which are attached to or logically associated with other electronic data and which serve as a method of authentication" (Mason 2012, 115). In other words, the code replaces the trace in the role of the supreme authority for authentication. Before a sender can use digital signing, she must obtain a code named a key pair, which is produced for this purpose. The key pair, consisting of a public key and a private key, can be created by the sender's employer or obtained from the certification authority. After the sender is issued a key pair, a process is followed to complete signing and ensure the integrity of messages. The message to be signed is processed by a hash algorithm. A hash value, or digital fingerprint, is calculated for the file to be signed. Hashing is a technique by which electronic information can be reduced to a unique fixed-length code; if even a single character in the file is modified in transmission or storage, the resulting hash value will change.

Dekeyser mentions that "the original digital fingerprint must be safeguarded against manipulation if it is to be compared later on with a newly calculated hash value. This is where encryption comes in. Encryption entails that a plain text message is transformed into a cipher text that seems meaningless" (Dekeyser 2006, 81). The resulting hash value is used to check whether the content of the message changes after the message is sent. By comparing the original hash value with the current one, one can determine whether a document has been altered or not. There is one caveat to this story of a new kind of mediation: a digital seal replaces the handwritten signature. Neither the hash value nor the private or public key refers to the sender's identity in any way, as they are just numerical values. In this sense, the term "digital seal" is more accurate for this technology. The receiver must use other means to identify the rightful owner of the public key. This is why, according to Dekeyser, "in open network environments, like the Internet, a public key infrastructure must be in place in order to tie public keys to the identity of their rightful owners" (Dekeyser 2006, 81). This technological change initiates a complex semantic transformation. It is no longer a physical trace, but an arbitrary code that is supposed to guarantee the authenticity of electronic signatures, because the metaphysical concept of similarity (and the aporia that it produces) cannot be defined in a logical way and understood by a computer.

However, even this logic can be abused: there is nothing authentic beyond metaphysics. In my view, the reliability of signatures is even more doubtful today because new digital media are variable in principle and open to further modifications. According to Neef and Van Dijck's "Sign here! Handwriting in the Age of Technical Reproduction," contemporary electronic culture operates based on constant remediation: "Our current media culture is full of 'ReMediated' handwriting. We find it etched, photographed, Xeroxed, and digitally scanned. Intelligent Fond Analysis allows us to write our own handwriting via a keyboard, to perform handwritten e-mail correspondence, indeed, even to write someone else's 'hand' " (Neef and Van Dijck 2006, 13). In this situation, new media can be used and abused to achieve various transformations of original traces including breaching copyright and forging signatures. How authentic and reliable is a digital signature as a new medium capable of constant remediation?

To answer this question, we need to specify that there are two kinds of digital signature technology based on encryption that is either symmetrical or asymmetrical. In the symmetrical version, the encryption key is only shared between the sender and receiver of the message. This protects against manipulation by third parties, but both the sender and receiver can impersonate one another by using the common key. Asymmetrical encryption avoids this problem by giving each party their own pair of keys, one of which must remain secret while the other may be made public. A text encrypted with one of the keys can only be decrypted with the corresponding key from the pair. Particularly in legal contexts, asymmetrical encryption technology has been declared the ideal electronic substitute for the handwritten signature and the best digital signature technology. Nevertheless, the reliability of this method is never totally guaranteed. As Dekeyser points out:

> Asymmetrical encryption works on the assumption that it is practically infeasible to crack the code by trying all the possible key combinations because the necessary computer power is not available. As time goes by, however, ever more powerful computers are developed, and eventually trying all the key combinations becomes a distinct possibility. Alternatively, flaws may be found in the encryption or hash algorithm, opening up new avenues of attack. . . . To alleviate these problems, the length of the encryption keys is increased to match the pace of computer development and new encryption algorithms are introduced. Of course, this does not offer a solution for the legacy of digital signatures. Once the key or the algorithm is broken, fake digital signatures, indistinguishable from genuine ones, can be created. (Dekeyser 2006, 85)

Put otherwise, in the case of electronic signature, the interpretation of arbitrarily attributed code is rid of the metaphysical belief in authentic physical presence of the signer: there is no authenticity guaranteed anymore by manual work. Handwritten and electronic signatures thus differ in terms of the types of authenticity they represent. The difference in discursive expectations reveals two different types of mediation, legitimizing two different conceptions of authenticity.

This section showed that there is a hierarchy of discourses on signature: digital cryptography is seen to be more reliable than forensic analysis of handwritten signature, which is more reliable than graphology of handwritten signature. In contemporary digital cryptography, the arbitrary code of electronic signature is considered more reliable than the personal trace of the handwritten signature. Contrary to the discourses of graphology and forensic analysis, the discourse of digital cryptography no longer deals with the precarious concept of style: it expects the electronic signature to be identical to the arbitrarily attributed digital code, which no longer relies on the physical trace of the signer's handwriting. This difference in our expectations of manual and electronic mediations can be better understood if we focus on our legal uses and expectations of handwritten signature. What is this medium like?

What Can Be Expected of Handwritten Signature?

The handwritten signature as a conventionally determined medium is used in legal interpretation of various criminal acts and definitions in different ways. First, the handwritten signature can be understood as a sign of natural expression of the signer's essential psychological qualities. Second, the handwritten signature can be taken for conventional, but strictly personal, visual trace certifying the signer's authentic presence in a given time and place. Finally, a combination of these two expectations with the belief in recognizable personal style, which allows—natural and authentic—repetition of the manual expression in time, enables us to use handwritten signatures as our legitimate delegates. This way, handwritten signatures stand for our personal confirmation, agreement, or engagement with the text written in contracts, invoices, testaments, or other legally important documents. Why do so many different uses and expectations coexist? Are they compatible? Are they incompatible? Are they deconstructable?

In the philosophy of both language and picture, the handwritten signature is an ambivalent sign: it is both a word and a picture. Handwritten signature is a contradictory writing/drawing of the signer/drawer's own civic name, of necessity done by her own hand. As the signature's content is usually fixed, it is the form of the signature that varies and matters. The form of this drawing must be simultaneously *constant* (permanently repeatable by the same signer) and unique (authentic, unrepeatable by no one else). On various occasions, representatives of banks and other institutions invite us to write and register the officially first or exemplary specimen signature, which will have the form of a referential sign, easily recognizable by others. Once we choose the written form of the signature, which is institutionally registered, we are obliged to keep it formally constant, unchanged in every further act of signing. In legally important documents, we must repeatedly manually draw the exemplary picture of the name, imitating our previously registered trace. That is the legal politics of handwritten signing: every time we are asked to sign, we have to draw the conventionally prescribed written form of our civic name and confirm our physical presence at the particular place where we performed the act of signing.

However, as Sherwin says in *Visualizing Law in the Age of Digital Baroque*, "Images do not speak for themselves, what we bring to them help give them voice" (Sherwin 2011, 41). Handwritten signature—the picture of its signer's name—does not speak, it just displays particular shapes and lines of handwriting. Experts from the disciplines of graphology and forensic analysis of handwriting speak instead of both the signature and the signer. In their interpretations, forensic experts turn the picture of signature into the word of signer's name. By means of this translation of the picture into word, they also approve or disapprove the supposed authorship of the signature, they pronounce a verdict.

These contradictory expectations of handwritten signature as a manually produced medium are partly explained by technologically oriented theoreticians of media studies. In this field, McLuhan and Flusser try to legitimate their conceptions of handwriting by their understanding of the historical evolution of mediation. Vilém Flusser, who calls himself a communicologist,[7] conceives a periodization of Western culture according to the communication medium that dominated in each period. Contrary to Derrida, Flusser states that writing is just one of the media that appears and disappears in Western history. In his book *Gestures*, he claims that writing does not mean bringing material to a surface but scratching at a surface, "writing still means making an in-scription. We are concerned not with a constructive but with a penetrating, pressing gesture" (Flusser 2014, 19). In his media conception, the characteristic Western gesture of linear writing introduced a new kind of communication, which determined "a whole dimension of our existence in the world" (Flusser 2014, 20). According to Flusser, "We enter into it as a form that is historical, logical, scientific, and progressive and also as a form whose specific linear character has made our gesture of writing irreversible" (Flusser 2014, 20). Although he claims that the invention of writing made possible the invention of history and science, he also claims that the writing technology itself is motivated by a universal human need for expression. In Flusser, the gesture of writing is naturally expressive, not constructive. This conception of writing is very different from Derrida's. Ahistorical deconstruction and historicizing media theory cannot differ more, not only methodologically, but also terminologically. Each of them speaks about another writing: while Derrida comments on *arche-writing*, Flusser comments on *phonological writing* he finds historically revolutionary. While Derrida puts the writing in opposition to the voice (for him, picture and writing pervade), Flusser puts writing in opposition to the picture (for him, voice and writing pervade).

Another example is the Toronto School's technological determinism. If we accept McLuhan's claim that cultural differences are more importantly determined by the dominating technology of communication than by the communicated content, we should also admit that each medium produces a particular kind of message, which requires its own kind of understanding and interpretation. The more the legitimate medium is instituted and spread in society, the more it becomes natural for people to use it and to think through or with it. Although the medium can be so familiar for their everyday communication that it becomes unreflected, unseen, and transparent, it remains present in their practices and continues to shape their perception, cognition, and communication. As McLuhan said in one of his interviews,

> most people, from truck drivers to the literary Brahmins, are still blissfully ignorant of what the media do to them; unaware that because of their pervasive effects on man, it is the medium itself that is the message, not the content, and unaware that the medium is also the message—that, all puns aside, it literally works over and saturates and molds and transforms every sense ratio. The content or message of any particular medium has about as much importance as the stenciling on the casing of an atomic bomb. (McLuhan 1997, 227)

According to McLuhan, every specific kind of interpretation is conditioned and determined by specific expectations. Each legitimate technology produces its own medium of communication, effective only if people believe in its persuasiveness, if they share the same kind of expectations. This belief in new semantic and persuasive disposition of a new medium must be pushed and procured politically: as a socio-technological revolution. From this historicizing theoretical viewpoint, handwriting is a specific medium of communication, which persuades because of the discursively determined expectation of mediation based on the specificity of manual work.

McLuhan's revolutionary characteristic of the technology of *alphabetic writing* differs from Derrida's conception of *generalized writing*, which could as well be a photograph, a tattoo, a drawing, or a sentence typed on a computer as a handwritten signature. Derrida's concept of *writing* is semantically larger than the specific way of writing based on alphabet; as he puts it: "By means of this double, and precisely stratified, dislodged and dislodging, writing, we must also mark the interval between inversion, which brings low what was high, and the irruptive emergence of a new 'concept,' a concept that can no longer be, and never could be, included in the previous régime" (Derrida 1981d, 42). Moreover, Derrida does not operate with the same definition of the concept of *medium*; he does not share McLuhan's strictly epistemological and technological determination. Derrida's understanding of this concept is motivated by his double interest in rhetorical dispositions of the medium as representation and as technology. Contrary to McLuhan, Derrida focuses not only on the chosen technology, but also on the content of exchanged messages. From a deconstructive point of view, technology is not the only determinant of representation; not only "the medium is the message" (McLuhan 1994, 7). In "Signature Event Context," Derrida explicitly disagrees with McLuhan's claim that the technology dominating in a certain historical period totally determines the way of perceiving and reasoning characteristic for that period. He goes even as far as considering to argue that McLuhan's periodization of media "galaxies" is ideological:

> We are not witnessing an end of writing which, to follow McLuhan's ideological representation, would restore a transparency or immediacy of social relations; but indeed a more and more powerful historical unfolding of a general writing of which the system of speech, consciousness, meaning, presence, truth, etc., would only be an effect to be analyzed as such. It is this questioned effect that I have elsewhere called logocentrism. (Derrida 1977b, 20)

From Derrida's point of view, there is no immediacy of media. It would be an oxymoron. Media are mediators, which are always and necessarily in the middle, in the medium zone, between what they connect. "Immediate" means without media, without mediation, without representation, without signs. In this respect, no culture has ever known immediate communication. There is no communication without mediation. McLuhan's "tribal," orally oriented culture did not know it either. As Derrida does not believe in the essential difference between media, the history, or the epistemology, his deconstruction may not seem useful for media semiotics inspired by Flusser's communicology or by McLuhan's technological conception of the medium.

In contrast, the generality of Derrida's concept of *archē-writing* makes all types of mediation—of which handwriting in the strict sense would be one example—both possible and necessary. Yet, by reducing all phenomena to archē-writing, Derrida homogenizes technologies of mediation. This homogenization is a double bind: on the one hand, it is crucial for his deconstructive conception of *generalized writing*; on the other hand, it does not mean that Derrida is not aware of the specificity of various media. Concerning Derrida's interest in the specificity of different technologies, one could point to *Of Grammatology* (Derrida 1997, 57–60) where Derrida praises Hjelmslev's glossematics for taking a substantial step toward grasping the specificity of phonetic writing in a way inaccessible to the Saussurean linguistics that inspires it. The same goes for Derrida's work on delayed time and metonymic substitution in relation to photographic technology, as he describes it in *Athens Still Remains* (Derrida 2010a, 3), and also the story of telecommunications in *The Postcard* (Derrida 1987b, 3)—both cases indicate his interest in rhetorical determination of different technologies. This problematic was also commented on by Derrida himself in his interview with Bernard Stiegler (Derrida and Stiegler 2002b, 113–17).

And yet, although Derrida does not deny the specificity of handwriting (or any other media), he also does not help to understand its specificity. Derrida's viewpoint of deconstructable meta-mediality considerably differs from the *media analysis* I need to do. Therefore, at some point in my research, I have to combine it with a scientifically positivist approach.

Following Derrida's thoughts on faith and knowledge, Michael Naas claims that every religion uses its privileged technology to spread among believers. As he puts it in *Miracle and Machine*,

> Because there is—as I believe—no proper place to begin reading Derrida on religion or anything else, because all one can do is prepare, calculate, strategize, and then give it a shot, I would like to begin with a religious tale that is rather far away from Derrida's interests, idiom, and culture, an American prophesy followed up by an American tale of faith and knowledge, testimony and technology, the miracle and the machine. (Naas 2012, 13)

The same goes for handwritten signature, which is a physical trace of the presence of signer's soul. In this respect, I do share Naas's claim, but I propose to prolong it to the legal sphere by saying that every legal belief needs its legally reliable medium. To define such a medium on the example of handwritten signature, I propose to grasp two kinds of prejudices linked to this belief—the discursive expectations (here I reveal the differences between graphological and forensic knowledges) and the metaphysical expectations (here I distinguish the presuppositions the two discursive knowledges have in common). This combination of discursive knowledges and metaphysical presuppositions determines the legal mediation politics dominating in particular periods. Although legal mediation politics affect the preferences for a certain medium, its legitimation and privilege in a particular cultural area or epoch, metaphysical expectations do not disappear when the political role of one medium is suppressed. Contrary to historically relative and changing discursive expectations, metaphysical expectations remain unchanged. Therefore, they are deconstructable. Derrida warned that there is no thinking and no meaning outside language or other mediations producing representations. Thus, if handwritten signature, as we know it today, did not exist in some historical period, it does not mean that human reasoning was not shaped by metaphysical expectations of nature and of authenticity in that period. In the legal mediation politics of some other period, this expectation would be applied in another way—through temporarily legal magical and ritual objects, relics, talismans, signets, imprints, casts, postmortem masks, or by some other means. If in the future, handwritten signature is not preferred as a reliable medium for identifying citizens, the founding metaphysical expectations of nature and of authenticity will not necessarily perish with it. These expectations will be applied in another—politically preferred—mediation.

Legal mediation politics preferred different media in different periods. This can be observed even nowadays, in the discursive turn from handwritten to electronic signatures. This shift is due both to the digitization and virtualization of communication and to the questioning of reliability of the result of manual work for identifying citizens. Electronic signature seems to be a far more reliable *sign of identification*, because of its exactness, instantaneousness, and delocalization. Furthermore, the virtual signature can work in online communication, which is now becoming the politically preferred way of administration. What occurs here is not only a change of discourse on the correct use of the same medium, as in the turn from graphological to forensic analysis of handwritten signature, but also a discursive change to prefer the use of a technologically different medium. The metaphysical expectations of the naturalness of personal expression and of the authenticity of personal trace, typically linked with the handwritten signature, are no longer associated with the electronic signature. The politically organized media turn, which occurs nowadays, can be described by means of McLuhan's positivist media theory of technological determinism, but cannot be reflected from the aporetical position of Derrida's deconstruction.

The question of media is crucial for my conception of legal handwritten signature, which I conceive as a specific medium. However, my reading reveals Derrida's distance from sociologically or historiographically oriented media theory—such as Flusser's and McLuhan's classification of historically successive eras of different politics of mediation. From his position questioning such positivist media theories, Derrida's deconstruction cannot help to distinguish specific discursive expectations of particular media, which founded legal mediation politics in particular historical periods. Therefore, I consider necessary to complete Derrida's deconstruction with double methodological consideration: with the discursive analysis of handwritten signature as a specific representation, and with the semiotic analysis of handwritten signature as a specific medium.

Contrary to McLuhan, I do not examine the contemporary technological preferences alone. I also focus on the metaphysical presuppositions linked to manual work and to one of its results, which is the handwritten signature. In accordance with Derrida, I suppose that metaphysical presuppositions cannot be eradicated from our reasoning by any new legal mediation politics—neither by a discursive, nor by a media change that would be required by such politics.

These metaphysical expectations can be found not only in scientific discourses, but also in philosophical discourses, such as Martin Heidegger's phenomenology. In his lecture *Parmenides*, Heidegger claims that man acts through the hand that is, together with the word, the essential distinction of man. Moreover, "writing, from its originating essence, is hand-writing" (Heidegger 1992, 85). Therefore, when writing was transferred to the machine, "a transformation occurred in the relation of Being to man. . . . The typewriter veils the essence of writing and of the script. It withdraws from man the essential rank of the hand, without man's experiencing this withdrawal appropriately and recognizing that it has transformed the relation of Being to his essence" (Heidegger 1992, 85).

Derrida notes in *Heidegger's Hand* (Derrida 2008a, 31–46) that Heidegger distinguishes the essence of man from the essence of animal by the advantage of the hand, which gives man the unique disposition to think. Nevertheless, this disposition is characteristic for only one hand, the right one, the writing one. Because the singular writing hand shapes words into images, saying, showing, and *hand*writing are essentially related: the writing tool "is not a simple present-at-hand object" (Harman 2002, 80). David Farell Krell points out that, in Heidegger's view, the writing machine degrades word and speech: "When everything is typewritten, all human beings become an indistinguishable and undistinguished mass" (Krell 2015, 54). The only thing that could restore their individuality would be handwriting, which is treated as *phonetic* writing: "the proximity of word, monstration, inscription, and the shaped letter has its home in the voice that hears and understands itself while speaking" (Krell 2015, 54).

In my further work on handwritten signature, I do not follow phenomenologically oriented readings of Derrida. Phenomenology is not my chosen methodological approach. I prefer to focus on Derrida's understanding of *metaphysical violence*, which is actually the vigilant, aporetical, melancholic side of his relation to both phenomenological and positivist methodologies. Because I propose to deconstruct the Western metaphysical expectation of handwritten signature as a civic sign, rather than phenomenologically, my own approach is semiotically oriented.

In the scope of my semiotically shaped research, I seek to answer two questions. What does it mean to sign by hand? What is the role of Western metaphysics in understanding this manual trace as a reliable sign of civic identity? I understand the handwritten signature as a handmade picture of the civic name of the signer. This picture is produced in the following way: the signer writes her own name by her own hand on a document designed for it, and she writes it visually identically to the specimen signature that she wrote beforehand. Signing is not any natural or spontaneous writing of the signer's own name in the signer's own hand: it is a regulated and iterated instantaneous plastic expression, led by the ambition to reach the most credible reproduction of the specimen signature. In this respect, I find it important to distinguish handwritten signature from other manual plastic expressions combining writing and drawing. Handwritten signature is an intentionally styled plastic trace, which is supposed to be reproduced by imitation of previous handwritten traces, and which become in iteration a recognizable personal pattern.

Because I try to uncover the double discursive expectations and the triple metaphysical expectations of the visual sign of legal handwritten signature, I do not follow Derrida's work on the "proper name." To focus on the legal signature in relation to one's proper name is beyond the scope of my work. Based on my previous analysis of graphological and forensic discourses, I take the sign of legal handwritten signature as a picture or a self-portrait, a plastic medium traced every time by the signer's proper hand. While this picture represents always the same thing, which is the civic name of the signer, the shape of this representation is involved in constant changes. My own work focuses on these multiple changes of signature's shape rather than on the signer's proper name that remains unchanged.

What I find particularly important in the conventional iterable gesture of signing is the ritual of specimen signature: occasional apposition of one random sample of the handwritten signature, which is institutionally registered and archived. Just like the individual signature, the specimen signature is supposed to be written by the signer's own hand. Its registered shape becomes referential for any further handwritten signature by the same signer; its content corresponds with the signer's civic name indicated in her identity card and passport. Nowadays, the specimen signature is used mostly for financial transactions in banks. Banks usually suggest that their clients create specimen signatures that differ from their current way of signing in order to protect them against forgery.

A handwritten signature is not calligraphy—it is no singular and unrepeatable drawing/writing of a picture/text by one concentrated move of a paintbrush. In the Western cultural tradition, the handwritten signature is expected to repeatedly produce identity between the civic name of the signer and her manual plastic expression, which is supposed to remain recognizable because it is both formally and unchanged and characteristic for the author. In the Eastern cultural tradition, calligraphy is an art of event of the singular plastic gesture in the singular moment, which simultaneously produces pictures and texts; the picture means here the text and vice versa. The meaning of the word and of the picture are not strictly unified. There is no imperative of eternal return of a fixed content, which is the arbitrary word (the civic name of the signer) in a fixed form, which is the picture of the name (specimen signature).

A handwritten signature is not a calligram, for two main reasons. Firstly, the content of the signature is the signer's name and is given in advance. Second, the written text of a signature is less legible. A calligram uses clearly recognizable, legible letters as a graphic material to construct a picture, which can signify something other than the written text. Therefore, the calligram offers simultaneously two different and clearly distinguishable meanings: pictorial and textual. The text of a signature is often recognizable but illegible: the individual letters of the signer's name are not clearly recognizable. This illegibility does not matter, because the letters of signature are used as a plastic material to compose a picture of the signer's name. The signer should be recognized by her supposedly characteristic—unique and repeated—plastic style of writing, not by her legibly written name. Contrary to a calligram, a handwritten signature has only one possible meaning: the picture of the name means the text of the name. The handwritten signature fuses the civic name of the author with her individually conceived and the manually performed plastic abstraction of her civic name into one united, legally important compound.

Typography and graphic design have the same problem with illegibility of a graphic font or a plastically conceived text. These fields prioritize the legibility of writing over the plastic conception of writing. According to Samara, regarding its communicational goal, graphic design is either good or bad: any illegible text is a "failed"[8] graphic work. From a designer's viewpoint,[9] "type that cannot be read has no purpose" (Samara 2014, 20).

Therefore, a handwritten signature cannot be considered as a work of graphic design and is not written in a graphic font. Individual plastic conception of the handwritten form and its manual varying differ from the font—technically and terminologically standardized graphic product,[10] which can be not only used as an exact mechanical or digital reproduction, but also created directly on the computer. Despite it, a kind of similarity could be observed between the handwriting and the graphic font: theory of graphic design shares with graphology the thesis on the natural expression of the author's soul.[11] The only difference is that the author of the unique handwriting is the signer herself, while the author of the font is a professional graphic artist offering her own unique style of mechanical writing to other signers.

For similar reasons, the handwritten signature is neither a cartouche nor a brand logo. Signature, cartouche, and logo should be recognizable and repeatable, plastically characteristic abstractions of the name of a person or a group they represent. As Derrida puts it in *The Truth in Painting*, the function of cartouche is more variable than that of handwritten signature: "We will be able to read this cartouche both as a title and as a signature. It is not a stranger to the cartellino or the cartel, even if it cannot be reduced to that. This latter can identify and sign the picture, whether or not it is integrated into it, whether or not it is separated from the image in very diverse topological configurations" (Derrida 1987c, 214). Contrary to signature, which is a strictly personal sign designed by the signer herself, a logo is a professionally designed brand sign, which strategically emphasizes the best qualities of an enterprise that is usually based on collective efforts.[12] In turn, contrary to logo, which is an exactly mechanically repeated picture and therefore can reach formal identity, handwritten signature cannot be repeated without formal variation. The manual work of handwritten signature cannot be manually repeated. It can only produce—more or less similar—variations of the original shape of the registered specimen signature. Signature is a personal sign of identification, but unlike logo, its manual repetition can reach only similarity, not identity of the repeated form.

Finally, signature is neither a signet[13] nor a stamp. Contrary to a stamp, which exactly reproduces a shape by mechanically generating imprints out of it, signature characterizes the originality of manual work. So a handwritten signature must be added to the mechanical imprint of a stamp. I suppose that the authenticity of handwritten signature can be understood in the sense of Benjamin's theory of the "aura" of work of art,[14] based on the belief that precision of a mechanical copy cannot be reached by means of manual reproduction. Every manual repetition produces copies as unrepeatable originals. Therefore, it is believed that all copies of handwritten signatures and of manually created works of art that are not done by the author herself can be recognized as unoriginal or fake works, as simple forgeries, as falsum.

Understanding the signer's traces as a copy of the signer herself depends on belief in ontological persuasiveness of remains. As Alexandra Walsham puts it in *Remains and Relics*, remains could be understood as a material manifestation of the act of remembering, or remembrance. Remains are ontologically specific representations, actual physical incarnations of the absent person, "each particle encapsulating the essence of the departed person, pars pro toto, in its entirety" (Walsham 2010, 12). Politics of identification by means of personal remains, including manual writing, comes from the rhetoric of relic: it is believed not only that the personal trace naturally and authentically replaces the signer's presence in her absence, but also that it is her past component, her personal fragment. If the handwritten signature, like any other existential remains, is separated from its specific cultural environment, it stops being intelligible and understandable.[15] This conception of handwriting as a continuous work of self-imitation by repetition of personal manual traces belongs to the modern tradition of understanding the author as a natural composer of her original style.

We have different expectations of different media: the difference in credibility between analog and digital media depends on the different ability of these technologies to identify citizens. Nowadays, digital mediation is seen as more reliable: while individual traces of a signer's personal style may be difficult to recognize in a handwritten signature, the identity of the arbitrarily distributed code used in an electronic signature appears more secure. Why is there a difference in credibility between forensic and graphological analysis, then, if both disciplines deal with the same analog technology of handwriting? Why do we have different expectations in the case of the same medium?

What Are Metaphysical and Discursive Expectations?

As we have already seen, graphology and forensic analysis examine the same medium of handwritten signature from a different approach, ambition, and expectations. Why do they differ so? Why did graphology become relegated to the pseudo-sciences, while the forensic analysis of handwriting remains scientifically "in?"

I propose to answer these questions by recalling the difference between two incompatible ways of semiotic thinking and applying them to signing. Charles S. Peirce's (and Jacques Derrida's) interest in metaphysical determination of interpretation can be understood as a concern for the metaphysical expectations of different media (or technologies) of signing. In contrast, Umberto Eco's (and Michel Foucault's) interest in discursive determination of interpretation can be understood as a concern for discursive expectations of different knowledge related to the same medium of signing.

To answer the questions concerning different knowledges about the same medium, I turn to Umberto Eco's theory of conventional limits of interpretation. Eco's semiotics of conventional realism is more useful to this discursive examination of signature than the metaphysical realism of Peirce. Eco, who both follows and revises Peirce's conception, allows us to understand that, although both disciplines propose to analyze signatures, each one of them mobilizes a different discursive expectation. While graphology expects that the handwritten signature is naturally identical to the signer's soul, forensic analysis of handwriting expects that the handwritten signature is authentically identical to another handwritten signature.

There are key differences between Peirce's metaphysical semiotics and Eco's discursive semiotics that are relevant to my research. In Charles S. Peirce's metaphysical conception of sign, his conception of semiosis is based on a complex relation between the Object, the Interpretant, and the Representamen. The *Interpretant* is a kind of metaphysical belief and the *Representamen* is a selected perceivable input. Peirce's definition of the *Object* is more complicated: he distinguishes between the *Immediate Object*, defined as a semiotic object represented by a sign, and the *Dynamical Object*, defined as a real object, which remains semantically unreachable. According to V. M. Colapietro in his *Peirce's Approach to the Self*, Peirce's conception is both immanent and transcendent: "Although the sign determines its Immediate Object, the Dynamic Object determines its sign. Moreover, in determining its Immediate Object, a sign creates the possibility of being determined by its Dynamic Object. With respect to the process of semiosis itself, the object of semiosis is, thus, both immanent and transcendent" (Colapietro 1988, 15). From the viewpoint of Peirce's semiotics, the handwritten signature as a sign represents the signer's recognizable psychological qualities, which makes it a perceivable Immediate Object that remains determined by an unperceivable Dynamical Object, the soul of the signer herself.

Peirce's decision to construct semiotics on his triad of metaphysical categories of Firstness, Secondness, and Thirdness is also interesting.[16] This triad of metaphysical categories could help me to understand the metaphysical reasons to believe in handwritten signature's ability to identify its signer. Thus, handwritten signature can be understood as a Representamen with a triple mode of interpretation, which is led by a triple belief, triple habit, and triple Interpretant. As Peirce puts it, "My view is that there are three modes of being. . . . They are the being of positive qualitative possibility, the being of actual fact, and the being of law that will govern facts in the future" (Peirce 1955, 75). If one applies Peirce's metaphysical conception to the handwritten signature, one notices that the supposed signer's qualities, which were supposed to be similar to the formal qualities of her signature, are founded by the *Firstness* of the signature as sign. The same signer's qualities, expressed on the existential level of signature in a form of authentic handwritten traces, are founded by the *Secondness* of the signature as sign. Finally, the same repeatedly expressed signer's qualities, registered as the rule for civic identification, are founded by the *Thirdness* of the signature as sign.

Based on his triad of metaphysical categories, Peirce introduces three trichotomies of signs. In my further analysis of signature as sign, I focus on the second trichotomy,[17] where Peirce situates his concepts of *Icon, Index, and Symbol*—there are perceivable signs related to the Object. In Peirce, these three signs generate the triple metaphysical belief, while "The essence of belief is the establishment of a habit; and different beliefs are distinguished by the different modes of action to which they give rise" (Peirce 1955, 29). First, handwritten signature as an image generates the iconic belief that the formal qualities of signature naturally resemble psychological qualities of the signer, which characterize qualities of the signer's soul. Second, handwritten signature as a trace of manual writing generates the indexical belief that existential contact between the signer's soul and signature is mediated by the signer's characteristic hand movements, which enable readers to verify the authenticity of the signer's trace. Third, handwritten signature as a rule generates the symbolic belief that there is an equivalence between the signer's soul and the picture of the signer's civic name performed by the signer's hand, which enables her to repeat the previous traces, and others to recognize the identity[18] of the signer as a citizen.

Thus, Peirce's ontological semiotics does not allow us to speak about any knowledge generated by the normative power of discourse in Foucault's sense. It only enables us to speak about various actions, which are privileged in various disciplines. In this respect, Peirce's semiotics explains both graphology and forensic analysis, on all levels of metaphysical production of meaning. Although graphology examines the qualities of the signer and forensic analysis verifies the authenticity of the signer, both disciplines work with signature as with icon, index, and symbol. Thus, graphology does not understand signatures only as icons, and forensic analysis does not understand signatures only as indexes.

Marcel Danesi uses Peircean terminology in his semiotic introduction to a new discipline: *Signs of Crime: Introducing Forensic Semiotics*. As Danesi puts it, in forensic semiotics, signatures can be understood as signs of personal identification that the murderer left at the scene of the crime, like specific positions and wounds in the bodies of victims, specific inscriptions on the walls or mirrors. While Danesi understands as "marks of violence" (Danesi 2014, 122) left on victims as iconic signs, he considers fingerprints and DNA samples to be indexical signs, and he takes inscriptions and signatures for symbolic signs. With reference to Peirce, Danesi claims that "signature clues are symbols, because they reveal some aspect of the killer's personality that is sensitive to cultural or upbringing factors of some kind. Using lipstick to write warped messages is clearly symbolic, since lipstick itself is a symbol of womanhood" (Danesi 2014, 123). Only ritual and serial murderers, who intentionally leave a stylized message at the scene of their crime, "link or discard a particular crime scene with others, because they are iconic and thus resemble previous crimes" (Danesi 2014, 123). Signatures of murderers can also "help determine if there is a theme among the crime scenes and what the state of mind of the perpetrator might be" (Danesi 2014, 123).

Not only forensic semiotics could apply this Peircean triple belief. Peircean iconic, indexical, and symbolic belief could be also useful for the semiotics of graphology. Despite their differences, both these analyses of handwritten signature rely on the possibility of uncovering the signer's soul, which is understood as the only generator of all of the signer's personal traces. Both disciplines believe that it is possible to identify the signer by means of her authentic traces of her style of handwriting that naturally characterizes her soul.

Because in Peirce, positivist scientific disciplines are based on the same metaphysical belief, his metaphysical semiotics is not suitable for distinguishing conventional discursive expectations of handwritten signature in graphology and forensic analysis, which could explain why contemporary forensic analysis keeps its distance from graphology. But Umberto Eco's semiotics of conventional realism is suitable for this purpose. In Eco's semiotics, graphology and forensic analysis can be seen as two different discourses. The possibility of recognition is given conventionally: one can recognize the signature as authentic or as forged only through common respect for a certain conventionally set limits of interpretation. In this viewpoint, graphology and forensic analysis do not share the same mode of interpretation, because they are shaped by two different discourses. While graphology compares the shape of a given signature to the psychological classification of handwriting shapes corresponding to the signer's qualities, forensic analysis compares the shape of one signature to the shape of another signature to decide whether the style of handwriting in both is the same. Each discourse expects a different type: while in graphology, the expected type is the signer's soul, in forensic analysis, the expected type is the signer's style of handwriting. Their discursive expectations differ: while graphological discourse skips the role of the signer's style, forensic discourse skips the role of the signer's soul. But both discourses share the metaphysical expectation that the shape of handwriting is not random. In both cases, the signature's shape is expected to be generated by the signer's personal style, which is generated by her unique soul.

In his early work, Umberto Eco declared his independence from structuralism. In *A Theory of Semiotics,* Eco notes that structuralism is a static semiotic project, governed by "a sort of verbocentric dogmatism" (Eco 1979, 213) reducing language to a fixed system of dyadic articulations. Eco disagrees with the structuralist claim that the structure of these connections is based on natural structures of a universal human mind. Therefore, he suggests turning from structuralism to more active interpretational input from the receiver. Although Eco prefers Peirce's pragmaticism to structuralism, he suggests a modification of it. The fundamental difference consists in Eco's claim that the sign universe is not natural, but conventional. Therefore, Eco does not work with metaphysical categories, but rather with the discursive limits of *sign-functions*. In *The Limits of Interpretation*, Eco requires limiting Peirce's conception of *unlimited semiosis* by a certain discursive setting:[19]

> There is something for Peirce that transcends the individual intention of the interpreter, and it is the transcendental idea of a community, or the idea of a community as a transcendental principle. This principle is not transcendental in the Kantian sense, because it does not come before but after the semiotic process; it is not the structure of the human mind that produces the interpretation but the reality that the semiosis builds up. (Eco 1994, 48)

Eco's shift away from Peirce is even more visible in his late monograph *Kant and the Platypus: Essays on Language and Cognition*, where Eco paradoxically declares his intention to approach Peirce's semiotics by emphasizing the ontological side of the semiosis, but repeatedly emphasizes the discursive conditions of possibility of recognition. On the one hand, Eco claims that the cultural and the natural produce concrescence that can be grasped by the concept of the Dynamical Object:

> as soon as we get back to the Dynamical Object and start speaking about it again, we are once more at the point of departure, and so we have to rename it using another *Representamen*, so that in a certain sense the Dynamical Object always remains a Thing-in-Itself, always present and impossible to capture, if not through semiosis. Yet the Dynamical Object is what drives us to produce semiosis. We produce signs because there is something that demands to be said. To use an expression that is efficacious albeit not very philosophical, the Dynamical Object is Something-that-sets-to-kicking-us and says "Talk!" to us—or "Talk about me!" or again, "Take me into consideration!" (Eco 2000, 14)

On the other hand, unlike Peirce, Eco constantly comes out from a discursively determined position (or Encyclopedia). Every observer produces another *cognitive type* of the object she observes. Once its description is accepted by a community, the community shares the *core content* of such description, which enables it to recognize the object. According to Eco, the problem with scientific recognition is that each expert notices a slightly different composition of qualities of the observed object: by describing it, in her mind, she produces another cognitive type and tries to share another core content of the object in her scientific community. To generalize these perceptional variations, the scientific community produces a convention about the accurate content of the object's cognitive type. Eco calls the result of this convention the *molar content* of the object and characterizes it as a discursively acceptable meaning—a meaning that is proposed and accepted by a community of experts. But, as Eco noticed, the expert's viewpoint can hardly bring something new: "The perceptual process was tentative, still private, while the Immediate Object, insofar as it is interpretable (and therefore transmissible), is on its way to becoming public. It can even, as a cognitive schema already consigned to me by the community, act not to encourage but to block the process of perceiving something new (as was the case with Marco Polo and the rhinoceros)" (Eco 2000, 116–17). Taking the examples of failure to recognize the rhinoceros or trouble with the platypus's biological classification, Eco demonstrates that the cognitive process of recognition—in his terms, *perceptual judgment*—is not an evaluation of perception that corresponds to the perception itself. The process of blocking of perception of something new paradoxically means that one perceives not only selectively, but also conventionally. Eco notices that the learned scientific convention prevents experts from perceiving new aspects.

This means that, observing my handwritten signature, every expert would notice different qualities of my soul and would produce another cognitive type with another core content than I would produce. Moreover, according to the rules of her discourse, every expert would determine another molar content of my handwriting. Therefore, every expert in every discipline would necessarily produce another essential characteristic of my soul and of my style of handwriting. Discursively predetermined rules force the expert to generate the molar content of observed objects correlatively to the discursive regulations of the given expertise. Thus, the goal of the expert's description of empirical objects is to concentrate attention on some of its discursively acceptable aspects, to unify various personal observations, and to fit them in the legitimate discursive setting.

Eco's theory of discursively accurate *metaphysical sign-functions* could be helpful in clarifying the problem of discursive expectations of handwritten signature. Below, I rethink three metaphysical sign-functions of the medium of handwritten signature, which are shared by the discourses of graphology and forensic analysis.

In Peirce's metaphysics, the rule of the Thirdness comes from the action of the Secondness, which comes from the quality of the Firstness. In this respect, the metaphysical expectation of the identity of signature and signer can be explained by the degenerated ontological rule of the Thirdness: Peirce's rule of the regular repetition (Thirdness) is generated from the authentic handwritten traces (Secondness), where the natural psychological qualities (Firstness) are expressed. From Eco's viewpoint, all three metaphysical categories—Firstness, Secondness, and Thirdness—are pervaded by a conventional realism, which makes it possible that these categories testify to reality. As Eco says in *Theory of Semiotics*, and later in *Kant and the Platypus*, the Firstness and the Secondness are coded. Thus, qualities or actions cannot be understood or recognized without the metaphysical categories generated by a universal human mind. Eco's conventional realism points to this construction of the real in a universal human mind, which generates collectively negotiated, concluded, and shared meanings of the reality registered and archived in discursively accurate Encyclopedias. In this respect, Eco turns to Peirce's realism only seemingly. He maintains Kant's schematism,[20] and he even completes it by the discursive delimitation of possible recognition. In Eco's semiotics, the a priori conditions of possibility for a conventionally determined interpretation are not universal and ahistorical in Kant's sense, but rather relative and historical in Foucault's sense.[21]

Therefore, the graphological and forensic interpretation of handwritten signature are determined by the same metaphysical expectations explainable by Peirce's semiotics, but they are not determined by the same discursive expectations explainable by Eco's semiotics. These two semiotic theories can be used to provide a double semiotic answer to the question about the difference between forensic and graphological discourses. While Peirce would see both discourses as legitimate, because they are metaphysical, Eco would notice a difference, because their legitimacy is given conventionally. Graphology was downgraded to pseudo-science, while forensic handwriting analysis was not, because of the new discursive convention of experts about what should be scientifically examined, and how. While forensic practice declares that it only compares handwritten documents with other handwritten documents, graphological practice admits that it compares handwritten documents with the souls of the signers. According to Eco's position in *Interpretation and Overinterpretation*, the economy of discursive limits determines which reader's interpretation is (or is not) "reasonable" (Eco 1992, 48–49). Nevertheless, because each discourse has a different focus and limits, their reasonable interpretations vary: while graphology declares that it aims to analyze the qualities of the signer's soul, forensic handwriting analysis declares that it examines only the authenticity of the signer's trace.

Eco's discursively oriented semiotics can be applied to point out the difference between graphological and forensic analysis of the discursive expectations of handwritten signature. In the discourse of graphology, the shape of the signature is considered to be a natural mirror of the qualities of signer's soul. In the discourse of forensic analysis, true signatures are considered to be authentic if they are compared to previous traces of the signer and situated in the interval between identity (mechanical copy of the trace) and difference (someone else's trace). Because of this forensic discursive expectation of the *interval of similarity*, obtained from comparing traces to other traces, the actual setting of discourse on signature seems to be more reliable than the graphological discursive expectation of the *effect of mirroring* between the qualities of the signer's soul and its natural expression in the shapes of handwriting. Even if the forensic discourse may appear more precise and subtle in its reasoning, its credibility could be treacherous: forensic analysis of handwriting secretly shares with graphology the metaphor of mirroring the signer's soul in her handwriting. If an examined trace is considered sufficiently similar to the previous traces, this is attributed to the effect of mirroring between the supposed constant qualities of the signer, supposedly constantly expressed in her manual writing. If one relies on the forensic analysis of handwriting, one does not quit the metaphysical expectation of nature, but only works with another definition and verification of this nature.

The difference between graphology and forensic analysis of handwriting consists in the normative setting of the discursive expectations of handwritten signature, because both discourses share the same set of metaphysical expectations. Digital cryptography is a complex technological change that impacts both discursive and metaphysical expectations of the signature as a sign of civic identification. For the benefit of exact distant identification, electronic signatures give up both the expectation of natural personal style of handwriting and the metaphysical expectation of authenticity of the manually written traces. The sign of signature undergoes technological transformation from a handwritten trace to an arbitrary digital code, which is already linked to another metaphysical expectation. This change of medium causes a fundamental change in discursive expectations of the discipline of cryptography. As it deals with the digital signature, considered more reliable in civic identification than the handwritten signature, cryptographic knowledge becomes hierarchically superior to graphological and forensic knowledges. Compared with its handwritten counterpart, the digital signature has all the advantages of arbitrariness and convention, which makes it a reliable sign of distant civic identification.

Eco's semiotics can be used to solve the problem of *conventional legitimization* of discursive expectations of handwritten signature. I have already explained why Peirce's semiotics is not suitable for solving the problem of discursive expectations of signature, while Eco's semiotics is suitable for this purpose. Also, using Eco's discursive semiotics, I have demonstrated the difference between the discursive expectations of signature in psychological graphology (which expects the signer's nature) and in forensic analysis of handwriting (which expects the signer's authenticity).

Discursive and metaphysical expectations differ because of the metaphysical belief founding the analog mediation of handwritten signature. This belief is no longer relevant for digital mediation of electronic signature. With the rise of electronic signatures, we are relying more on the identity of computer codes than on the authenticity of physical traces. The identity of electronic signatures should be guaranteed by an arbitrarily attributed code. Contrary to the handwritten signature, the electronic one cannot certify the citizen's physical presence at the place of signing. Because the signer is only present electronically or online, her electronic signature is no longer an authentic manual trace: it is an arbitrary code generated by computer.

Although one can explain the turn from the metaphysics of analog mediation toward the metaphysics of digital mediation, one should not deconstruct the metaphysical thinking—or mediation—as such. Neither analog nor digital mediation is totally reliable, because its identity of their mediation is metaphysically constructed. In this situation of complex discursive and media change, I find important to deconstruct the growing dependence on the binary code and on the supreme authority of computer logic and mathematics. Both conceptions of identity should be deconstructed. Both should be liberated from the naive belief in identity between living beings and the signs they construct.

As the electronic signature and the handwritten signature are technologically two different media, they are linked to different metaphysical expectations. Once I have characterized the metaphysical expectations of the electronic signature, I can concentrate on the metaphysical characteristics of handwritten signature and on the possibility of their deconstruction. Below, I focus on the three metaphysical expectations of handwritten signature—similarity, authenticity, and identity—that I understand as deconstructable, aporetic, paradoxical legal requirements. This triple metaphysical expectation is no longer linked to the electronic signature, for which only the metaphysical expectation of identity persists. But in this case, the expectation of identity is based on the arbitrariness of randomly attributed numbers, not on the signer's essential psychological qualities or physical traces.

The similarity, authenticity, and identity of the handwritten signature are expected in two coexisting scientific discourses. In the next chapter, I draw a detailed distinction between the discursive expectations of psychological graphology and forensic analysis of handwriting. Each expertise legitimates its own discursive expectation, which sets its discursive limits of acceptability of formal variations in individual performances of signing. This way, every discourse sets an acceptable extent of dissimilarity, which is intentionally neglected, and which enables receivers to understand the similarity of handwritten shapes as a proof of the signer's identity, of their natural and authentic relation with the expected signer.

Chapter II

The Discursive Expectations of Handwritten Signature

What is handwriting? Is it a transcription of vocal expressions? Or an inscription of thoughts? Do we read handwriting? Or do we look at it? Who is its receiver? A reader? Or a spectator? I find that answers to these questions vary according to those who answer these questions. There are different conceptualizations of writing: on the one hand, Derrida's philosophy of writing, *grammatology*; on the other hand, historical science of writing, *paleography*.

Let us start by focusing on the approach to writing in the discipline of paleography, as illustrated by Margaret R. Finn's "A History of Latin's Paleography." Finn's aim was to explain the historical patterns of handwriting according to periods and areas of the Latin-speaking and -writing world. She defines paleography as "the study of the ancient scripts to be found on soft pliable substances that had been especially prepared for writing, such as sheepskin (parchment), calfskin (vellum), leaves (papyrus) and less commonly, the bark of trees" (Finn 1950, 11). But, according to Finn, paleography is more than this: "orthography, abbreviations, peculiar ligatures, the signatures of quires, and format (i.e., the arrangement of both words and columns) all feature prominently in the work of a paleographer" (Finn 1950, 12).

The paleographer's definition of writing therefore does not include drawings, dances, tattoos, laces, and so forth—its scientific concern is not the deconstructed writing Derrida speaks about. Correlatively to ethnocentric claims of Western metaphysics, in paleography, writing is understood as the historically determined conventional setting of phonetic alphabetic inscriptions, which can be historically described, compared, and sorted. As Finn puts it, a paleographer works "for the purpose of enabling the student to arrive correctly at the dates and points of origin of all manuscripts which may come under his scrutiny" (Finn 1950, 13).

Rosemary Sassoon, an expert in contemporary paleography, understands handwriting as a double historical mirror[1] reflecting both the signer's individual character and the way in which the population was educated. The main purpose of Sassoon's *Handwriting of the Twentieth Century* is "to create a historical record" (Sassoon 2007, 9) of details of teaching of handwriting skills during the twentieth century, which is important because "everyday handwriting is ephemeral and schoolbooks soon disappear" (Sassoon 2007, 9). In her historical narration of graphic patterns and policies changing in the twentieth century, Sassoon demonstrates that, progressively, writers were released from the rigid handwriting movement taught in the previous centuries. She finds that in this century, writers broke away to develop an efficient personal hand, an individual style of handwriting:

> Within the short space of the period covered by this present study, the changing educational policies, economic forces and inevitable technological advance radically altered the priorities and form of handwriting. These changes show in the models and examples throughout this book as an inexorable (though not entirely smooth) journey toward speed and efficiency. The downgrading of skill training and the freeing of children's creative talent have done the rest. (Sassoon 2007, 9)

Legitimization of the personal style of handwriting, supported by the metaphysical expectation of recognition of the signer, goes hand in hand with development of forensic interest in individually stylized handwritten signatures, signs of civic identification. For paleography, this is a historically new situation: instead of studying the collectively followed norm of the given pattern, every single signer is supposed to become her own norm setter, the only designer of the strictly personal pattern of specimen signature.

Contrary to these narrative achievements of paleography, Derrida's philosophical grammatology does not work with historical narration and does not understand writing as a progressively evolving social practice of the Western cultural tradition. Derrida views such a conception of writing as derived from the ethnocentric term of being literate, which means being able to write in a phonetic alphabet of Western cultural tradition that is considered supreme. At this point, deconstruction could help us to raise disturbing questions, such as: If Western culture is characterized by alphabetic phonetic writing, why are pictograms and ideograms used on traffic signs instead of words? Why does graphic design exist? Why do we illustrate books? Why do journalists and scientists use pictures in their demonstrations? These questions can be answered only if we accept a broader definition of writing than the ethnocentric one, which is proposed by experts in paleography. Derrida's deconstruction proposes such broader conception. And it offers something more—explanation for why these questions are so controversial. Derrida shows how phonocentrism and logocentrism are linked to ethnocentrism, which is noticeable in the paleographic approach to writing.

Derrida defines Western metaphysics as a primarily European cultural tradition of reasoning that postulates a contradictory ontological and semantic presupposition of the *total presence* of meaning, which is enforced and violently organized in simplifying binary oppositions. The Greek and Jewish-Christian tradition of thinking is *phonocentric*, placing the voice above the writing. While the "divine" voice, the *phoné*, is the transcendent origin of meaning, phonetic writing is just its "human" derivation, a mere representation. Derrida considers it problematic that the represented meaning is taken for something less than the original meaning, although we are not able to produce anything else than the represented meaning. To cover up this inevitable "insufficiency" of human communication, the materiality of the sign is traditionally sidelined. According to Derrida, the hidden hierarchy of the superior original ideality of the voice and the inferior representing materiality of the writing emerges in the work of various philosophers from Plato to present times.

Systematic logocentrism, considered by Derrida to be a Western phenomenon,[2] developed from phonocentrism. Logocentrism requires totally present or immediate meaning of things communicated by signs, which is a semantic requirement that is simultaneously ultimate and impossible. Sign replaces the thing it communicates; it is its supplement. The sign, presented as a meaningful representative of the thing, will never be equal to the represented thing, because it adds something more; its own being. Our expectation of identity of the sign and the represented thing generates aporia that establishes the Western metaphysics (the legitimate way of semantic and political thinking in Europe and in the area of its cultural influence). As Derrida puts it in an interview with Richard Kearney, "logocentrism is, in the whole range of its philosophical sense, inseparably linked to Greek and European tradition" (Derrida and Kearney 2012, 17).

Based on his conception questioning phonocentrism and logocentrism, Derrida postulates continuation of the contradictory metaphysical thinking in Western cultural tradition, which simultaneously generates and hides the process of representation: the meaning added to the thing by the process of representation is traditionally presented as the original meaning of the thing. As this continuation in the Western metaphysical thinking does not allow any essential historical or epistemological changes of rhetoric, Derrida questions the benefit of differentiation of conceptions of meaning in the history of philosophy. Together with history and epistemology, which postulate essential changes over time and do not focus on the continuation of Western metaphysical thinking in various periods, Derrida questions both semiotic and discursive analysis, which describe and sort signs without considering the risks of metaphysical aporia of the sign.

Derrida addressed this problem several times but was especially concerned with Marin's semiotic and political conception of representation. As few philosophers devoted such systematic reflection to the problem of representation as Louis Marin, it is worth looking at it in more detail. In *Politiques de la représentation,* Marin states that representation is a practice of governorship that gives both appearance and presence to the absent and is the basis of the double relation of agency and misprision. There are two main meanings of representation in Marin: the substitute and the screen. The first understanding of representation is principally based on the prefix "re" in the word represent, which has the value of substitution, replacement, and agency. Thus, the first role of representation, which mobilizes its function of substitute, consists in its ability to replace an original with a copy and to make legitimate the presence of the copy. Representation as substitution means making present something absent by its replacement. By means of this substitution, while being absent, one can reach a partial mode of presence. From this viewpoint, the representation is a substitute of the presence of a whole piece by means of the presence of some of its parts: competences of the whole piece can be delegated to these selected elements. The second role of representation consists in its function as a screen. To represent means both to double the original presence and to expose the doubling. As Louis Marin puts it, this sense is completely different from the first one: to represent an object means not only to exhibit the object that was put into storage, but also to expose a legitimization to exhibit it, because "to represent means always to represent oneself or to present oneself as representing something" (Marin 2005, 73). Thus, the second understanding of representation needs the constitution of a subject of reflection, which produces an intensified presence. Because of this particular mode of presence, the chosen representative elements dispose of competences that the power delegates to them. By doubling the object, not only the absent object is doubled, but also the power of the act of representation: in the practice of representation, doubling of the original reality produces a new reality. If this practice of simulation is not admitted, it is because the representation should function as a *screen of signs*.

Representation, defined as a screen and a substitute, is characteristic of its double duality: duality of the representing and the represented, and duality of the imagination and legitimization. Two effects of representation constitute its double power: the effect of imaginary presence and the effect of legitimization of this presence. Marin claims that the power always tries to appropriate the representation, because "representation itself is power" (Marin 2005, 73). Representation and power are of the same nature. Therefore, it is impossible to define the power as an "effect of dispositive of representation, which introduces force to signs and to discourse; representation produces power as an effect of its operations. Put otherwise, the power-effect of representation is the representation itself" (Marin 2005, 75). A representative picture does not only reproduce the absent power that it proposes to substitute. The picture itself is a power confirmed by itself, legitimated by itself: it doubles its presence and reflects it, to be able to double its own authority.

According to Derrida's *The Work of Mourning*, in Marin, the "Representation is here no longer a simple reproductive re-presentation; it is such a regaining of presence, such a recrudescence or resurgence of presence thereby intensified, that it allows lack to be thought, the default of presence or the mourning that had hollowed out in advance the so-called primitive or originary presence, the presence that is represented, the so-called living presence" (Derrida 2001b, 149). By this double turn, "Marin protects the question of the image from the authority of ontology, and this is already a question of force and of power" (Derrida 2001b, 147). Derrida shares with Marin the force of powerlessness, the "melancholia"[3] that utopian representation tries to cover up by its fetish. In Marin's conception of representation, the concept of fetish has neither Hegelian nor Marxist connotations—it rather follows Freudian definition as a replacement of displaced memory. According to Marin, every representation is inevitably fetishist in the sense that it gives presence to what is absent; it produces a fragmentary substitute of the absent totality of memory. Derrida comments on Marin's interpretational ethics of humbleness and respect for alterity of the picture, which actually is not what it represents: its vocation is "a work of mourning of the absolute of 'force,' says Louis Marin, keeping the word 'force' between quotation marks that will not let go. It is a question of the absolute renunciation of the absolute of force, of the absolute of force in its impossibility and unavoidability; both at once, as inaccessible as it is ineluctable" (Derrida 2001b, 144).

Derrida emphasizes that Marin's understanding of representation as mourning for the lost whole contrasts with a limiting, framing ambition of every historical document, archive, and memory. History needs to produce and to share some legitimate photographic representation of reality to build a collective memory and to recall the reality in a politically and technologically determined way. As he puts it in *Psyché,* recording technology is necessary to "translate" the parts of the event of perception into perceivable and archivable representations: "to be in representation, *être en représentation,* for an envoy, also means in our language to show oneself, to-represent-oneself-on-behalf-of, to-make-oneself-visible-for, on an occasion that is sometimes called a *manifestation* so as to recognize, with this word, a certain solemnity" (Derrida 2007, 96).

Derrida understands historiography in terms of how it selects and describes singular events. His aim is to dismantle this historiographic representation, not to describe, name, and list events in a historically positivist manner. This dismantling is not motivated by ambition to offer a new version of the legitimate version of historical narration—deconstruction is neither an archeology nor a genealogy. On the contrary, Derrida systematically searches for persisting methodological aporias of impossible projects, which come across various historical periods and appear again and again—metaphysically unchanged. Derrida's deconstruction produces neither a positivist analysis of discursively based expectations of particular media nor a positivist historical narration of the way they change over time.

However, this does not mean that Derrida would have no interest in history, in the historicity of meaning. If I argue that Derrida's concept of *arche-writing* is meta-historical, I mean that Derrida is very careful in the case of historical positivity. He suggests rethinking history as *historiography* with its metaphysical conditions of *historicity.* Thus, his *arche* does not mean *historical* origin—it exists *along with* handwriting (in the sense of *together,* not *before* or *after* its historical invention as a form of human communication).

Derrida is not particularly interested in the problematic of discourse, because his aim is to deconstruct the metaphysical expectations that persist across various discourses and over time. His deconstruction of metaphysical expectations questions the remaining belief in natural difference and identity, as well as the reasons for enforcing a hierarchy of discourses.

Despite its difference from deconstruction, discursive description of the current legal mediation politics helps me to understand the scientifically pertinent ways in which handwritten signature is enunciated today. I analyze the discursive expectations in two discourses of handwritten signature, which coexist in contemporary mediation politics: in the psychological discipline of graphology and in the forensic discipline of handwriting analysis. My own analysis of discursive—as distinct from metaphysical—expectation is inspired by Foucault's conception of discursive regulations.

In *The Order of Things* (1989), Foucault finds that words and things are essentially separated. Examining three historical periods in Western Europe, he observes that words were arranged into three different, mutually impassable, strictly separated formations, attributing to the same things a triple, strictly differentiated rhetorical meaning: resemblances in the Renaissance, identities and contrasts in the Classical era, or causes in the era of Modernity. The goal of Foucault's investigation was to describe and theorize the discursive politics of meaning, which caused this triple rhetorical redistribution of words and things in history. His archeology of humanities aimed to uncover the hidden layers of the epistemologically relative organization of verbal interpretations of things and to reveal the conditions of possibility of their inception in history. Foucault presents the discursive formation organizing knowledge in various historical periods as various semantic systems, all of which follow one organizing principle. As in Foucault, the conditions of possibility of discursively truthful enunciation are relative and temporary; they can only differ by setting. This organizing principle allows Foucault to compare the practice of enunciation in various discursive formations. The common principle is the representation of things by words enabling discursive sharing of meanings. Such a politics of meaning can have various settings conditioned by various epistemes, but cannot break free from the principle of representation, which constructs and maintains it. The representation of things by words is epistemologically relative and discursively binding. Without this practice of representation, there would be no discourse, no discursive formation, and no archeology.

Foucault does not question the reason for the epistemological organization of meaning: he defines the *episteme* as historical conditions of possibility of enunciation but does not solve the broad philosophical problem of the relation between things and words. Foucault defines representation only in relation to his classical episteme, and in a structuralist way. For him, the representation is an arbitrary cover, which is supposed to replace the absent thing with the discursively present word for it. In structuralism, the signifying sound is an arbitrary conventional cover of the signified concept, which is hierarchically superior to the sound. Foucault's archeology and French structuralism have the same politics of shared meaning: both generate representation of representation without theorizing this semantic practice of their own.

Contrary to structuralism and archeology, deconstruction dissociates the conventional correlate of the *signifier* and the *signified* to give the signifier a new semantic and political freedom. If Derrida subverts the hierarchic relation between the signifier and the signified this way, it is because he wants to occasionally make the writing original, not just a representing sound of voice, which represents the concept. He notices that without the *arche-writing*, we would not be able to produce words and to share their meaning with others. The transcendental signified and conventionally shared concept needs to somehow be produced and registered in the minds of people in the given speaking community.

Moreover, as Derrida demonstrated in "Cogito and the History of Madness," Foucault the archeologist does not only observe the discursive generating of verbal representations of things, he also produces these representations, creating the historical knowledge that he claims to uncover in the archives. By means of his own alternative selection and description of representative historical documents, Foucault produces his own representation of historical representations, which he considers to be characteristic for the politics of meaning of the respective historical periods. This way, Foucault produces his archeological representation of how the historical politics of meaning proceeded. The result is a new history of an old history, a new politics of meaning of an old politics of meaning, a new representation of things by words representing an old representation of things by words. Yet archeological representation of representation is no meta-representation, because Foucault does not reflect on his own historical practice of representation. As Derrida puts it, representation is a semantic necessity: it "is not a defect or mystification linked to a determined historical structure, but rather is an essential and universal necessity from which no discourse can escape, for it belongs to the meaning of meaning. It is an essential necessity from which no discourse can escape, even the discourse which denounces a mystification or an act of force" (Derrida 1978a, 65). Foucault's archeology is based on rejecting such a conception of representation. He tries to denunciate it, but he cannot succeed because he cannot escape the reach of its influence, because the logos and its principle of representation enable Foucault to call for understanding from any scientific community.

In this respect, the early Foucault did not quit structuralism. Although he declares it in his interviews, he does not do it in his own practice. As Jean-François Bert reminds us in "Y a-t-il un structuralisme chez Foucault?," Foucault borrows from structuralism mostly its negative aspects: its negation of history, genesis, and subject. Correlatively to structuralism—and contrary to humanities, obliged to "refer to the concept of subject, to his psychology and his representation" (Bert 2004, 207)—Foucault eliminates these concepts from his terminology. Nevertheless, he keeps the same representational practice: when Foucault arranges his own version of rhetorical history of knowledge and presents it as the accurate version, he continues to use the same representational procedures as structuralism did. Derrida notices in "Cogito and the History of Madness" that Foucault's structuralism consists in his ambition to present her own representation of history as their total representation: "The attempt to write the history of the decision, division, difference runs the risk of construing the division as an event or a structure subsequent to the unity of an original presence, thereby confirming metaphysics in its fundamental operation" (Derrida 1978a, 48). I propose to call this consideration by the producer of representation about her own practice of representation—absenting in the early Foucault—the *ethics of meaning*. And I propose to call the principle of creative self-consideration, correlatively to which the ethics of meaning acts, the principle of meta-representation. Ethics of meaning produces meta-representation by drawing attention to the politics of meaning and its production of representation.

In their later work, Foucault and Derrida share this intentional move toward the ethics of meaning. The main goal of their semantic ethics is to critically point out the semantic violence in everyday communication, which is considered both necessary and inevitable. Both thinkers assume pathos, which enables their ethical questioning of the semantic violence of the highly problematic conception of human nature. In this respect, both act as poststructuralists: structuralists open to reconsidering the political limits of semantic structure and proposing an ethics denouncing the falsity of every politics of truthfulness. They only think about signs as elements organized in a fixed structure of relations that they denunciate. The late Foucault tries to get out of this via relativism, pointing out the semantic violence of all discursive regimes of enunciation. Derrida deploys textual strategies of semantic grafting and putting under erasure to get closer to margins of the logos. Therefore, he occasionally subverts the established natural hierarchy in binary oppositions and points out the violent nature of this metaphysical construction. But at the same time, he vigilantly claims that metaphysical construction of the hierarchy in binary oppositions cannot be totally rejected without falling into the madness of contradiction.

As in structuralism, in Foucault, the word corresponds to the shared idea of the thing. But this idea of the thing is relative: the meaning of any sign is a discursive construct, which depends on episteme, on historical conditions of the possibility of its emerging. Because every meaning is determined by the historical episteme, it cannot be understood in any universal sense. Already the early Foucault considers it necessary to dare to tell the non-discursive truth about the violence of all semantic regimes that present their discursively relative meaning as natural. This ambition leads him toward systematic uncovering of the politics of meaning in historical discursive ways of enunciation, which he later theorizes from the position of his genealogy. In "La parrhesia chez Foucault," Frédéric Gros proposes to term this ethical dimension in Foucault's late work as *parrhesia* (Gros 2002, 155–66). As he reminds us, in his course at Collège de France from 1982 to 1984, Foucault distinguishes between parrhesia and rhetoric: while parrhesia "speaks truthfully," rhetoric "speaks well." Contrary to rhetoric, which has logos and politics of representation on its side, parrhesia has pathos and ethics of meta-representation on its side. The speech of such an ethically motivated critic is personally engaged, politically risky, and led by the courage to be honest even for the price of a conflict or a misunderstanding, as Foucault himself mentions in his severe critique of Derrida's work titled "Mon corps, ce feu, ce papier" (Foucault 2001, 35). If the late Foucault and Derrida have something in common, it is precisely this pathos, produced by the ethics of fight against the hypocrisy of all undeclared semantic construction.

For this reason, it is—and is not—easy to criticize Foucault. It all depends on whether one accepts the ethical dimension of pathos in his work. If the critic rejects the ethical pathos of the true representation as a defect of Foucault's philosophical work, her situation is easy. But if the critic accepts Foucault's pathos—and the ethical dimension it carries—her situation is more difficult, because she falls into the contradictory practice of reproaching the one she criticizes. That was the case for Jacques Derrida.[4]

In Derrida's view, the writing semantically precedes the voice: actually, the writing produces a description of being, the *grammé*, while the voice produces a science of being, the logos. Derrida intentionally subverts this seemingly natural hierarchy in the binary opposition of voice and of writing, pointing out that it multiplies contradictions inside the philosophical conception. The politics of knowledge described by Foucault is animated by his own logocentric gesture that aimed to construct an alternative history and to uncover the relativity of every knowledge—of everyone, except his own.

This methodological trouble led Derrida to ask his well-known disturbing question: where does Foucault the archeologist speak from? As he puts it, one can inquire

> about the source and the status of the language of this archaeology, of this language which is to be understood by a reason that is not classical reason. What is the historical responsibility of this logic of archaeology? Where should it be situated? Does it suffice to stack the tools of psychiatry neatly, inside a tightly shut workshop, in order to return to innocence and to end all complicity with the rational or political order which keeps madness captive? The psychiatrist is but the delegate of this order, one delegate among others. (Derrida 1978a, 41)

And Derrida continues:

> if Foucault's book, despite all the acknowledged impossibilities and difficulties, was capable of being written, we have the right to ask what, in the last resort, supports this language without recourse or support: who enunciates the possibility of nonrecourse? Who wrote and who is to understand, in what language and from what historical situation of logos, who wrote and who is to understand this history of madness? (Derrida 1978a, 44–45)

Put otherwise, where does Foucault situate himself when he tells us his alternative, non-historical, non-discursive truth? If he claims every scholar speaks from inside her historically conditioned scientific discourse, what about Foucault himself? Can his archeology announce any historical truth that would be relieved of epistemological determinations of knowledge? Can it avoid representing a discourse, being conditioned by a historical a priori? Is there such an epistemologically neutral place, from which true history could be finally written?

Derrida doubts it. In his view, every philosophical project that denounces representation by producing representation is an impossible project: "Order is then denounced within order" (Derrida 1978a, 42). Foucault the archeologist seems to opt for such an impossible project when he sets out in two divergent directions: by introducing his conception of *historical* and *epistemological ruptures*, he refuses causality in historical narration and simultaneously acts as a historian, an expert giving reasonable meaning to the past events he describes. As Derrida puts it, "an archaeology against reason doubtless cannot be written, for, despite all appearances to the contrary, the concept of history has always been a rational one. It is the meaning of 'history' or *archia* that should have been questioned first, perhaps. A writing that exceeds, by questioning them, the values 'origin,' 'reason,' and 'history' could not be contained within the metaphysical closure of an archaeology" (Derrida 1978a, 43). Historiography is first of all a metaphysical work: it turns unique events into positivist representations.

Derrida himself does not opt for writing any positivist history; he takes the event differently. In his interview with Borradori, he does not understand it as an occasion for introducing a new philosophical concept or scientific explanation, but as an unpredictable invasion, which "should be so unforeseeable and irruptive that it disturbs even the horizon of the concept or essence on the basis of which we believe we recognize an event as such" (Derrida and Borradori 2003, 90). The deconstructed *event* resists scientific positivism:

> The event is what comes and, in coming, comes to surprise me, to surprise and to suspend comprehension: the event is first of all that which I do not first of all comprehend. Better, the event is first of all that I do not comprehend. It consists in that, that I do not comprehend that which I do not comprehend and first of all that I do not comprehend, the fact that I do not comprehend: my incomprehension. (Derrida and Borradori 2003, 90)

Derrida's "minimal definition of event" determines "the unappropriability, the unforeseen ability, absolute surprise, incomprehension, the risk of misunderstanding, unanticipatable novelty, pure singularity, the absence of horizon" (Derrida and Borradori 2003, 91). From this ultimate viewpoint of deconstruction, the event can be neither understood nor named, let alone explained in its totality, as chronological history, epistemology, and archeology attempt to do.

Because there is no critique beyond metaphysics, the main problem of this exemplary confrontation between Derrida and Foucault remains unsolved:[5] one cannot criticize metaphysics in order to quit it. No critic escapes metaphysics: Foucault does not escape by criticizing the history of ideas, nor does Derrida by criticizing the archeology. To criticize means to mobilize a particular semantic politics of means inside the metaphysics. That is the destiny of Derrida criticizing Foucault: one could ask "where does Derrida the critic speak from?" Because relations of signs and things are metaphysical, neither Foucault's nor Derrida's alternative semantic politics can escape it; their critique produces meanings that call for common understanding. Put otherwise, every critique postulates a semantic equivalence between the criticized thing and the critic's description of the thing. Every critic puts herself on the side of the metaphysics of totally present meaning: she situates herself in the position of the one who knows, who exactly understands the true meaning of the criticized thing. Moreover, every critic believes themselves to be its discoverer and its speaker. Every critique is supreme. If Derrida is being critical, it puts him into a hierarchically superordinated position in relation to what he criticizes: he leaves writing and becomes voice. In such circumstances, can he criticize Foucault without falling into the trap of his own critical strategy?

Only a quasi-critique daring to tell the precarious, risky truth, which has no discursive legitimation, can do this. Such critique does the parrhesia, tells the ethical truth of the political truth, produces the meta-representation. The ethics of meaning nourishes the "just" anger of the individual fighting against prejudices constructed by discursive politics of meaning. In this respect, the rhetoric is political and the parrhesia is ethical; the one follows the discursively acceptable representation, the other produces and simultaneously theorizes its own critical representation of the discursively acceptable representation. Because of this double vigilance of *quasi-representation*, the ethics of meaning can act. Although Foucault's parrhesia cannot get rid of the metaphysical tools of rhetoric[6] and representation, it neither gives up the fight for his own critical truth, which again can be reached only by means of representation. Nevertheless, as Derrida supposed, this unfinishable quasi-representational fight against semantic violence inside Western metaphysics only seems to be vain. Each semantics, which gives it up, loses its alertness, its ethos, and heads toward totalities.

The parrhesia in the later work of Foucault, the courage to tell the truth outside discourse, is noticeably similar to the meta-historical ethos of thinking and writing in the later work of Derrida. As Derrida puts it in his last interview, "One can be the 'anachronistic' contemporary of a past or future 'generation'" (Derrida 2007a, 27). But, if you want to share with others, what you need is the "an *ethos* of writing and of thinking, an intransigent or indeed incorruptible *ethos* (Helene Cixous calls us the 'incorruptible ones'), without any concession even to philosophy, an *ethos* that does not let itself be scared off by what public opinion, the media, or the phantasm of an intimidating readership might pressure one to simplify or repress. Whence the strict taste for refinement, paradox, and aporia" (Derrida 2007a, 27–28). Because deconstruction brings no solution to the problems mentioned above—it only indicates the places, where the same problems could be hidden—its major contribution consists in untiring warning, in its role of ethical memento.

In my philosophical project, I operate a double methodological switch. The positivist discourses of both history and media studies tend to avoid problematization of their work of representation of events—they do not play the "double jeu" of deconstruction. Their work consists in positivist analysis producing discursively truthful representation; it consists neither in its critical questioning nor in considering the problem of meta-representation. Therefore, their own work of interpretation and narration of events is deconstructable, and it can be done the same way Derrida deconstructs the positivist work of archives. My own approach to handwritten signature is not only discursive, not only positivist, but focuses also on the way history, media studies, and semiotics *produce* their representations of events.

However, in order to deconstruct the common metaphysical prejudices shared by these discourses, I need to start by positivist examination of these discourses. To do so, I cannot follow deconstruction right away. To begin, I have to use a positivist method. This is my first methodological switch. At this point, I intentionally turn to historical discursive analysis of both graphological and forensic knowledges of legal handwritten signature.

Once this rigorous methodological work uncovering discursive expectations of handwritten signature is done, I operate another methodological switch. By comparing knowledges of the given scientific discourses, I search for a common ground of their discursive beliefs, which I propose to call metaphysical expectations of handwritten signature as a specific sign. To help understand metaphysical expectations of this specific sign, I introduce another positivist method of analysis, which is Peircean scientific semiotics of logical realism. To reveal all of these expectations of signature as metaphysically conditioned prejudices, I finally turn to deconstruction.

In my last methodological switch, I follow Derrida's work on these problems, but not in a positivist way. Based on the positivist research I have done, I can start the double play of deconstruction, which is common metaphysical expectations of specifically handwritten signature as metaphysical prejudices shared by the discourses of graphology and forensic analysis. By using this combined methodology, I formulate two kinds of expectations—discursive and metaphysical—of legal handwritten signature help to understand the precarious event of signing.

I am aware of the risk I am taking by combining these three different and in many ways incompatible methodological approaches. Derrida's own conception of history as a deconstructed meta-history, as a historiography with its proper conditions of historicity, is not compatible with the positivist sociological and historical method of discursive analysis. Because Derrida's work is primarily concerned with the general system of Western metaphysics, it is limited to a perspective that does not match with positivist historical analyses of discourses on handwritten signature. However, to understand what experts claim to know about signature, at some point of my own research project, I cannot avoid positivist discursive analysis linked to the scientific conception of historical facts. My methodological call for a positivist historically oriented discursive analysis, then justifies my turn to thinkers like Foucault or Kittler. Let us have a closer look at crucial differences between these two working strategies in relation to history.

What is Derrida's conception of history? On the one hand, one can say Derrida has profound philosophical interest in history-related questions. His interest in systematic perspective does not necessarily commit him to a strictly ahistorical perspective. Derrida himself relates his work to historical perspective in three different ways. Two of them are affirmative to historical approach. Either Derrida follows Heidegger's *Destruktion* to work on etymological and genealogical sedimentation of interpretations of being, or he writes a "history" in the sense of a story composed of personally important events and comments, which is the case of his equivocal history of "telecommunications" (Derrida 1987b, 3) in "Envois," in *The Postcard*. The third way is a meta-historical approach. In *Echographies of Television*, Derrida suggests a meta-inquiry questioning the positivity of historiographical projects: "memory includes forgetting. If there is selectivity, it is because there is forgetting" (Derrida and Stiegler 2002, 64). Moreover, by pointing to the connection between Freudian death drive and selective strategy of memory in *Archive Fever* (Derrida 1998, 28–31), Derrida explicitly problematizes the positivist historical work of archivation from a psychoanalytical position. Finally, he distinguishes deconstruction from epistemology in *Positions* by stating that he does not believe in decisive ruptures, in an unequivocal epistemological break, as it is called today. Breaks are always, and fatally, reinscribed in an old cloth that must continually, interminably be undone. This interminability is not an accident or contingency; it is essential, systematic, and theoretical. And this in no way minimizes the necessity and relative importance of certain breaks, of the appearance and definition of new structure. (Derrida 1981d, 24)

On the other hand, Derrida often stresses the Western metaphysical system of thought that remains continuous across various shifts in the history of ideas. For instance, in his paper "The Linguistic Circle of Geneva" (Derrida 1982a, 137–75), adopting a systematic position allows him to bring together Rousseau and de Saussure across centuries. Derrida himself positions himself at the margins of philosophical discourse, which allows him to be engaged both inside the genealogical work with metaphysical concepts and to take a critical step. As he puts it in *Positions*, "To 'de-construct' philosophy, thus, would be to think—in the most faithful, interior way—the structured genealogy of philosophy's concepts, but at the same time to determine—from a certain exterior that is unqualifiable or unnamable by philosophy—what this history has been able to dissimulate or forbid, making itself into a history by means of this somewhere motivated repression" (Derrida 1981d, 6). Petra Gehring calls Derrida's intermingling of historical and systematic philosophical approaches the "intersection of contrary, paradox double perspectives" (Gehring 2008, 65). As she notices, Derrida explains his *auto-hetero-deconstruction* particularly in "Force of Law," where he comments on two methodological styles along which deconstruction equally proceeds: "there are logical-formal aporias and there is the reading of texts with a view to the historical dimension, a careful interpreting which Derrida calls 'genealogical' (which I do not think should be regarded in the proximity of Michel Foucault's genealogie)" (Gehring 2008, 65). In this sense, deconstruction strategically moves back and forth between active intervention (a destructive, random intervention in texts that is directed against their declared meanings) and an intervention that the text itself does itself, by itself, on itself (Gehring 2008, 65–66).

This double-binded strategical position in relation to history and historicity, repeatedly emphasized by Derrida himself, is not methodologically compatible with the positivist historical discourse I need to partly follow in my work. Therefore, in my own research into metaphysical expectations in legal mediation politics, I wish to maintain this deconstruction's dimension of the *memento*. To problematize this politics of mediation and to speak about its deconstructable metaphysical dimension, I have to start by clearly describing it and explaining its main intentions and effects. I thus first make a temporary shift away from deconstruction, to which I return later. In my conception, this logocentric shift is necessary. Without it, it would not be possible to explain what is to be deconstructed. Derrida's melancholic conception of signature as the idiom of the signer[7]—which resists any positivist understanding, translation, and interpretation—cannot be used as a starting point for determining the legal politics of signature as a medium, which is linked to some scientific expectation.

Because "Derrida adopts a resolutely anti-positivistic stance" (Legrand 2009, xxiii), I combine the positivist history of Western practice and knowledge of manual signing (which, in its chronological explanation of events, is not distanced from paleography) with discursive analysis (which, with its two coexisting discourses of handwritten signature, is not distanced from Foucault's ambition to differentiate individual orders of enunciation). Both scientific approaches, problematized by deconstruction, allow me to describe general issues in legal mediation politics. My description focuses on the circumstances of emergence and mutual relations of the two discourses of signature, which currently coexist in the Western cultural space. For the moment, I leave aside Derrida's distrustful consideration of positivist historical narration and discursive analysis, because I consider both to be partly inevitable for the scientific constitution of the object of my research, which is the legal mediation politics of handwritten signature.

In the next section of this chapter, I understand the discursive expectation of legal handwritten signature as a range of its acceptable interpretations shared inside a particular scientific discipline. My conception of discursive expectation of technologically determined media is inspired by Friedrich A. Kittler, who describes his project in terms that invoke both McLuhan's technological determinism and Foucault's genealogy of discourses; his "descriptive and nonevolutionary model favoring sudden ruptures and transformations at the expense of genetic causalities is derived from Foucault, but it takes on a certain edge because epistemological breaks are tied to technological ruptures" (Winthorp-Young and Wutz 1999, xxxiv). Moreover, Kittler's focus on the mechanical technology of typewriting is inspiring—he strictly distinguishes from the previous technology of handwriting. As he puts it in *Gramophone, Film, Typewriter*, "Voice and handwriting treacherously could fall subject to criminal detection; hence every trace of them disappears from literature" (Kittler 1999, 228), which is mechanically typed. Contrary to typewriting, handwriting is based on the "psychological conception that guaranteed humans that they could find their souls" (Kittler 1999, 188) through their analysis of handwriting.

Following Kittler's discursive analysis of technologies, I try to demonstrate that handwriting is expected to enable to identify the signers. Nevertheless, my hypothesis is that discursive expectations in psychological graphology and forensic analysis of handwriting are adjusted differently; these two kinds of expertise systematically generate two different interpretations of signature. What do these experts know about handwritten signatures? How do they explain the reasons for their belief in signature's ability to represent the signer?

Discourse of Graphology: The Transparent Expression

In graphology, the discursive expectation of equivalence introduces equivalence between the observed similarity of individual shapes of handwriting and their supposed identity with characteristics of the signer's soul. Psychological and graphic identity fuse here into graphic-psychological identity. Moreover, although the shapes of the letters can be seen as constantly repeating themselves, in reality, they permanently vary. Therefore, in manual writing, it is impossible to reach the identity of invariant shapes of letters: one can only reach variability, or varying similarity of variants. The same is valid for characteristics of the signer's soul, which should be expressed in her writing. The identity of individual expressions of the soul cannot be reached. Because the signer is a living individual, not an identically programmed machine, her expressions are not constantly identical. For these reasons, it would be more accurate to speak not about relation of identity, but rather about relation between these two similarities: between particular shapes of handwriting, and between expressions of the signer's soul. In its practice, graphology determines an interval of the discursively acceptable degree of similarity, where every expression of similarity is understood as an expression of identity.

Using samples from contemporary graphological discourse, I try to demonstrate the ambition of graphologists, who put themselves in the supreme position of accurate interpreters of the meaning of the given signature's shape. They believe that, without their reading, this meaning would not be discovered, not only by other readers, but also by the signer herself. In this respect, the ambition of their interpretation is compatible with the ambition of psychologists and curators of art exhibitions, who describe the souls of patients and works of art from the same supreme position of the expert. From the graphologist's position, signature is a metaphysically inevitable and natural expression of the signer's unconsciousness, which can be examined, understood, and diagnosed only by an expert in psycho-graphology. It is the expert—speaker of her discourse—who determines the meaning of each signer's expression. In the interaction between signer and graphologist, the graphologist is the true holder of the vocabulary necessary for translation between the expert's consciousness and the signer's unconsciousness.

In *Handwriting: A Key to Personality*, graphologist Klara G. Roman emphasizes the need for non-linguistic reception of handwriting: to minimalize disturbing influences on handwriting analysis, graphologists should learn how to examine the writing without reading the text. Graphologists have to pay attention to the pictorial side of the handwriting to uncover personality traits that are not expressed in words and are partly unknown even by the signer herself. As Roman claims, "handwriting is a brain writing" (Roman 1962, 108); every signer's personality is inevitably revealed in the features of handwriting. Graphological discourse also emphasizes this pictorial aspect of handwritten signature, which is usually composed of first and last names, and in many cases of a final supplement, which can be a simple dot or a conclusive stroke, but also complicated ornaments, decorative curls, or a characteristically composed configuration of other traces.

When Roman comments on the form of handwriting, she proposes to focus—besides letters, tying, and rhythm—on the signer's personal *psychogram*, understood as a self-expressive picture generated by the signer's characteristic personal graphic stylization. In this respect, she states, the graphologist's "judgment turns on whether the expressive picture is natural or stilted, individual or conventional, linear or pictorial in quality" (Roman 1962, 126). Klimoski and Rafaeli write that Roman was able to use individual "script characteristics to create a profile of the writer's personality" (Klimoski and Rafaeli 1983, 192). However, Roman does not explain how she distinguishes natural from forged writing, or how she recognizes what is natural for the given signer and what is not.

Roman's explanation of the scientific method of graphology seems contradictory. On the one hand, she humbly claims that "there can be no standard key for reading off personality traits, living features cannot be sorted out by formula and assigned to a type pattern on any one plane" (Roman 1962, 130). But, on the other hand, she claims the opposite when she writes that psychological interpretation of graphic indices is rigorous synthetic work: "the graphologist must interpret them as expressions of personality, i.e., he must correlate the graphic indicators he has found with the personality traits they stand for" (Roman 1962, 130). The last step of every psychological analysis of handwriting consists in construction of the entire picture: from predetermined psychological components, the graphologist composes a total, complex representation of the supposed signer's personality (Roman 1962, 130).

I propose to illustrate this graphology's contradictory approach to its own object of examination with the contemporary setting of graphological discourse presented by several experts in this field.

In *Handwriting Analysis: The Complete Basic Book*, Karen Amend and Mary S. Ruiz state that graphologists study handwriting as a means to discover other people's qualities. If they can use any writer's handwriting to create a psychological portrait, it is because

> they know that exaggerations in writing formations suggest similar exaggerations in the personality of the signer. Character traits that deviate from the norm will show up in the handwriting. The graphologist learns to analyze the difference between normal and abnormal traits in the writing. Both fundamental knowledge and interpretive skill have their importance in an accurate analysis of a handwriting sample, and all interpreters unavoidably bring their own personal shadings and colorings to the portrait. (Amend and Ruiz 1980, iv–v)

Although the authors admit that no two writings are exactly alike,[8] they suppose that these various manual expressions can be classified and examined as fitting into several a priori psychological categories corresponding to several predetermined cases of the possible signers. As they expect that every signer has her own personal, "unconsciously"[9] determined way of handwriting, despite occasional fluctuations, every signer's personal style is consistent enough to be recognized: it is a true mirror that "reflects"[10] the essential qualities of the signer's soul. Therefore, they claim, "it is possible through thoughtful observation to penetrate the disguise and reveal the inner character behind the mask" (Amend and Ruiz 1980, iii).

In *Handwriting Analysis: Putting It to Work for You*, graphologists Andrea McNichol and Jeffrey A. Nelson understand the style of handwriting, similarly to fingerprints, as the signer's unique "brain print." As they claim:

"when we produce any graphic movement, such as handwriting, we are actually 'brainwriting' and leaving our 'brain prints' behind on the paper" (McNichol and Nelson 1994, 24). These brain prints "reveal who we are and how we think, feel, and behave. They are an x-ray of our mind. And, like our fingerprints, they remain uniquely our own forever. No two people ever have the exact same brain prints" (McNichol and Nelson 1994, 24). They also believe that the signer's expressive identity is essentially fixed, which is why a signer can distinguish her own handwriting from any other: "For example, if I hid your writing in a hundred samples of other people's writing and asked you to find the one you wrote, no matter when you wrote the sample, no matter what the slant, size, or look of your particular sample, you could pick it out from the pile. That is because, although your moods may change, part of your writing always stays the same, just as part of you always remains the same" (McNichol and Nelson 1994, 25).

A similar approach, promising to uncover the hidden secrets of signers' emotions, can be seen in Bart A. Baggett's graphological work. Even the "cerebral" terminology is similar: in his definition, handwriting is "brain writing."[11] In *The Secrets to Making Love Happen! Mastering Your Relationships Using Handwriting Analysis & Neuro-Linguistic Programming*, Baggett proposes to understand handwriting as a "secret weapon" (Baggett 1998, 11) in social interactions. By teaching his readers how to handle this weapon, he promises to improve their relationships.[12] To keep this promise and make graphological analysis work properly, Baggett explains that it is necessary to understand one's handwriting as unconsciously stylized painting.[13] This true self-portrait can be understood and explained because "handwriting simplifies the personality into individual traits identifiable in specific handwriting strokes" (Baggett 1998, 14). According to Baggett, the signer's own simplification of handwritten strokes uncovers and exhibits her essential psychological characteristics.

Graphologist Paula Roberts promises similar analytical achievements to those who learn how to read or unmask the visual side of handwriting. In *Love Letter: The Romantic Secrets Hidden in Our Handwriting*, she proposes to understand handwriting "as reflecting the complete, true personality of the person we are studying" (Roberts 2002, 129). Graphological ambition to understand the signer totally—to uncover their "full personality"—can be seen particularly in her chapter on signatures. Although Roberts claims that handwritten signature is the most important thing[14] one can ever write, "the signature alone cannot be used to reveal the full personality. Rather, the signature will tell you how your partner is projecting himself to the world in general (the ego statement) and how he would like to be seen by others" (Roberts 2002, 129–30).

Michelle Dresbold and James Kwalwasser, in *Sex, Lies and Handwriting: A Top Expert Reveals the Secrets Hidden in Your Handwriting*, emphasize these evaluative and advising goals of graphological expertise. They even go as far as proclaiming its total credibility: "The truth is, appearances can be deceiving, but handwriting never lies" (Dresbold and Kwalwasser 2006, 17). The authors share the previous claim that "handwriting is really 'brain writing,' and the marks you place on the paper are your 'brain prints'" (Dresbold and Kwalwasser 2006, 17). They also share the conception of handwritten signature as a public self of the signer. While handwriting in general "reveals the way you privately think and feel" (Dresbold, Kwalwasser 2006, 47), the handwritten signature is not private: "when you write your name, you are putting your public self on the page [which] shows how you want to be seen by others, how do you think others see you, and how you feel about yourself and your position in the world" (Dresbold and Kwalwasser 2006, 47).

As the previous examples demonstrate, the discipline of graphology is so certain about accuracy of its knowledge that it understands the results of its examination as naturally appearing. The graphologist believes that she can uncover the hidden secrets of signers' souls. She even believes that she knows the signer's psychological qualities better than the signer herself. As a holder of the accurate mirror of the disciplinary knowledge, the graphologist believes that the signer has no clue about her own psychological qualities, because she plays the discursive role of outsider to psychological knowledge. The expert in graphology does it for her, according to the standardized categories of psychological judgment. Because the graphologist believes the signer is not competent enough to judge herself, the signer cannot refuse graphological examination, which can lead to a change of her post or specialization at work, or even to a juridical sentence. Contrary to the expert's decision, the signer, who remains outside the discourse that judges her, cannot prove her own truth concerning her own psychological qualities and/or the authenticity of her own signature.

Experts in psychological graphology expect the handwritten signature to be a transparent expression of the signer's soul. As they suppose an essential resemblance of qualities, by analyzing a signature's shape they take themselves to be analyzing the signer's soul. Graphology shares these discursive expectations with anthropometry, bertillonage, and eugenics, disciplines that founded standardization of human shapes in the late nineteenth century. Contrary to these authors, I suppose that personal handwriting is neither totally natural nor totally unconscious: partly, it is a result of a conscious strategy to stylize, to perform oneself. What the signer lets us see in her signature is her own pictorial self-construction. The ambition of graphological discourse cannot be reached, because the trace of the signer's physical and psychological presence is unrepeatable. One can repeat only the elements of a style that is born and developed in shared expectation of the eternal return of the same, but that is, in fact, just a variation. Contrary to what graphologists believe, the handwritten signature does not reflect its author's character as a mirror. Rather, handwritten signature covers the signer's nature by her premeditated and stylized construction, which is in a state of permanent transformation. Therefore, I find that it is impossible to define the signer's psychological qualities by means of graphology.

Discourse of Forensic Analysis: The Original Style

Contrary to graphology, forensic analysis of handwriting declares that it does not opt for determining the signer's psychological qualities; it does not compare the analyzed handwriting to the signer's soul or *psyche*. Forensic analysts compare writing samples to determine whether they are written by the same or different authors. Apparently, each analyst treats the problem of handwritten signature as a sign in a different way. Because forensic analysis conceives of writing as authorial work, it keeps its distance from the graphology. In this new discursive light, graphology appears to be a contradictory "pseudo-science"[15] based on empathy, which is not useful for the rigorous needs of forensic handwriting analysis.

The forensic analysis of handwriting deals with the problem of the authenticity of a given signer's handwriting or, more particularly, of a given signer's signature. In the context of expertise, an unauthentic trace of writing means a forged trace, a trace left by means of a fake imitation of previous authentic traces. Imitation is not declared here, because the imitator does not want the trace to appear authentic. The imitator does not wish to be indicated as the author of traces she has left. She wishes her trace to be identified as the authentic trace of some other signer. Thus, a forged signature is an unauthentic trace that is presented as an authentic trace. It is a copy, not of the original, but a copy that—for essential reasons of identification—cannot replace the original. All individual signatures performed manually by the same author are copies that have identical legal value. But even if the signature performed by someone else's hand was similar to the author's specimen signature, or even more similar than all of the individual signatures performed by the author, it would not have the same legal value. Similarity between the individual expressions of author's personal style is not enough; it should be also linked to the authenticity of author's manual traces. However, as Sonja Neef and Jose van Dijck claim,

> the concept of "authenticity" is currently undergoing a substantial overhaul now that computers are becoming the preferred tools for (written) communication. Signatures, for instance, were supposed to be authentic, idiosyncratic signs of selves, intimately tied to the hand that produced them; now that they are gradually replaced by memorized codes and biometrical scans, the former handwritten sign of identification is no longer considered foolproof. (Neef and van Dijck 2006, 8)

The forensic ambition is to distinguish between the authentic and the unauthentic personal signs. What do the world authorities in forensic analysis of handwriting say in their methodological textbooks? Harralson indicates in *Developments in Handwriting and Signature Identification in the Digital Age* that one of the most important principles of forensic analysis of handwriting is the allowed variation of the signer's personal handwriting style. No two (or more) signatures of the same person can be written identically. "If a handwriting expert finds an identical signature to the one that is being questioned, it is an indicator that one may be a copy of the other which may be based on a tracing, a copy, or a scan of one signature that is placed on another document" (Harralson 2013, 4–5). Another forensic principle mentioned by Harralson is that each personal style of handwriting contains a combination of traits, which are unique and recognizable in each signer. Not only is the same signer unable to write two signatures totally identically, but no other signer can write identically to the given signer.

> This principle is also based on the examination of multiple handwriting features as this could not be supported if the examiner relied upon one or two handwriting features. Handwriting is not only unique but its various features are interrelated, creating a complex handwriting formula for each individual signer. The principle that no two handwritings are written exactly alike is

related to the concept that each signer has a natural range of variation. As such, handwriting is pattern based and rather than relying on isolated handwriting features, handwriting experts examine patterns in handwriting . . . Because handwriting is not static and is subject to change over time or due to other variable conditions, handwriting samples written during a comparable time period and under the same conditions applying to the questioned writing material are also necessary. (Harralson 2013, 5)

Finally, according to Harralson, "This naturally leads to the next point involving natural and unnatural handwriting. One of the first steps in a handwriting examination involves the assessment of the handwriting samples under inspection. The examiner needs to evaluate the samples and determine if they possess the characteristics of natural handwriting. Natural handwriting has an unimpeded flow of movement" (Harralson 2013, 6).

This discursive expectation of forensic analysis of handwriting is also confirmed by forensic analysts Caligiuri and Mohammed. As the authors claim in *The Neuroscience of Handwriting*, "Decades of laboratory research in handwriting have given us the tools necessary to elucidate normal and pathological processes underlying handwriting and signature production" (Caligiuri and Mohammed 2012, xiii). At the same time, the authors regret that these principles are still not integrated into the forensic analysis of signature. They try to inform the reader about relevant neuroscientific principles conditioning normal and pathological control of hand and handwriting motor skills. From the viewpoint of my examination of the forensic analysis discourse, it is particularly interesting that they summarize the advances in quantitative approach to *signature authentication*. Caligiuri and Mohammed notice that "while the vast majority of research regarding signatures has focused on static traces, modern technology has enabled researchers to quantify the kinematic features of signatures at the level of an individual pen stroke" (Caligiuri and Mohammed 2012, xiv). Historically, they claim,

> visually detectable features in handwritten signatures formed the basis of evidence supporting whether a questioned signature was genuine, disguised, or forged. . . . Today, research into static features associated with different signing behaviors can be supplemented by dynamic studies where kinematic data are collected from subjects' signing on digitizing tablets. This technique has been used to report on the effects of disguise and

simulation behaviors in terms of pen pressure, stroke formation, and movement duration. (Caligiuri and Mohammed 2012, xiv)

The authors also introduce an abundant overview of *kinematic approaches* to signature that issues from studies of the neuromuscular system, which controls hand movement and allows analysts to measure the speed response in individual pen traction.

Cognitive scientists Gerard P. Van Galen, Ruud G. J. Meulenbroek, and Henk Hylkema deal with similar problematics. In "On the Simultaneous Processing of Words, Letters and Strokes in Handwriting," they concentrate attention on invariants or motor patterns in handwriting: their objective is to trace the time boundaries of processing motoric demands at different levels of the handwriting process. Their strategy "to measure precisely latencies and movement characteristics and to relate these values to the dimensions we used for the construction of the tasks" (Hylkema, Meulenbroek, and Van Galen 1986, 17) is finally revealed as successful. Based on their research, the authors claim that "motor execution in handwriting is done at a fairly constant manner. The standard deviations of strokes for individual subject produced in different contexts are extremely low" (Hylkema, Meulenbroek, and Van Galen 1986, 19).

Besides these physical methods of authentication, I find it important to mention the computer programs using algorithms to verify handwritten signature, which compare samples of signatures according to criteria set beforehand. As Impedovo indicates in "Frontiers in Handwriting Recognition," criteria can include "parameters like global length of the signature, local characteristics, or functions like position, velocity, acceleration or pressure of the tip of the pen during the whole writing process" (Impedovo 1994, 35). Meanwhile, in "Algorithms for Signature Verification," Pirlo writes: "the comparison process in a signature verification system tries to evaluate the authenticity of the test specimen by matching its features against those stored in the reference data-base" (Pirlo 1994, 443). This procedure of verification is not totally reliable; rather, it uncovers the problems with verifying the handwritten signature. As Impedovo puts it,

> in general, the approaches based on functions show greater efficiency, but they are also time-expensive. Moreover, it is still not clear if it is better to use a local approach, generally requiring a binding preprocessing phase, or a global one, which seems to be more sensitive to the variability in signing. In both

cases, the detection of one or more optimal thresholds is still a problem to be solved, that will certainly improve the verification performance of the current systems for signature verification. (Impedovo 1994, 35)

At this point, I would like to mention several terminological gaps and methodological contradictions that pervade the forensic analysis of handwriting. Contrary to the scientifically doubtful graphology, forensic analysis, which became a legitimate scientific practice in the twentieth century, declares that it no longer expects the mirroring effect between the signer's psychological qualities and the pictorial side of her signature. What made this new science of handwriting legitimate? At first glance, the goals proclaimed by forensic analysis seem to be humbler than the goals proclaimed by graphology. To discover the author's personal writing strategy and to distinguish the authentic signatures from the forged ones that can be produced by imitation or by simple mechanical copying of previous signer's signatures, the forensic analysis of handwriting compares the appearance of one signature with appearances of other signatures supposedly done by the same signer. While the psychological discipline of graphology compares the handwritten documents to the soul of their signer, the forensic analysis of handwriting claims that its only goal is to compare handwritten documents to other handwritten documents. Is it really possible to compare some handwritten documents with others without expecting some particular characteristics of their signer's soul? Not only graphology, but also forensic analysis of handwriting expects the supposed signer's soul to be a generator of naturally similar handwritten traces and to be a guarantee that these traces are authentically expressed. Does the only real difference between these two disciplines then lie in the normative setting of their discourses? Are graphological and forensic interpretations of signatures determined by the same metaphysical expectations, while they are determined by different discursive expectations?

In both discourses, it is equally expected that—because of the signer's natural, unique, and recognizable style of handwriting—one of her handwritten signatures can be identified with another. The signer's psychological qualities are reflected naturally and continually in her handwriting expressions and, simultaneously, prove the authenticity of her stylized expressions as her authentic traces. Graphology and forensic analysis of handwriting observe the same traces of the signer's natural style of writing, because both of their knowledges are rooted in the same metaphysical belief that the signer produces and confirms her natural style of handwriting in each of her repeated gestures. To confirm the given signature's authenticity, forensic analysis must reliably recognize the natural style of the given signer's handwriting. But this style cannot be recognized without having recognized the qualities of the signer's soul, which forces the signer to constantly express herself in the same recognizable manner. Thus, forensic analysis of handwriting shares with graphology its own object of examination, which is the signer's soul. Whether they proclaim it or not, both disciplines expect to understand and define the characteristics of the signer's soul, mostly in relation with its natural similarity with the stylized shapes of handwriting and with its authentic expressions in handwriting. The two disciplines differ only in the apparent focus of their analysis and in the emphasis they put on the authenticity of handwritten traces.

My overview of the essential textbooks of both discourses on handwritten signature shows differences in their normative knowledge. Contrary to graphology, which takes the natural shape of the signature for a mirror of the signer's soul, forensic analysis of handwriting compares authentic signature with previous writing expressions of the given signer and situates it in the interval between identity (of mechanical copy) and difference (of manual trace). Experts in forensic analysis expect that signature will allow them to distinguish authentic traces from fake ones. Their ability to recognize the original style of handwriting allows them to recognize forgeries. Forensic analysis of the *interval of similarity* (obtained from comparing traces to other traces) appears to be less naive and more reliable than the effect of psychological mirroring in graphology (obtained from comparing the signer's soul and traces). In this interval of similarity, it is necessary to trace a conventional picture of name that would be sufficiently similar to be recognized (by degree of similarity) as an authentic handwritten signature. In this interval, forensic analysis of handwriting finds the reason for credibility and legitimation of its discourse. Understanding the difference between discursive and metaphysical expectations is important for my further work on the metaphysical beliefs that make it possible to legally communicate by the medium of handwritten signature.

In the following chapters, I focus on handwritten signature to deconstruct the metaphysical expectations of nature, authenticity, and identity that legitimize both the graphological and forensic analysis of handwriting. Deconstruction of these expectations is correlative with the metaphysical goals of Peirce's categories of Firstness, Secondness, and Thirdness. My reading of Derrida helps me to point out three aporias, which are linked to these metaphysical expectations related to the medium of handwritten signature.

Therefore, from now on, I focus exclusively on the manual medium and the metaphysical expectations we have of it. I also explore the metaphysical presuppositions shared by the discursive expectations in graphology and in forensic analysis. In the next chapter, I consider these shared presuppositions of handwritten signature, using the concept of metaphysical expectations.

Chapter III
The Metaphysical Expectations of Handwritten Signature

Let us have a closer look now at the metaphysical dimension of the mediation politics of handwritten signature. Following the positivist description of the two discourses of graphology and forensic analysis in the preceding chapter, I try to deconstruct the triple metaphysical expectation—of nature, of authenticity, and of identity—that these two kinds of expertise of handwritten signature share. By *metaphysical expectations,* I understand the inevitable shared prejudices and presuppositions that allow experts in the mentioned disciplines to understand the handwritten signature as a medium generating a specific meaning.

This negative definition of handwritten signature makes it evident that signature written by hand is an analog medium with several contradictory qualities. In comparison with its electronic counterpart, handwritten signature is a conventional picture of the signer's own civic name, which should be manually repeated by the citizen herself each time she is asked to sign. As such, handwritten signature is considered to be an authentic trace, a visual proof of the signer's both physical and psychological presence at the place and time of signing. Every time a citizen is asked to sign, the legal mediation politics forces her to repeat by her own hand the already performed and conventional shape of writing recorded in her registered specimen signature. Once its graphic form is officially registered, the specimen signature obtains the status of a referential and strictly personal civic sign. Every citizen is required to remember and repeat this original shape of manual writing on every occasion when she signs. It is supposed that without it, her signature would not be recognizable and identifiable.

Thus, identifying the citizen in every new written signature requires an identity of personal style between the picture of the specimen signature and the picture of the newly written signature. Nevertheless, there is an essential double bind that metaphysically forces the signer to do the impossible: to repeat an unrepeatable event, to write again, from memory, the previously registered specimen signature. Let me explain the clash of two contradictory metaphysical expectations that shape the apparently simple conventional act of signing. According to the first metaphysical expectation, it is believed that the signer, caring for her civic identification, will trace the pictorial form of her signature in an identical way. And yet this identical way is not allowed to be mechanically exact: handwritten signature is not a mechanical copy or stamp. According to the second metaphysical expectation, it is believed that no signer can write two signatures by hand that have exactly the same shape. Having two exactly formally identical signatures would—ironically—mean that one of them is forged: it would identify not the authentic signer, but the criminal, unauthentic one. The result is an aporia: every signer is required to perform manually a trace that is simultaneously occasional, authentic, and thus unrepeatable, and natural, constant, and thus repeatable.

This contradictory situation is complicated by the fact that handwritten signature has no legally mandatory definition. As Delphine Majdanski puts it in *La signature et les mentions manuscrites dans les contrats*, "this absence of any definition can be explained, on the one hand, by the fact that signature appears as a concept being able to have several forms. On the other hand, and mostly, because it connotates the concept, which belongs to collective unconscious that the majority of people experiences and does not reflect" (Majdanski 2000, 43). This legal explanation does not clarify why legislators base their legal proofs on collective unconsciousness, which has contents that cannot be defined. Can we rely on such proofs, especially in such precarious cases as the identification of a signer when important documents are suspected to have been forged? What do we expect of these existential remains? Why do we need them to be both natural and authentic?

To answer these questions, I try to determine the metaphysical expectation of handwritten signature, which organizes the legal mediation politics of manual writing. I propose an innovative reconsideration of the metaphysical dimension of psychological graphology and forensic analysis of handwriting, which is founded on the scientific belief in the ability of a signature to identify the signer, if it is grasped as a natural and authentic sign. I suppose that this belief goes across various areas of expertise, from the forensic analysis of handwriting, which is considered to be scientifically legitimate nowadays, to the psychological discipline of graphology, which is now considered to be pseudo-scientific.

Concerning the metaphysical expectation of authenticity, it is important to emphasize that a handwritten signature is not a mechanical imprint or stamp. Contrary to a stamp, which can mechanically reproduce the given picture by generating its imprints, a handwritten signature is a single manual imitation of the remembered signature specimen. This is why a handwritten signature is usually added to the mechanical imprint of a stamp. As Sonja Neef and José van Dijck indicate, this is the reason that the handwritten signature is supposed to dispose the metaphysically legitimated force of proof that a mechanically imprinted picture lacks:

> handwriting is traditionally regarded as an autograph, as an un-exchangeable, unique and authentic "signature" that claims to guarantee the presence of an individual signer during a historically unique moment of writing. This claim for authenticity distinguishes handwriting from its cultural opposite, mechanical writing, in the sense of print or typed writing. After all, the cultural significance of mechanical writing resides in its capacity to be iterated and reproduced. The reproduction of authentic handwriting, on the other hand, risks being considered a forgery. (Neef and van Dijck 2006, 9)

Also, Harralson shows that the legal term forgery is usually used in relation with the effort to identify the author of a given piece of handwriting, while it refers "not only to the imitation of a handwriting or signature but also to the intent on the part of the forger to defraud" (Harralson 2013, 6–7).

Forensic expert Stina Teilmann-Lock mentions in *The Object of Copyright* that the word "copy" traditionally implies a relation of strict causality. "A copy repeats its object with accuracy. But it works according to a serial principle: every new copy can potentially function as a substitution of its source and could therefore take its place as the 'original'" (Teilmann-Lock 2016, 117). This traditional understanding of the copy is the opposite of Benjamin's conception of aura as uniqueness and authenticity of the work of art, which cannot have the same value as any mechanically produced copy. As Teilmann-Lock mentioned, the modern determination of authorial work and its legal copyright made it necessary to distinguish authentic originals from forged copies:

> the exercise of defining the modern object of protection, the original work, was closely tied to the cultural context of the philosophical debate over authenticity in art, literature, and philosophy; as Walter Benjamin realized, authenticity confers an aura. The new polarity between authenticity and inauthenticity provided a conceptual framework within which copyright law could establish a distinction between an "authentic" original work and an "inauthentic" copy. (Teilmann-Lock 2016, 121)

Following Teilmann-Lock, I suppose that this unmechanical authenticity of handwritten signature can be understood in the sense of Benjamin's aura of manual work. Contrary to manual copy, which is a remain of the signer's life, mechanical reproduction repeatedly reaches mimetic precision, but loses the aura of authentic occurrence.[1] Because manual work produces a *new work* every time, copies of artworks and handwritten signatures done by someone other than the declared signer can be recognized as forgeries. In contrast to manual reproduction, it is impossible to distinguish between the original work and the forgery in mechanical reproduction: all mechanical copies are identical. Benjamin's belief in authentic traces of life is also emphasized by McFarland, who notices the importance of mourning in his work: "What is mourned and remembered by loyal survivors Benjamin calls the person" (McFarland 2013, 58). The person's authentic signature remains even after the living body dies and "disperses into anonymous history as nature" (McFarland 2013, 58).

Understood in this Benjaminian vital sense, the vital aura of the handwritten signature expresses a paradoxical "present distance" of its signer, its unrepeatable and unreplaceable here and now, which is usually accompanied by information about the place and date of the act of signing. As Rodolphe Gasché notices in *Of Minimal Things*, "the auratic is thus linked to the being present as object, or thing, of the distance. It is a function of this materialization of distance, its being effective in the shape of the present object" (Gasché 1999, 89). This referring to the distant origin of sign, although permanently present in its sign, makes of Benjamin's aura a "phenomenon of natural order."[2]

This could explain the metaphysical belief in handwritten signature as natural and authentic remains of the signer's past presence. Because signature is born through the physical contact between the writing instrument held by the signer's own hand and the document to be signed, scientists believe that this unique picture of a name enables us to believe in the real presence of the given signer in a given place and time of signing. In this respect, the metaphysical force of the signature can be understood as a symptom of aura, which leads our thinking to the question of authenticity and irreplaceability of the signer's natural presence. This understanding of handwriting belongs to the tradition of persuasion by authenticity that is at work in various disciplines, mostly in criminology and judicature, but also in history and theory of arts, which deal with the recognition of artistic styles and authentic works.

Nevertheless, contrary to Benjamin, who puts great emphasis on social and cultural aspects of the decay of aura in the conditions of mass culture, the goal of my work is not to criticize the danger of ideological misuse of automatization, which generates the cultural industry. But, as I suppose, his idea on the decay of aura as standardization of the unique caused by mechanical reproducibility remains valid for each manual work, including signature. Although it is a sign, which should be recognized and repeated in order to communicate, its reproduction must be strictly manual, because the handwritten signature as a sign of identification is not mechanically reproducible.

In order to follow Benjamin, and to solve the problem of interpretation of the handwritten signature as natural, authentic remains of the signer's presence attesting to the signer's civic identity, we need to deconstruct our metaphysical expectations. As I demonstrate in the next section of this chapter, such a deconstruction will help us to understand our inevitable prejudices that enable every interpretation based on a legitimate belief in knowledge. This double bind of deconstruction enables us to see the handwritten signature as a sign of identification.

Contrary to semiotics, which traditionally offers a positivist conception of the sign as an accurate representation of the being, deconstruction gives the term representation a meaning that is aporetic, supplementary, and never totally accurate to the represented being. In his subversive reading of the most referential texts of Western philosophy, Derrida points out that things are not semantically transparent: their meaning is neither perpetually present, nor given naturally or immediately, but always by a certain mediation or representation, by means of a substitute, by the deferral of meaning generated by reading. To deconstruct the metaphysically violent determination of semiotics, Derrida proposes his concept of trace, which is self-effacing and haunting, without any traceable origin. As Legrand puts it, Derridean trace is

> ephemeral, something always in the process of disappearing into the absorbing whole: each trace is dissolved in the whole, as the trace in the sand leaves but sand. Likewise, the traces that constitute the law constantly alter themselves as traces to become the law that they are constituting: they are never "present" in the sense in which one colloquially understands 'presence' . . . It is present, but not as the self-same history or ideology that was: it is present as a "remainder effect." (Legrand 2009, xxiii)

In Western (or traditionally European) metaphysics, as Derrida understands it, the concept of representation is a typical construction of meaning, which can be deconstructed. As he puts it in *Learning to Live Finally*, "what I call 'deconstruction,' even when it is directed toward something from Europe, is European; it is a product of Europe, a relation of Europe to itself as an experience of radical alterity" (Derrida 2007a, 44–45). By systematically deferring the inherited way of speaking and reasoning, Derrida prevents the meaning being presented as totally evident, entirely natural, or fully present. In this respect, his deconstruction is a philosophical attempt to dismantle the metaphysical construction of total presence of meaning. And yet his philosophical strategy questions metaphysics in its basic operations without having recourse to its devastating critique. Because Derrida is aware that each critique of metaphysics uses metaphysical concepts, which keeps the movement of thinking in a vicious circle, he does not seek to liberate himself from metaphysics: as soon as he uncovers the metaphysical schemas of thinking in analyzed texts, he lets them go on as uncovered. This way, Derrida uses the metaphysical principles that pervade and organize every philosophical discourse to introduce mutual connections between the apparently incommensurable philosophical projects of his chosen thinkers.

Derrida is well-known for his philosophical explanation of infinite deferral of meaning, which can be understood as a permanent semantic *drift* in a continuous series of representations of representations. In the situation of infinite series of deferred representations, the meaning of individual representation is neither present nor absent. Therefore, Derrida speaks of the origin of their meaning neither as of existing nor as of non-existing, but as of deferred. What is original is actually the deferral: there is no other meaning than deferred. If we accept supplementarity as a cultural and communicational inevitability and propose to systematically trace the elusive meaning in infinite series of representations of representations, *deferral*, he calls for this very philosophical vigilance and ethical mobilization in relation to "totalitarian" expressions of the metaphysics inside the philosophy itself.

To better understand this surprising claim, I examine Derrida's own conception of meaning. By means of his strategic reading of other philosophers, I show the thinking operations that deconstruction seeks. When Derrida reads other philosophers, he systematically focuses on their remaining in the *metaphysics of presence* without reflecting on their own position and the philosophical consequences it has. Derrida himself choses another position and another project. By deferring meaning, he introduces a double gesture of interpretation, which allows him to balance the metaphysical certainty of total presence of meaning and the metaphysical certainty of total absence of meaning. The movement of deferral brings him to a semantically unstable marginal zone of Western metaphysics, to the very margins of the philosophical zone of meaning.

Jacques Derrida opens the text to instability of linguistic meanings: he builds a new tactic to challenge the violence of Western metaphysics that determines the total presence or total absence of meanings in the text. In Derrida's deconstruction, the text contains every meaning: it is tractable, telescopic, and porous. There is nothing outside the text: everything is in the text, which prolongs itself through other texts by means of its various supplements. All of the text's meanings are contained in the context, which is unlimited; the intertextual meaning drifts in an infinite context.[3]

Derrida conceives of the text simultaneously as a place of semantic productivity and as a movement of representation, which signifies itself. Because of these qualities, text in deconstruction acts against the "referential delusion" of language, which is the way Western metaphysics traditionally governs the reading of texts. This understanding of the text produces an unstable web of meanings, where every element is constituted on the basis of traces of other elements. Such a text is not semantically enclosed in itself, because it is produced continuously, by transformation of other text: there is nothing outside text that would not already be a text. The quest for the proper meaning of text is impossible, as deconstruction reveals: text is readable because there is a permanent movement of sense in it that continuously leaves traces.

Derrida tries to grasp this mobility or happening of sense by means of his strategy of dispersion or interspersion of a text's meaning, which he proposes to call *dissemination*. Dissemination questions the idea that a text has an original core organizing its meaning according to a chosen idea, thematic unity, or truth, because the text always lacks something. Text is principally unfinished: it is a place of germinal meaning. In order to complete the text, we add various supplements to it, which helps us to make its meaning more precise and to compensate for its partial presence, which is never totally sufficient. Derrida warns that supplement is excessive: it overcomes the text by adding itself to it and by prolonging it with other texts. Because a supplement can be joined to every text, and because every text is a result of a series of supplementary prolonging with other texts, definitive competition of a textual meaning is indefinitely deferred.

By his theoretical strategy, Derrida aims to subvert the apparently natural hierarchical relation of binary oppositions, which was established in philosophy as metaphysical evidence. For instance, Derrida finds the metaphysical of voice's natural superordination over writing problematic: the metaphysics forces philosophers to privilege voice as the primary source of meaning and to marginalize writing as a mere semantic derivation of the voice's meaning. As Derrida puts it in *Of Grammatology*, "In linguistics as well as in metaphysics, phonologism is undoubtedly the exclusion or abasement of writing" (Derrida 1997, 102).

Ferdinand de Saussure, one such thinker, hierarchically superordinates the voice over the writing in his *Course in General Linguistics*. In the sixth chapter, dealing with the representation of language by writing, de Saussure determines the relation between spoken language and writing in the following critical way:

> Language and writing are two distinct systems of signs; the second exists for the sole purpose of representing the first. The linguistic object is not both the written and the spoken forms of words; the spoken forms alone constitute the object. But the spoken word is so intimately bound to its written image that the latter manages to usurp the main role. People attach even more importance to the written image of a vocal sign than to the sign itself. (de Saussure 2011, 23–24)

Derrida emphasizes that, in de Saussure's conception, writing is derived from the spoken language, depends on it, and serves only to represent it. In his reading, this aspect of de Saussure's linguistics confirms his alliance with the history of Western metaphysical thinking, which systematically marginalized writing.

Derrida's far-reaching conclusions have met with a critical reaction by Russel Daylight, who writes in *What if Derrida Was Wrong about Saussure?*:

> What we know about Saussure is that he *does* treat writing as external to linguistics proper, and that writing is "empty" in the sense that it does not form part of the double articulation of sound-pattern and sense. Written signs *follow* an original production of linguistic semiology, and do not add anything to meaning. At least, if they *do* add something to a linguistic sign, they do so as part of language-in-its-totality, not as an element of the language-as-a-system. (Daylight 2012, 77)

However, continues Daylight, "the remainder of Derrida's assertions here are more contentious: that Saussure determines 'non-intuition' as a crisis of truth, that writing obscures the clear evidence of the sense. What drives Derrida's approach to the division between speech and writing, and the privilege accorded to the former, is the apparently 'natural' relationship between sense and sound that Saussure takes for granted in the *Course*" (Daylight 2012, 77). Daylight supposes that Derrida does not read de Saussure correctly, because de Saussure himself does not claim what Derrida points out when he rethinks the consequences of de Saussure's conception of writing. However, as I wish to emphasize, the problem of their misunderstanding does not consist in the correctness of one's reading of de Saussure, but in the fact that Derrida, from the beginning, is not discussing the conception of writing that both de Saussure and Daylight speak about. While Derrida deals with the problem of *arche-writing*, which conditions both the voice (*phonê*) and the phonetic writing derived from it, de Saussure (and Daylight) speak only about phonetic writing derived from voice (*phonê*). Derrida regrets that Saussure did not consider how meaning is formed at the stage before it was leveled off and conventionally established in commonly shared linguistic meanings. Therefore, Derrida asks him: how did the concept—the Saussurean mental image—get into people's minds? How is it possible that an immaterial idea became collectively shared? For those who do not believe in telepathy, this raises an elementary question: how was the language constructed, from what metaphysical, transcendental, prelinguistic matter? Derrida answers: the voice (*phonê*) was produced from arche-writing. Nevertheless, the arche-writing Derrida speaks about is not the mere phonetic writing that de Saussure speaks about. Derrida is not interested in phonetic writing, which was derived from the shared voice, its sound units. As Daylight misses this conceptual drift, his critique misses Derrida's effort to thematize a new philosophical problem, which emerges from his own strategic reading of de Saussure. Derrida's interest in linguistics consists in the parallel he sees between the linguistic law and the juridical law: both become valid by declaration, but the origin of both is mystical. This mysticism of unknown origin covers the construction and shifts attention to what legalizes their validity—the transcendental idea of communication in the case of national language and the transcendental idea of justice in the case of civic rights.

But de Saussure was not alone in conceiving of writing as a mere derivation from voice. According to Derrida, this metaphysical humiliation of writing is characteristic for such thinkers as Jean-Jacques Rousseau or Claude Lévi-Strauss. Both multiply contradictions inside their own conceptions, because they do not work with the possibility of sharing *arche-linguistic* meaning. When Derrida claims that the writing semantically precedes the voice, he turns this traditional hierarchy of voice and writing upside-down.

Nevertheless, Derrida's definition of writing differs from the traditional conception. Derrida parasitically keeps the old form but fills it with new content: it is not the conventionally fixed phonetical inscription of words that children learn at primary school that makes them literate. Derrida's deconstructed writing can be understood as arche-writing that precedes not only the conventional phonetical inscription of spoken words, but also the spoken words themselves—*arche-writing* is the condition of possibility of any empirical production of traces. It is particularly in this sense that Derrida can say that no culture exists without writing. As he puts it in *Of Grammatology,*

> if writing is no longer understood in the narrow sense of linear and phonetic notation, it should be possible to say that all societies capable of producing, that is to say of obliterating, their proper names, and of bringing classificatory difference into play, practice writing in general. No reality or concept would therefore correspond to the expression "society without writing." This expression is dependent on ethnocentric oneirism, upon the vulgar, that is to say ethnocentric, misconception of writing. (Derrida 1997, 109)

As Derrida explains in "Table ronde sur la traduction," the writing is exposed to the reading, to the voice, that comes to interpret it, to explain its meaning. Interpretation of a text is just a production of vocal supplements of writing that extend the text toward other texts and move its meaning elsewhere. In this respect, every explanation is also a translation of the text's meaning generating a new supplementary text: "Writing is read, and 'in the last analysis' does not give rise to a hermeneutic deciphering, to the decoding of a meaning or truth" (Derrida 1982d, 329). Thus, contrary to the metaphysical demands of total presence of meaning, the meaning of each text is deferred, postponed, and transformed. In Derrida, these demands are to be deconstructed: one does not have to deal with a sign, but with a trace of meaning, which dismantles the apparently solid and united meaning of the text into a fragmentary representation of representation. As Borradori puts it, when Derrida claims that the meaning of the text is disseminated, he says that identity is not a homogeneous and self-enclosed totality: "a given identity may not be perfectly homogeneous because it includes traces of what it explicitly excludes. Deconstruction searches for these traces and uses them to give voice to that which does not fit the dominant set of inclusions and exclusions. Deconstructive interventions de-totalize self-enclosed totalities by placing them face to face with their internal differentiation" (Borradori 2003, 147).

Derrida's objections relate to the central figures of structuralism. But he is not alone in taking a critical stance against this semiotic movement. What are the reasons for poststructuralist critique of structuralism? Although they specialize in different fields, poststructuralists share a critical attitude toward structuralism, for several reasons. First, they find that structuralism is a static semiotic system with fixed relations that do not allow any creative treatment of the problem of interpretation. Second, in their opinion, structuralism allows a relational change only at the price of transformation and possible breakdown of the whole system, because every relational change is complex and fatal for the structuralist system of signs. Third, because structuralism works only with arbitrarily determined signs, there is no represented object involved in structuralist semiosis. Because there is no ontological standpoint, no phenomenology of the observed object is possible inside structuralism. Therefore, poststructuralists see structuralism as based on panlingualization of semiotic thinking: structuralist signs do not refer to any existence outside the conventional system of language. Finally, poststructuralists denounce the absence of the pragmatic approach in structuralism: they try to accentuate its role in every creative interpretation and to free the signifier from its hierarchical relational fixation to the signified.

Because of poststructuralist thinkers, during the 1970s and 1980s Charles Senders Peirce's texts became an attractive, frequent, and influential reading. Poststructuralist rediscovery of Peirce's semiotics seemed to offer a possible cure for the totalitarian "disease" of structuralism. Trying to find a way out of "dying" structuralism, the poststructuralists raised Peirce to the status of a main source of their philosophical inspiration. They interpreted Peirce's texts in various ways to fit it in the poststructuralist context. The divergent interpretations of Peirce's texts presented by leading philosophical figures of poststructuralism in the 1970s and 1980s, such as Jacques Derrida, Gilles Deleuze, and Umberto Eco, have one common point: they all want Peirce to help them treat the metaphysical violence "diagnosed" as structuralism. But is Peirce's metaphysics really able to do this?

In the next few pages, I seek to show that it is not. Curiously, Peirce became a poststructuralist hero because of a collective interpretational misunderstanding. As I showed in "Hopes of Derrida's Reading? On Emergence of Peirce's Texts in the Poststructuralist Context" (Fišerová 2017), Peirce's work was rediscovered by French poststructuralists in the late 1960s. Although every poststructuralist proposes an alternative reading, they share several reasons for turning to Peirce. First, these semioticians suppose that the meaning of a sign can be seen as motivated by its object. More precisely, they consider that the real existence of an object forces us to rethink its qualities and effects, which is a kind of metaphysical thought refused by structuralism. Second, they find that temporality is an important component of the semiotics, which was completely omitted by structuralism. Third, poststructuralists turn from structuralism to ontology and phenomenology by accepting the importance accorded to our perception and description of perceived phenomena. Thus, they postulate an open, transitive, instable network of meanings. Finally, they prefer discovering pragmatic and performative aspects of communication to studying fixed systemic relations of meanings.

Peirce himself did not have these ambitions. He founded his ambitious semiotics of scientifically objective idealism[4] on a triple metaphysical belief: "The essence of belief is the establishment of a habit, and different beliefs are distinguished by different modes of action to which they give rise" (Peirce 1955, 29). Peirce believed that science was capable of discovering metaphysical principles organizing the perceivable reality. For Peirce, belief "involves the establishment in our nature of a rule of action, or, say for short, a habit," which helps to appease "the irritation of doubt" (Peirce 1955, 28). Peirce himself proposed basing philosophical thinking on positive ontological knowledge of the natural sciences, even governed by the laws of logic. Like many nineteenth-century scientists, Peirce was not afraid of metaphysical violence, the foundation of this belief in a kind of knowledge that identifies ontological and logical explanations of reality. Peirce's definition of philosophy as a logical science makes him unable to understand the art, which is one of the goals of poststructuralism. Poststructuralists are aware of these difficulties in the structuralist attempt to semantically grasp the nature of the world. Why are they not so aware in Peirce's case? Why did not they pay enough attention to his texts?

It is possible to find several answers to this question in the larger context of poststructuralist work. First, I would like to mention the problem of the hoax of Peircean "unlimited semiosis"—poststructuralist thinkers believe that this "new" theoretical orientation allows them to free the meaning for pragmatic and creative issues and to open up the process of semiosis, which has been fatally limited by structuralism. But in Peirce, there is no such thing as freedom in *semiosis*: it is limited by both the Immediate Object (itself determined by the Dynamic Object) and by the epistemological setting of its interpretant.

Second, there is the ontological problem of the object and its recognition. The solution proposed by poststructuralism consists in criticizing Western metaphysics for its construction of totalitarian ontotheology. In poststructuralism, representation and identity are scientifically constructed. But in Peirce, all the reals are already signs: Peirce is realist in this sense. We think only in signs, which are reals for us: Immediate Object is naturally determined by Dynamic Object; there is no social construction of real thing involved in Peirce.

Third, it is necessary to mention the epistemological problem of pertinent comprehension: the right understanding of a thing is compatible with it, and both versions are supposed to be identical. Such a reading is possible in Peirce, whose unfailing logic dominates the fallibilism of empirical science, which cannot avoid phaneroscopy of the Immediate Object. Poststructuralism, in contrast, systematically introduces subversion into the relations of identity: in poststructuralism, logic is considered as a supreme way of thinking only as a supreme act of violence, because there is no such activity as an always truthful reading.

Compared to Derrida's vigilant work with metaphysical concepts, Peirce's philosophical ambitions are less vigilant regarding the totalitarian side of metaphysics: he understands logical constructions as hierarchically superior to experience. In my opinion, this is the main reason why Peirce remains so ethnocentric: he even takes Western metaphysics for an anthropological universal. Such an affirmative law of logic gives birth to political violence, which was described by Derrida as a founding ethical aporia of the law.

In his "Force of Law," Derrida pointed out that the politics of meaning, which is the basis of every law, does not allow us to negotiate the meaning: it forces us to accept its constructions without any polemics. Fighting for the establishment of justice as law can happen only by means of the violence of metaphysics, which generates the law as order.[5] But this violence, proper to the law, is strange for justice. Derrida is aware that every fight for justice, which is necessarily situated out of reach of the law, is violent:[6] one violence fights another violence, the one that enforces the currently valid law. A fighter for justice does not understand her fight as violent, when she—because of the act of *founding violence*—legalizes her own law that will be again enforced by violence. Justice inevitably disappears in new legal practices and remains beyond their limit. The movement of supplementation causes Derrida's justice to be a revenant coming from the limit zone of the law. As a semantic and ethical *specter*, justice will never be totally present; it is always to come. The specter can never be made totally present without letting it vanish in its legitimate—total—presence. The result of any fight for justice is always establishing a new law, not justice. In the process of legalization, the justice inevitably vanishes. It is not by chance that, in both graphology and forensic analysis, the founding violence of specimen signature is also hushed up.

Finally, it seems that Peirce is not the best helper in the poststructuralist fight with semantic totalities. Peirce's "naive" belief in logical "scholastic realism"[7] even has potential for ideological abuse. Derrida, well known for his deconstruction of the metaphysical promise of justice, would never have agreed with Peirce's modernist opinions on the role of nation and justice. As Philip P. Wiener writes in his introduction to Peirce's *Selected Papers*, Peirce defends a form of scholastic realism in which general principles, laws, universal qualities, and relations are imbedded in individual realities. Therefore, in Peirce, "A nation or people that failed to see that truth and justice were living realities, as objectively real as the hardness of diamonds or laws of the physical world was doomed to live in confusion" (Wiener 1966, xvi). Peirce's nationalist and moralist conception of justice is incompatible with Derrida's ethically careful and vigilant formulation of the metaphysical aporia of justice.

So what is the proper reading of Peirce? Does it exist? Most of Peirce's texts were published posthumously, based on transcription of his handwritten notes. If one admits that transcription is the first interpretation of edited texts, which both legitimates and defers their original meaning, no reader can reach a totally or universally accurate reading. It is an aporetic specter, which haunts all rigorous reader wishing to get immediately into the Peirce's mind by means of their own readings of his texts.

This methodological problem might be seen as an example of Peirce's fallibilism and as an occasion for abductive testing of a reader's hypothesis, which could unfold the reader's inattention. Such a reading could be condemned for logical reasons as absence of total order in the reader's activity. But such a reading could be welcomed—for other, anti-totalitarian reasons—as a fruitful manifestation of the reader's creativity. The second option shaped poststructuralist readings—and systematic transformations—of Peirce's texts. Thus, paradoxically, Peirce became a specter of poststructuralism that repeatedly reappeared to announce the poststructuralist project of metaphysically nonviolent philosophical thinking. More precisely, in their creative enthusiastic reading, poststructuralists made Peirce reappear and announce it: he became a poststructuralist hero via this willful collective misunderstanding.

In the next section, I try to do what Derrida did not: deconstruct Peirce's three metaphysical categories—Firstness, Secondness, and Thirdness. These categories generate three metaphysical expectations that both of the discourses on handwritten signature have in common: first, expectation of the signer's natural qualities expressed in the signature; second, expectation of signer's authentic presence imprinted in the signature; third, expectation of legitimate identity between the signer and the signature. Handwritten signature can be positively determined in a triple way: first, as a shape of writing (similarity), second, as a trace of writing (authenticity), third, as a style of writing (repetition). This triple metaphysical expectation of handwritten signature—corresponding to the three categories—can be deconstructed. All three mentioned metaphysical expectations, understood as common prejudices that structure the two discourses of handwritten signature, legitimize both graphology and forensic analysis. My further reading of Derrida's work helps me to question the prejudices of natural resemblance, authentic tracing, and identical repetition that pervade these discourses.

"Natural" Resemblance

The first metaphysical expectation of handwritten signature is *confirmation of natural qualities*: a signature is a handmade picture of the signer's civic name, which is expected to naturally express the signer's soul. Because this expression is understood as naturally similar to the essential personal qualities of the signer, handwritten signature is expected to be able to legally replace the signer's physical presence. Nevertheless, who can reliably recognize someone's essential personal qualities in a performed trace? Is not handwritten signature haunted by a quasi-presence of the signer's natural qualities?

In my own analysis of metaphysical expectation of natural mirroring between the signer's psychological qualities and her handwritten signature's pictorial qualities, I follow Avital Ronell, who, in *American Philo*, proposed to analyze "scientific persecutions" and to "localize the screams of specters in the very history of science" (Ronell 2006, 178). As she claims,

> this method is not really strange to philosophy, which silently listens to and refuses to believe in positive stories, which are divested of parasitical noises coming from underground chains of History. Every technical era calls its specters, communicates urgently, behind the limits of pure empiricism. Every time I write, I listen to, I answer one specter, which is enclosed in its solitude and has not been heard yet. (Ronell 2006, 178)

Such a specter is the personal style of handwriting, which is expected to shape the graphic form of every individual handwritten signature. The problem is that the style of writing disappears in mechanical reproduction. The style exists only in constant variations of imperfect manual imitation of her own previous traces. The handwritten signature is expected to allow the signer to repeatedly manually express her psychological nature in her characteristic graphic gesture.

Derrida's understanding of signatures can be related to his understanding of portraits. In deconstruction, there is no technology of inscription, no archive without construction of inscription. Technology of inscription transcribes, translates, rhetorically transforms someone's memory of the event of writing into its memorable and archivable object, its material representation. Without it, remembering would have lost every support. But it is a "mere" support: in the spectator's gaze, technology of recording produces *revenants*, which return displaced fragments of perceptions to the memory, and *arrivants*, which promise, but do not satisfy, the memory's expectation. The effect of both is a result of fragmentary representation, or incomplete attempt to make present again what is no longer here. As Derrida puts it in *Trace et archive, image et art*, every portrait generates *différance*: because the painter sees the person to depict each time differently, there is no "truthful portrait" (Derrida 2014, 39). Because a painting cannot expose the essence of what it depicts, it gains its own value when it stops trying to equate to the depicted object. If a picture accepts its *différance*—visible, but ungraspable, unsayable difference regarding what its depicts—it "gets rid of what it is supposed to represent, of its referent" (Derrida 2014, 37). Such a deconstructed portrait "represents nothing but itself, presents itself" (Derrida 2014, 38).

In this respect, it is worth considering Derrida's reading of Jean-Luc Nancy, and Nancy's own deconstructed ontology. In *Being Singular Plural*, Nancy proposes a curious reflection of "Being singular plural: in a single stroke, without punctuation, without a mark of equivalence, implication, or sequence. A single, continuous-discontinuous mark tracing out the entirety of the ontological domain, being-with-itself designated as the 'with' of Being, of the singular and plural, and dealing a blow to ontology—not only another signification but also another syntax" (Nancy 2000, 37). Nancy's being-with or co-being has a common essence, a "coessence" that "puts essence itself in the hyphenation—'being-singular-plural'—which is a mark of union and also a mark of division, a mark of sharing that effaces itself, leaving each term to its isolation *and* being-with-the-others" (Nancy 2000, 37).

Their common topic is an interval between total loss and total conservation of past being, which cannot be sufficiently supplemented by the picture, but which is partly kept in the picture. Derrida agrees with Nancy because of his systematic "vigilance" toward metaphysical violence and his mistrust in technological metonymy, which rhetorically promises physical contact, but which provides it only in an imaginary way. According to Derrida, the same way one cannot directly touch fire, one cannot touch the soul. The soul, or *Psyché*, cannot be touched. As he writes in *On Touching—Jean-Luc Nancy*, thinkers can only gather around the soul, gather their knowledge around her: "They are there subject to her. They now hold onto her subject. They hold a session, a council, a conference on the subject of her. Just as they take up the places around this locus where nothing takes place but place, that is, extension, one can also sense that they take the place of—but of whom? Of what? What does this metonymy announce? For whom and for what is it in mourning, if every metonymy remains a sign of mourning?" (Derrida 2005c, 17). If one links Derrida's own response—that "Metonymies are in mourning, at least, for a proper sense or name" (Derrida 2005c, 17)—to handwritten signature, one should say that handwriting is a technology of production of authentically stylized traces that recalls the signer's style; it provokes mourning of loss of the whole, which is not fragmented. As Derrida writes in "The Double Session," every medium is the *hymen* (Derrida 1981c, 220)—its materiality dooms the interpreter to restraint, to suspend the desire to penetrate further. In his view, the interpreter's undecidability is due to this impossibility of grasping the meaning of the represented object: it is the "between, whether it names fusion of separation, that thus carries all the force of the operation" (Derrida 1981c, 220). Signature does the same: in a fetishistic way it suspends the "hungry eyes" and forces them to turn away. Its austerity does not provide more than a fragmentary representation, which becomes total only metonymically.

As a legitimate representation of the event of writing, handwritten signature is tricky also by its provoking of a double metaphysical expectation. One is a hopeful promise of a total representation and *recognition of the lost event*; the other is a hopeless understanding of the *loss of event, which cannot be recognized* in its representation.

In "Artifactualities," Derrida mentions that the first expectation can be grasped by his term of the *arrivant*, the unexpected and unexpectable event, the reminder of "the unanticipatability of the future" (Derrida 2002, 21). I propose to call this a metonymic *ruin:* it is Nancy's melancholic impossibility to recognize his mother in her portrait, which is given by gaps in the picture,[8] its inability to make entirely present again what is no more here. As Derrida puts it, the event cannot be reduced to the fact that something happens: "The *arrivant* must be absolutely other, an other that I expect not to be expecting, that I'm not waiting for, whose expectation is made of nonexpectation, an expectation without what in philosophy is called a horizon of expectation, when a certain knowledge still anticipates and amortizes in advance. If I am sure that this is going to be an event, this will not be an event" (Derrida 2002, 13).

The second expectation could be grasped by Derrida's term, revenant. I propose to call this a metonymic *relic*. As Derrida puts it, technologies of recording and reproducing help the spread of spectrality; modern technological rationality does not stop it; on the contrary, technology amplifies it: "The revenant is not confined to the culture of the manor house or to the spiritualism and fantastic literature from the last century. Every culture has its phantoms and the spectrality that is conditioned by its technology" (Derrida 2010b, 39). According to Derrida, manual writing is not a pre-technological craft: it is already a technology of writing. Thus, when we write by hand, we are not in the time before technology; there is already instrumentality and iterability in our movements.

The practice of manual signing is legitimized by the expectation not only of a transparent signer's soul, but also of an eternal return of the same verbal content (an officially attributed and registered word, which is the signer's civic name[9]) in a recognizable pictorial form (as similar as possible to specimen signature, the originally written and officially registered pictorial form of handwritten signature). In this respect, the legibility of the signer's handwriting is irrelevant: it is unimportant whether the individual letters of the signature are clearly recognizable and legible. The concern is with not the name itself, but its personally stylized *picture of the name*. Put otherwise, illegibility of the manually written letters does not disallow recognizing someone's signature, because the letters are used here as pictorial material. The signer composes a formally recognizable picture of her civic name. What is to be recognized here is the singular, inventive way of shaping the letters. The signer should be recognized by her characteristic style of writing, which shapes her signature.

From a legal point of view, every handwritten signature has only one conventional meaning: the picture of the name means the word of the name. Signature links the author's civic name with her stylized plastic abstraction, supposed to be repeatable" by author's own hand, into a singular legitimate meaning. The first metaphysical expectation of handwritten signature—that the signature makes it possible to recognize the signer's psychological qualities—issues from the shared presupposition that the signer can only sign naturally. The metaphysical expectation of similarity as a picture (Peirce's icon[10]) of the signer's spiritual qualities in her specimen signature, and in each her further handwritten signature, opens the door to deconstruction of signature as a copula or technology of junction, based on the *aporetic metaphor of recognizable spiritual nature*. Deconstruction of the metaphysical expectation of natural resemblance warns that although a handwritten signature is supposed to have similar natural qualities to its author, to recognize the signer by their signature is a metaphysical demand of law that is impossible to satisfy in life.

"Authentic" Tracing

The second metaphysical expectation of handwritten signature is *confirmation of authenticity*: signature is a trace of authentic physical contact between a document to be signed and the signer's writing instrument held by her own hand. Handwritten signature is considered to be able to produce and maintain the original traces of the signer's presence in the moment and at the place of signing. That is why signed contracts and letters are usually accompanied by the date and place when and where the signature was done. That is also why fans worship their beloved celebrities' autographs as relics. Is this expectation not more irrational than rational? Is it not close to belief in the spectral life of relics, in an imaginary connection with something absent or directly unreachable?

My own analysis of the metaphysical expectation of the authentic traces of the signer's presence in her handwritten signature is inspired by Derrida's reflection about the surprising experience of the specter. The technology of manual work calls for mourning the loss of touch and fetishization of its remains. Such a medium rhetorically survives the touch. But this survival is only rhetorical: it is impossible to touch the signer's presence, just as it is impossible to touch a ghost that is both present and absent. Personal style expressed in signature disappears and reappears elsewhere. The possibility of perceptual interval guarantees the historical experience and collective memory in general. From this metonymic point of view, every signature can be understood as a specter, or technologically produced remains of the perceivable world. In "Artifactuality, Homohegemony," Derrida notes that our uses of media trouble the phenomenological conception of *living present*, our present divides itself: the living present is itself divided. From now on, it bears death within itself and reinscribes in its own immediacy what ought as it were to survive it. It divides itself, in its life, between its life and its afterlife, without which there would be no image, no recording. There would be no archive without this dehiscence, without this divisibility of the living present, which bears its specter within itself (Derrida and Stiegler 2002a, 51).

What does Derrida mean by *spectrality* in the spectator's gaze? First of all, as he states in "Spectrographies," the combination of metaphysical expectation of technology with the spectator's unique unconscious means that the spectator instrumentalizes her gaze to produce specters: the spectator's "gaze is spectrality itself" (Derrida and Stiegler 2002b, 122). Such an understanding of the specter overcomes descriptive and analytical possibilities of both phenomenology and semiotics, because the specter "regularly exceeds all the oppositions between visible and invisible, sensible and insensible" (Derrida and Stiegler 2002b, 117). The gaze producing spectrality is out of reach of the usual binary oppositions. "A specter is both visible and invisible, both phenomenal and nonphenomenal: a trace that marks the present with its absence in advance. The spectral logic is de facto a deconstructive logic"

(Derrida and Stiegler 2002b, 117). Instead of keeping this polarity as a binary opposition that is impossible to bridge, Derrida proposes to grasp it as two poles determining the interval of sight in which encounters with specters inevitably happen.

For Derrida, handwritten signature is an incomplete testimony, always limited by the randomness and singularity of recorded and archived traces. However, under the pressure of metaphysical violence, a signature can rhetorically turn into a total, generally valid proof. This transformation is enabled by metonymy, which is the basis of the double understanding of relation between the supposed totality of personal style and its incomplete, fragmentary presence in every trace. Handwritten signature is trapped in a *metonymical interval* exchanging a part of the whole for the whole, going from a singular, mere momentary manual movement to a spectacular legal proof of the signer's civic identity. Inside this interval, Derridean signature is already its own countersignature:

> It might authorise, endorse, ratify, sanction, and declare responsibility for that to which it was attached, but it might equally be a forgery, a counterfeit, a reappropriation, or a fraudulent parody of the text, with these two opposing manifestations sharing in the structure of iterability a common condition of possibility, without it being possible ever definitively to distinguish the one from the other, or immunise it against its counterpart. (Hill 2010, 317)

Derrida repeatedly referred to the metonymic force of representation as the condition of possibility determining the legitimate totality of chosen traces. On the one hand, the metonymically directed selection of what will be displaced and what will be remembered is inevitable, because one can neither represent the whole soul in any momentary hand movement, nor grasp the whole style in any written trace. Derrida indicates that we always have to border, demarcate, and frame the perceived event somehow, if we want to understand, share, and recall it: "all artifactuality, all the manipulations we were just talking about take place through intervention at the level of what is called framing, rhythm, borders, form, contextualization" (Derrida and Stiegler 2002a, 52). On the other hand, choices to frame and decisions to cut are "never neutral, whether they are made at the television or radio stations or whether they are already decided at the press agencies. All actuality negotiates with the artifice, in general dissimulated, of this filtration" (Derrida and Stiegler 2002a, 42).

Can one see something good in this politics of memory? Derrida's answer is positive. In his deconstruction, the main goal of the technology of reproduction and repetition is to enable to recall what has been fragmentarily registered. It makes it possible to generate an archive of technological recordings as a collective memory. Why is it important? Why do we have to remember collectively, and why do we have to imagine what happened without our presence? Mostly because collective memory is a collective memento. Derrida notices in "Artifactualities" that "a ghost can come back, like the worst, but without this possible coming-back, and if we refuse to acknowledge its irreducible originality, we are deprived of memory, heritage, justice, of everything that has value beyond life and by which the dignity of life is measured" (Derrida 2002, 23).

For this reason, Derrida's quasi-ethical thinking is vigilant in identifying historical events. In "Topolitics and Teletechnology," he mentions that "disidentification, singularity, rupture with the solidity of identity, de-liaison seem just as necessary to me as the contrary. I would not want to have to choose between identification and differentiation" (Derrida and Stiegler 2002c, 67). Derrida finds it necessary to be aware of selectivity, which grounds every memory and every history, because it is a political act of elimination: "The very fact that there is a politics of memory already poses a problem" (Derrida and Stiegler 2002c, 63). Although memory is needed, because it "is better than amnesia" (Derrida and Stiegler 2002c, 63), we can only remember correctly in the name of some political unit:

> This memory being finite, we are going to delegate this responsibility to a so-called state institution, that is to say to a system of powers which in fact always represents, in the name of the state—and history has taught us to think this—a fraction of the nation, if not a class, than at least something which is not the 'integral will' nor often the 'general will' of all citizens of this state, citizens past, present, and future? (Derrida and Stiegler 2002c, 63)

Although politics of memory is necessary, "we must awaken to critical vigilance with regard to the politics of memory: we must practice a politics of memory and, simultaneously, in the same movement, a critique of the politics of memory" (Derrida and Stiegler 2002c, 63).

How can one criticize the politics of memory? How can one construct a collective memory without losing vigilance? Derrida finds that it is not enough to be vigilant about the political selection of representative inscriptions; it is also important to evaluate the risks of the tools and instruments used to generate these inscriptions. Therefore, "we have to come back, here, to the question of instrumentalization. None of this could be done without instrumentalization and without a culture of instrumentality" (Derrida and Stiegler 2002c, 63). But, as Derrida adds, technology and instrument are two different things: language is the technique, but the inherited device, the ability to use and master it, is the instrument. Although every technique can be instrumentalized, "'mastery of language' does not simply signify a relation of objectivity or of objectification. There is something in memory that is neither objectifying nor objectifiable" (Derrida and Stiegler 2002c, 63–64). Put otherwise, techniques can be used in a completely general way for general intentions, while instruments can be handled in a very personal way, to attain a strictly personal goal. Vigilance toward recordings requires focus on three things: the politics of choice of the technology of recording and transmission; the handling or instrumentalization of the chosen medium enabling users to take pictures convenient to certain goals; and the politics of choice of the existing recordings.

In this respect, Derrida emphasizes that memory necessarily "includes forgetting. If there is selectivity, it is because there is forgetting" (Derrida and Stiegler 2002a, 64). Although forgetting is a part of every rational politics of selecting representants, the political gesture of their exclusion does not mean that they are gone for good. According to Derrida's "Artifactualities," psychoanalysis offers its explanation of return of the displaced, which is usually forgotten by philosophy, because its ontological nature tends to displace, or ward off the specter. In spite of the effort to rationalize the metaphysics, it falls into "repetition of the worst, which threatens all historical progress" (Derrida 2002, 22). Although displaced, the worst always threatens to return (Derrida 2002, 23). This happens because a conscious effort of memory can hardly win the inequal combat with the unconscious—with forgetting—where "one phantom calls another" (Derrida 2002, 23).

Such a specter is also the expected trace of original presence of the signer at the place of her manual signing. The expectation of authenticity of manual work is why personal handwritten signature is usually added to an institutional stamp. I consider that this authenticity of signature can be understood in the sense of Benjamin's metaphysical concept of the aura of manual work, based on the belief that it is impossible to reach the precision of mechanical reproduction by means of imitation and manual production. The metaphysical expectation of signature generates the belief that the practice of manual writing produces unrepeatable originals, or authentic works. Because it is believed that these originals cannot be exactly copied, it is also believed that all non-authorial copies of signatures and works of art can be recognized as unoriginal, or forged.

The metaphysical expectation that the signature can confirm the signer's physical presence is based on the presupposition that no signer can sign otherwise than authentically. Authentic trace is produced as remains of her strictly personal—replaceable by no one else—psychological and physical contact with the document. The metaphysical expectation of authenticity as originality of the signer's traces (Peirce's index[11]) opens the door to deconstruction of signature as a performative, disseminated trace, based on the *aporetic* metonymy of authentic presence and touch. Deconstruction of the metaphysical expectation of authentic tracing warns that although a handwritten signature is taken as proof of contact between the signed document and the writing instrument held in the author's hand, to certify the trace's authenticity is a metaphysical demand of law that is impossible to satisfy in life.

"Identical" Repetition

The third metaphysical expectation of handwritten signature is *confirmation of identity*. This confirmation is made possible by the specimen signature, which can be understood as a visual convention or rule (Peirce's symbol[12]) that arises from authentic traces coming from natural qualities of the signer's soul. It is this shared belief in motivation by reality that generates the specimen signature as a sign confirming the author's legal identity.

My own consideration of the metaphysical expectation that handwritten signature is the proof making it possible to legally identify the signer is inspired by John D. Caputo's *Deconstruction in a Nutshell*, especially by his note on spectrality of identity. "Derrida emphasizes the instability of the notion of 'identity,' that no so-called identity is, or should take itself to be, 'homogeneous' or 'self-identical,' that indeed it is dangerous to let a group—a family, a community, or a state—settle back down into self-identity" (Caputo 1997, 113). Such a specter is also the proof of the signer's legal identity. The form and content of the handwritten signature are individual and personal, on the one hand, and fixed and legally binding, on the other: once the citizen starts to repeat her specimen signature publicly and mandatorily, she cannot change it without previous notification. That is the main reason why, when doing financial transactions in a bank, every citizen is asked to conform her civic identity by means of her handwritten signature, which is sufficiently similar to her previously registered specimen signature. If someone forgets the originally registered pictorial shape of her specimen signature and occasionally signs very differently, her signature is not sufficiently similar to the specimen signature. In such circumstances, the bank authorities can consider that what she actually did is not her own signature. If such a signer is not able to confirm her civic identity by her signature, the bank representative does not allow her to access her own bank account, unless she officially registers a new specimen signature and signs again in a way that is judged by the bank representative to be sufficiently similar.

According to the metaphysical expectation of legal identity, the legal role of handwritten signature is to confirm that there is a relation of identity between the signer's civic name and her own pictorial expression by means of manual writing. It is expected that this handwritten expression is recognizable by others and considered to be characteristic only for the given signer. Nevertheless, despite the supposedly recognizable and repeatable nature of the specimen signature, the corresponding individual signature cannot be done without varying its handwritten form: each time, it is shaped in a slightly different way. As Sarah Gendron puts it,

> Derrida does not deny that repetition, by definition, is obliged to repeat something deemed "original," yet he likewise insists that there would be no conception of an "original" entity or an "origin" if there were no potential for its repetition. Because repetition hesitates somewhere between "re-presentation" (the so-called Platonic model) and pre-presentation (a notion that is already implied in the French definition of the word, since "répétition" also signifies "rehearsal"), it calls into question all so-called "absolute" and "primary" notions of an "original" entity or "origin." (Gendron 2008, 19)

No model can be manually reproduced without generating material differences that are expected to be legal identities. The result of every manual repetition is a performative difference, a deviation from the supposed origin, that exists only as an infinite deferral in rehearsal. The signer can only generate a—more or less similar—variation of the specimen signature, the supposedly original picture of her civic name.

Derrida's understanding of stylized signing can be compared to his understanding of training. Every signer has to train the style of every further handwritten signature, including the specimen signature. Every single signature performs the trained pose, which is suspended and monumental: it transforms the signer into stylized portraits written into signatures. But this normalization of sculpture-like poses is not only an imposed gestural rule, which must be followed by a posing person or a group of people. Pose really "works" only if the represented person acts it well: posing is also an acting performance, which exhibits the practiced form of affect. The posing person must presuppose and premeditate their effect on others. Before the pose is officially performed, one must prepare, practice, and rehearse it. By training—compulsive iteration—the shape is progressively tuned into one that approaches identity with the conceived posing strategy. The more the represented person succeeds in repeating the trained form of pose, the greater her satisfaction with her performance of the pose. As she gets rid of every unexpected, random spontaneity, she masters her social acting better and gains control over herself. In this sense, the specimen signature became an object separated from life, isolated from its random and unpredictable events. It is an extraordinary, particular object, relieved of current use, enriched by the added value of fetish, the founding object that we remember and believe in. This belief calls for the mechanical, automatic side of thinking. As Derrida puts it, "instead of opposing the machinic and the faith, as we do it almost all the time, we would have to think them together, as one and the same possibility" (Derrida 2000, 72).

Put otherwise, the tension between universality of technology and singularity of its instrumentalization, which makes heritage possible, is given by the fact that there is always more than one ghost, more than one heritage. It is necessary to choose from them the one who will be understood as the remembered ancestor, the legitimate reference: the one who inherits chooses one ghost rather than another. Derrida notices that every inheritor selects and filters the ghost's requirements, choosing which memory and memorial she will refer to. "Only when the assignations are multiple and contradictory is there inheritance, only when they are secret enough to challenge interpretation, to call for the limitless risk of active interpretation. Only then is there a decision and a responsibility to be taken or made" (Derrida 2002, 26). Surprisingly, even history—understood as responsible remembrance of events—is based on aporias: "When there is no *double bind*, there is no responsibility. Inheritance must retain this undecidable reserve . . ." (Derrida 2002, 26).

Memory is a collection of selected fragments. Their selection is legitimated morally, by a social and political necessity to limit the *sublime infinity* of events. Therefore, archive rises from censorship, which forces people to forget the large majority of past events. Filtration and sorting, the foundation of every archive, cuts imaginary contact with unwanted remains, makes their presence in the archive impossible (one cannot remain in contact with an erased, forgotten idea). The main role of the archive is to regulate the political setting of future memory: to choose which past events it will be possible to remember, to imagine, and to mourn. What remains collectively invisible cannot be touched or reached by the collective memory: traces of events that the archive makes disappear, disappear from the range of remembering minds.

Derrida notices that the metaphysical authority of the archive consists in the fight against amnesia, or loss of memory. Archiving itself is a work of sorting and selecting material remains of the past, which presupposes the historian's authorized trust in collective narration and dating (Derrida and Borradori 2003, 100). As Derrida mentions in *Trace et archive, image et art*, these remains are designated to last, to survive the period of their appearance as their legitimate representative: archiving is a "work of organization of a relative, the longest possible survival of some traces, chosen to dassein in the given political and legal conditions" (Derrida 2014, 61). Archive would not have its metaphysical force "without a quasi-ethical—in any case, legitimate and political—organization of such informed material that we give a form by interpretation and classification, hierarchization, selection. There is no archive without destruction, because we select, we cannot keep everything. If we kept everything, there would be no archive. The archive begins with selection and this selection is violence. There is no archive without violence" (Derrida 2014, 60). Moreover, this *violence of selection* is not just political: it "happens already in the unconscious" (Derrida 2014, 60).

The force of the archive is also its violence, culturally regulated amnesia, desire to forget, and death drive,[13] which threatens the desire to return to the past and to keep the idea of continuity. *Archive Fever* leads people to produce collections, albums, catalogs, and encyclopedias, but only at the cost of systematically eliminating what they do not want to remember and recall. Only after the primary gesture of exclusion of the unwanted can the archive start to construct the continuity of meaning of selected fragments of events, which are lined up in a meaningful chronological narrative. As described in *Archive Fever*, the archive "will never be either memory or anamnesis as spontaneous, alive, and internal experience. On the contrary:

the archive takes place at the place of originary and structural breakdown of the said memory. *There is no archive without a place of consignation, without a technique of repetition, and without a certain exteriority. No archive without outside*" (Derrida 1998, 11).

Surprisingly, archive is *hypomnesic*: it is constituted by lack of living memory, by rupture in traumatic memory: "if there is no archive without consignation in an *external place* which assures the possibility of memorization, of repetition, of reproduction, or of reimpression, then we must also remember that repetition itself, the logic of repetition, indeed the repetition compulsion, remains, according to Freud, indissociable from the death drive. And thus from destruction" (Derrida 1998, 11–12). Derrida finds that in the ambition of archiving that makes the historian's deposition and description of events possible, "we will never find anything other than that which exposes to destruction, and in truth menaces with destruction, introducing, a priori, forgetfulness and the archiviolithic into the heart of the monument. Into the 'by heart' itself" (Derrida 1998, 12).

Is it even possible to confirm the signer's legitimate identity, as is expected of the handwritten signature? How much does this metaphysical expectation correspond to the signer's immediate disposition to manually reproduce her specimen signature? This does not exclude the constant creative metamorphosis and becoming oneself in the process of writing, which is neither an occasional imitation nor a mechanical copying of the specimen signature. In handwritten signature, the signer's civic name is identified with the signer's stylized self-portrait. The mentioned metaphysical expectation of "identical repetition"[14] as a law, a rule (Peirce's symbol) opens the door to deconstruction of legal realism, one of the doctrines founding criminology and legal studies. Deconstruction warns that although a handwritten signature is considered to be a stylized personal idiom, which guarantees the author's legal identity, perpetual manual reproduction is a metaphysical demand of law that is impossible to satisfy in life.

In the next chapter, I focus on the three mentioned metaphysical expectations of handwritten signature corresponding to the three Peirce's metaphysical categories, and to three deconstructed aporias.

The first expectation is the aporia of natural resemblance. Based on Derrida's reading of Benveniste, I focus on the use of the copula in the act of recognition, which introduces a relation of equivalence between resemblance and identity. In Derrida, a signer's recognizable handwriting is built up by her repeated attempts to imitate her previous traces, which generates a fragmentary, partial, spectral resemblance. Deconstructed handwritten signature is not a natural expression of the signer's self, but rather a supplement to her self-imitation. This illegible remainder of her past presence is expected to appear identical across different contexts, but it never emerges in the same form, because it is ontologically impossible to reenter the same event by writing.

The second one is the aporia of authentic tracing. I demonstrate that, by contrast with Searle, Derrida grasps the performative as a pragmatic paradox. For Derrida, because of the inevitable parasitism of writing, each writing act generates a "disseminated tracing" operated by iteration, or unauthentic repetition of traces. Deconstructed handwritten signature operates in the interval between repeatable stylized imprint and unrepeatable original work. The metaphysical force of law is disseminated in the event of a signature act, which is not a citable speech act usable in communication, but a parasitical writing act produced by iteration of traces.

The third one is the aporia of identical repetition. I show that Deleuze's "variation of sense" and Derrida's "dissemination of meaning" suggest two divergent solutions to the problem of the logical repeatability of ontologically unrepeatable traces. Because of his awareness of metaphysical violence, Derrida does not share Deleuze's conception of expression and style as a product of immanent creativity, which has important consequences for his own understanding of signature. Deconstructed handwritten signature, operated by an iteration, is trace performed in the *interval* between life and law. As confirmation of the signer's civic identity depends on the legal side of this interval, its displaced vital side haunts every signer who wants to legally reproduce her specimen signature in her manual signing. Moreover, it is only within a discursively acceptable range of resemblance to previous traces that a handwritten trace can be recognized as authentic and, finally, able to legally represent the writer's civic identity.

Chapter IV
Deconstructing Handwritten Signature I

Derrida's deconstruction is characterized by its effort to reach justice at the margins of a principally violent semantics and principally unjust law. Deconstructed justice cannot be established because it is constantly in a state of promised arrival; it is to come. In Derrida, no one can both escape the violent law of Western metaphysics and require understanding from the metaphysical order. The one who quits metaphysics becomes incomprehensible. That is the price to pay for the exit of somehow naively promising semantic justice and freedom. If we want to be understandable, we need to accept the semantic violence of metaphysics, to appropriate it, and to reproduce it.

As Derrida claims in "Cogito and the History of Madness," it makes no sense to shake Western metaphysics by simply criticizing it—critical tools do not serve this purpose. Metaphysics cannot be criticized from within: "Order is then denounced within order" (Derrida 1978a, 42). Nor can metaphysics be criticized from outside, because it is impossible to get out the metaphysics by means of critique. Every critique keeps critics inside. If Derrida does not believe that "someday it will be possible *simply* to escape metaphysics" (Derrida 1981d, 17), it is because there are no reachable linguistic instruments to get outside metaphysics. Because of this resignation to the possibility of semantic liberation, Derrida resigns to critique as one possible tool for his deconstruction work. He sees the problem in authoritarian positivist critique, which he understands as a strong repressive instrument of Western metaphysics.

A melancholic moment of semantic resignation appears in Derrida at this point, when he refuses to build his strategy on definitions and other methodological, analytical, and critical instruments. In Derrida, deconstructed meaning is deferred to traces of text, of writing, which are in the limit zone of metaphysics, on its margins. Derrida does not believe that one can go outside metaphysics, but he does expect the *justice to come*, understood as a tracing of the law, which alone is unreachable. Derrida describes this unreachability in a melancholic way, as a necessity, which opens up space for undecidability.

Adversaries of Derrida's thinking surprisingly often believe that deconstruction introduces into philosophy a new type of critical reading. They usually agree in that this reading is a reproachful, even arrogant critique referring to naive mistakes in other philosophers' ways of thinking.[1] According to its varying attributes, Derrida's critique is taken either for instructive lecturing[2] or for confusing misinterpretation.[3] But they all agree on one thing: when Derrida does deconstruction, he does critique. But does Derrida really read works of other philosophers and writers critically? What does his reading concentrate on? What makes him write philosophically?

In this chapter, I explain why Derrida's writing is not a critique. In his own work, deconstruction is a melancholic eternal return of the same as other, oscillating between ethico-ontological revolt and politico-logical resignation, which makes positivist critique alone unstable and unsustainable. Derrida mobilizes his ethical vigilance against the totalitarian violence of the total presence of meaning that is claimed by any positivist critique. Contrary to the interpretational violence of signification, Derrida proposes his dissemination as a semantic process of a systematic deferral of meaning in a text's performativity. Dissemination is tracing deferred meaning, but not in an objective or historically legitimate sense. Derrida's concept of trace, which was constructed by grafting[4] a new layer of meaning on the traditional metaphysical concept of trace, is not motivated by the idea of a physical touch, so it does not refer to causality to explain its origin. Derrida's deconstruction is no positivist science; it refuses the positivist scientific mechanism of definitions and method production, as well as the scientific prejudices of identity and origin this generates.

Because Derrida is aware that one can criticize only from a precisely determined position, which is always positively situated inside metaphysics, he formulates the arche-ethical[5] demand to conceive of his deconstruction negatively: do not criticize and do not pontificate. In his "Letter to a Japanese Friend," Derrida writes that

> deconstruction is neither an analysis nor a critique and its translation would have to take that into consideration. It is not an

analysis in particular because the dismantling of a structure is not a regression toward a simple element, toward an indissoluble origin. These values, like that of analysis, are themselves philosophemes subject to deconstruction. No more is it a critique, in a general or in a Kantian sense. The instance of *krinein* or *krisis* (decision, choice, judgment, discernment) is itself, as is all the apparatus of transcendental critique, one of the essential "themes" or "objects" of deconstruction. (Derrida 1988a, 3)

Derrida's conceptual work introduces an unstable meaning—a meaning dealing with permanent self-transformation, dissemination, and drift from the supposed origin, which is unreachable and always already deferred. Contrary to both ontological and logical conceptions of totally present meaning, guaranteed by the eternal present tense of the copula used in definitions, Derrida's understanding of deferred meaning makes him work with such concepts as trace, remains, specter, deferral, supplement, graft, and parasite. Deconstructed margins of philosophy are made of aporias, which bring no satisfying solution to philosophical problems that are apparently easily resolvable inside Western metaphysics. If we wanted to imagine Western metaphysics in terms of Derrida's deconstruction, we would have to exchange the philosophical copula for the philosophical metaphor. In such a rhetorical view, the deconstructed logos would not be a fixed and solid system of meanings, but rather a porous, spongy structure full of cracks and grafts—that would be the very margins from which Derrida philosophically writes.

Derrida's deconstruction is not satisfied with settling down on the margins of Western metaphysics; its movement is more complicated. On the one hand, Derrida's vigilant movement of *différance* tries to disturb the prejudice of the supposed total presence of identity between beings and their representations. On the other hand, he understands that if he wants to speak about it, he must turn back and situate himself in the metaphysically present tense of speaking constructed of copulas. This resigned movement brings him to a melancholic play with language that he uses for other than critical purposes. A circular movement of *subversive translation of idioms* can be seen in his work: from his resistance to idioms back to his play with idioms. What I propose to call the *melancholy* of this circular subversive translation between the center and the periphery of Western metaphysics consists in understanding that the margins of metaphysics can be reached from inside metaphysics, by means of vigilant mistrust toward idioms.

Beyond these margins lies madness—the opposite of the logos—that is, a semantic emptiness. If Derrida does not want to enter the zone of madness and if he still wants to be heard in the logos, he must come back to the logos by means of experimental play with idioms.

His quasi-ethical *gesture of mistrust*[6] leads Derrida to a melancholic play with meaning, which cannot be interconnected with scientifically positive semiotic projects. First, because Derrida does not distinguish picture and writing; for him, nothing is outside the text: everything is inside it. This homogenization is characteristic for deconstruction. All writing (*grammé*) faces its vocal interpretation (logos), which defines and fixes the unstable meaning of writing. This conception of writing does not allow us to speak about differences in visual and verbal rhetoric and is not usable in scientifically positive media semiotics. Second, Derrida does not admit any limits of interpretation. Contrary to the traditional conception of traces, Derrida's trace is a subversive draft, which is not based on causality of imprint. This *quasi-trace,* or deconstructed trace, has no causal link to its origin and refers only to the process of deferral of this origin. Because he questions scientifically positive empiricism, Derrida's deconstruction cannot be used to achieve the goals of cognitive semiotics. Third, because Derrida does not believe in essential historical changes in Western metaphysics, he rejects the positivism of history. As Gasché puts it in *Deconstruction, Its Force, Its Violence*, "Derrida's thought consists in radically drawing the consequences from this generally overlooked complexity of Western thought" (Gasché 2016, xiii). Derrida describes Western metaphysics as an aporetic construction of meaning, which presents fragmentary and supplementary meaning as total and original. He understands this aporia as constantly passing through particular historical periods and remerging at different occasions. As Derrida's deconstruction considers the ahistorical[7] metaphysical conditions of possibility of historiography as such, it cannot be used for the purposes of any positivist historiographic analysis. Thus it is no surprise that Derrida's deconstruction is least understood and most criticized by scientific positivists.

Aporia of Natural Resemblance

The *pragmatic paradox* of any empirical research is based on the impossibility of equivalence between the being and its representation. Every empirical work is simultaneously legally obligatory and ontologically unfeasible. In this respect, I would like to emphasize the fact that Derrida situates his philosophical position neither inside nor outside Western metaphysics. Derrida repeatedly claims that to criticize the metaphysical order from the inside does not solve anything. It cannot really help us to criticize the Western metaphysics of total presence of meaning and, at the same time, use metaphysical instruments (such as concepts and definitions, examples and methods) to perform this critique. Such a strategy makes it impossible to quit Western metaphysics, because all discourses criticizing Western metaphysics are already taken into its vicious circle. As Derrida puts it in "Structure, Sign and Play in the Discourse of the Human Sciences," this circle describes the relation between history of metaphysics and destruction of the history of metaphysics: "There is no sense in doing without the concepts of metaphysics in order to shake metaphysics. We have no language—no syntax and no lexicon—which is foreign to this history; we can pronounce not a single destructive proposition which has not already had to slip into the form, the logic, and the implicit postulations of precisely what it seeks to contest" (Derrida 1978b, 354). The Western metaphysics of total semantic presence can be shaken by means of the concept of sign, but "as soon as one seeks to demonstrate in this way that there is no transcendental or privileged signified and that the domain or play of signification henceforth has no limit, one must reject even the concept and word 'sign' itself—which is precisely what cannot be done" (Derrida 1978b, 354).

Derrida finds the main problem of deconstruction—which is to rethink the metaphysical prejudices related to grasping the *grammé*—in the logos, the paralytical place, the blind spot of Western metaphysics. According to the aporetic principle of Derrida's work, it is inevitable that the final meaning cannot be grasped. In Derrida, inevitable parasites are the foundation of the melancholic play of supplementarity, which makes any revolt essentially vain. As he writes in "White Mythology," in deconstruction, one cannot think otherwise than in terms of aporia. The aporia of metaphorical definition cannot be separated from philosophy: "What is defined, therefore, is implied in the defining of the definition" (Derrida 1982c, 230). Therefore, deconstruction is no critique. Critique is deconstruction's proper metaphysical object.

If Derrida's goal is not to criticize Western metaphysics, what is his goal? Is it to establish a new, melancholic semiotics of deferred meaning? Is it a kind of semiotics motivated by an ethics of justice that never occurs? Where is the place Derrida speaks from? Are the margins of metaphysics signed by himself? Does it exist independently from his writing?

Derrida's *Margins of Philosophy* could help us find answers to these questions. Derrida notices there that playful writing occurs at the margins of violent logos, the center of Western metaphysics. As far as Western metaphysics aims to turn individual experience into universal law, it is philosophically violent: in its center, the similar (and particular) becomes identical (and general). Derrida's thoughts on the ontologico-logical function of copula and principial impossibility of emancipating philosophy from metaphor[8] compete here. Contrary to copula, metaphor does not produce equivalence; it can only produce similarity. In this view, the metaphor is metaphysically ungraspable, both ontologically and logically. Put otherwise, the metaphor is everything in philosophical language, except for the verb "to be," which belongs to both ontological and logical vocabularies. If a metaphysically violent connection between metaphor and copula occurs, it transforms the ontologically similar into the logically identical. Identity (equivalence) replaces similarity (approximation).

In "The Supplement of Copula," Derrida deals with the contradictory ontological and logical functions of the copula in Western metaphysics. Because of his deconstructive reading of Émile Benveniste's works, he finds the aporia following up the contradiction found by Benveniste himself. Benveniste noticed that some world languages do not contain the verb "to be," but they can produce a definition using an equivalent, which substitutes the absence of this verb. Such an equivalent can be a link between words, which are presented as semantically identical. Based on his reading of Benveniste, Derrida formulates the following questioning of Western metaphysical thinking:

> Is there a "metaphysics" outside the Indo-European organization of the function "to be"? This is not in the least an ethnocentric question. It does not amount to envisaging that other languages might be deprived of the surpassing mission of philosophy and metaphysics but, on the contrary, avoids projecting outside the West very determined forms of "history" and "culture." (Derrida 1982b, 231)

Derrida recognizes both Western ethnocentrism and attempts to overcome it in two of Benveniste's gestures. In the first gesture, Benveniste states that the verb "to be" cannot be translated into all world languages, because some languages have no sufficiently close equivalent—they have nothing with which to compensate for this lexical absence. In the second gesture, Benveniste claims the opposite, that such an equivalent can be found in all languages; not in the vocabulary, but in a particular function of interpunction or phrasing. Derrida finds a double metaphysical gesture—critically constructive and aporetically deconstructive—in this double answer to the question of metaphysical limits of translation.

From Derrida's viewpoint, this double gesture simultaneously displays a double metaphysical function of the word "to be" in Indo-European languages: ontological ("lexical" in Benveniste) and logical ("grammatical" in Benveniste). In Benveniste's first gesture, grammatical copula and lexical being essentially differ: the function of the copula or of the "grammatical mark of identity" is absolutely distinct from the word "to be" in its full-fledged use. But, in many Indo-European languages, these two functions have merged. Therefore, if one speaks about the verb "to be," it is necessary to define if one means the grammatical concept or the lexical concept (Derrida 1982b, 200). Derrida notices that Benveniste demonstrates the universality of the grammatical function of "to be" as the copula, even in a language that "does not possess the verb 'to be' in its lexical presence" (Derrida 1982b, 201). In Benveniste's second gesture, every language finds a compensation for the essential lack: every language has a function that supplements the lexical absence of the verb "to be." Nevertheless, as Derrida claims, this supplementarity can satisfyingly compensate for the absence only for those who speak a language where the two—grammatical and lexical—functions have "merged" (Derrida 1982b, 201). According to Derrida, this supplementarity entails fundamental historical consequences: "Is not what we perceive, outside the West, as a supplement of absence or as vicariousness in fact an original possibility which comes to be added to the lexical function of the verb 'to be'—and thus equally well does without it, indeed even dispensing with any reference to it? And does so even within Indo-European?" (Derrida 1982b, 201).

Derrida focuses on Benveniste's conception of the *compensation of absence* for the copula "to be" in other than Indo-European languages that do not have this verb. In Derrida, the copula is not absent and should not be compensated in other world languages. On the contrary, the Indo-European linguistic copula is not a compensation, but an excessive addition, a supplement. Thus, there is an important difference between the critique of absence of the verb "to be," understood as an important lexical lack, and the deconstruction of absence of the verb "to be," understood as an original linguistic state, to which the verb "to be" is only a supplement.

In Derrida's deconstructive reading of Benveniste, the ontologico-logical unity constructed in the verb "to be" appears as a metaphysical particularity of Indo-European languages. "Is"—the ontological word "to be" in the third person of singular and present tense—also signifies the relation of logical equivalence. These two meanings are violently kept together: while both functions pervade in one word, they mutually exclude each other. For Derrida, this is problematic: while identity can be required and reached logically, it cannot be reached ontologically—every empiricism that identifies ontology with logic inevitably faces the metaphysical risk of totalities. These two meanings are violently kept together: while both functions pervade in one word, they mutually exclude each other.

Therefore, in Indo-European languages, which generate the Western metaphysical thinking, the copula "is" should be grasped as an aporetic element. This aporia works particularly boldly in philosophy, where every concept needs a definition constructed by means of the copula "is." The copula introduces a metaphysical linkage between the previously separated meanings of two words. Moreover, this linkage establishes the relation of equivalence, or identity.

As Waldenfels notes in "For example," this requirement of identity in life produces a *gap*, which makes the legal definition of handwritten signature disappear: "The decisive point, what it all comes down to in indirect and paradigmatic description, is that a gap opens up between the general and the particular that can only be crossed by a leap. It makes no difference for this leap if one is ascending from the particular to the general or descending from the general to the particular" (Waldenfels 2015, 39). Derrida's deconstructive reading calls attention to this gap: despite the metaphysical expectation, between the logical (permanently present) and the ontological (temporary, drifting) meaning, no identity is reachable.

Let us return to "White Mythology," where Derrida points to how use of metaphor of natural language is transformed from philosophy into rhetoric. Derrida introduces his study with an idea borrowed from Anatole de France's book *The Garden of Epicurus* concerning the *usura*—aporetic use of rhetorical figures, which consists in wearing of images, and which also brings usurious profit from their over-evaluation. In de France's text, Polyfil, critic of metaphysics, discusses with Aristo, defender of metaphysics. As Derrida puts it, according to Polyfil, the original meaning, which is sensory and material, is not exactly a metaphor:

> It is a kind of transparent figure, equivalent to a literal meaning (sens propre). It becomes a metaphor when philosophical discourse puts it into circulation. Simultaneously the first meaning and the first displacement are then forgotten. The metaphor is no longer noticed, and it is taken for the proper meaning. A double

effacement. Philosophy would be this process of metaphorization which gets carried away in and of itself. Constitutionally, philosophical culture will always have been an obliterating one. (Derrida 1982c, 211)

In de France's text, this Western metaphysical culture of the metaphor is called white mythology: "the white man takes his own mythology, Indo-European mythology, his own logos, that is, the mythos of his idiom, for the universal form of that he must still wish to call Reason. Which does not go uncontested" (Derrida 1982c, 213).

Derrida comments on this fruitful dialogue from his position of deconstructing Western metaphysics, which he grasps in a more complicated way than the characters in Anatole de France's work. He asks: "The exergue effaced, how are we to decipher figures of speech, and singularly metaphor, in the philosophic text?" (Derrida 1982c, 219). In his own words referring to Kant, Derrida proposes a subversion: "instead of venturing into the prolegomena to some future metaphorics, let us rather attempt to recognize in principle the *condition for the impossibility* of such a project" (Derrida 1982c, 219). The uncrossable boundary, from which Derrida formulates this condition, is given by the fact that the metaphor is "a classical philosopheme, a metaphysical concept" (Derrida 1982c, 219). According to Derrida, it is impossible to classify all the metaphorical possibilities in philosophy, because one metaphor would still be eliminated and remain outside the system: to form the concept of metaphor it is necessary to start by a metaphor of metaphor.[9] Thus, every attempt to formulate a general philosophical metaphorology is vain: it makes no sense to both philosophically criticize the metaphor and philosophically use it to critique metaphor. No philosophy can produce a general taxonomy of philosophical metaphors because it constantly generates them. Such a taxonomy would presuppose that philosophy no longer exists; that all problems producing philosophy as a historical unity are already solved. Even the rhetoric of philosophy, or *meta-philosophy*, would not be relevant here, because whenever rhetoric defines metaphor, it implies the whole conceptual texture in which philosophy as such was founded.

Spectral Resemblance

As we have seen, Derrida's conception of metaphor postulates the exchangeability of two things that are similar. This means that it postulates logical equivalence between two things, which—from an ontological viewpoint—can never be the same. The metaphysical force of the metaphor enforces the ontologically individual and unique object to play the rhetorical role of an object, which is identical and exchangeable with other objects.

Geoffrey Bennington mentions in "Métaphore, méta-force," dedicated to several shifts in Derrida's understanding of metaphor, that Derrida's thinking is evolving. Although it goes through various modifications in time, for principial reasons, certain procedures remain unchanged. Bennington chronicles the period from the 1960s to "White Mythology" (1971) to show that the word "metaphor" later disappeared from Derrida's texts and was replaced by "analogy." The problem of analogy brings Bennington to rethink Derrida's deconstruction of Kant's concept of the regulative Idea and to introduce the neologism *meta-force*.[10] However, in all of his moments of deconstruction of similarity, Derrida does not perform any critique of the presence of metaphor and of analogy in philosophical practices. On the contrary, he takes it as a philosophical necessity—with all of its metaphysical possibilities and impossibilities.

In Derrida's approach to signature as an event submitted to iteration, one quits the ontological expectation of total presence of meaning. The pragmatic paradox of *exact iteration*—which is both legally obligatory and ontologically impossible—occurs inside Western metaphysics. Derrida repeatedly mentions that it is not useful to criticize the metaphysical order from the inside.

Derrida rejects discursive analysis because, for him, no meaning is historically original. He believes that no meaning can be generated outside the intertextual practices of grafting and supplementing that exceed any discursively acceptable limits. Therefore, from a deconstruction perspective, there is no context generating the original meaning that would not be possible to use in another context. As Ramond indicates,

> discourse is not definitively linked to the primary context, because it can always be "grafted" (or "cited") in another context. This possibility does not depend on contexts: there are not such contexts or discourses that are suitable to be "grafted," while others are not. Derrida claims that (the paradoxal and provocative dimension of his thinking can be found here) discourse is always graftable or, more radically, that discourse is *always already* a "graft" or a "citation." The thesis of "citability" or generalized "graft" is nothing but a new aspect of the theory of original *différance*. (Ramond 2001, 40)

In Derrida's dissemination, the signature is a trace prolonging and amplifying its meaning to other traces. If we admit that signature becomes here a metonymical representation of representation, we also admit that the meaning is produced performatively. Such a conception of signature disperses each metaphysical origin of sense, or the prejudice establishing legal ontology of the total presence of meaning. Derrida uses the metaphysical concepts that fund and organize discourses to show that there is no direct—immediate, not mediated—access to the original meaning. The process of writing is not supplementary work that dislocates the signer from the origin of meaning. On the contrary, in Derrida, the written supplement remains the only possible approach. If Derrida suggests accepting the fact of supplementarity as a communicational necessity, and if he suggests following the disseminated meaning, which keeps on escaping in infinite series of representations of representations, he calls for philosophical vigilance and mobilization against the totalitarian expressions inside the philosophy itself. Thus, in Derrida, the handwritten signature can only be grasped as a subversive performative, which enables both recognition and overcoming of the constructed identity. The deconstructed handwritten signature refers to both the alterity and the identity of the signer.

Deconstructed handwritten signature is an aporetic trace of style. The signer's recognizable style of writing is shaped by the effort to imitate her own previous traces. It is expected that the signer's systematic effort to repeat her own traces produces a certain personal style, which is recognizable by others. The more the signer tries to imitate her previous traces, the more she tries to identify her traces with herself: in the continuous work of self-imitation, she becomes her own style. Is it possible to determine a reliable limit separating the admissible similarity from the inadmissible dissimilarity of one's handwritten traces? Where does the similarity begin? Where does it end and become dissimilarity? When is the handwritten signature considered to be sufficiently similar to the signer's previous signatures to be able to reveal the signer's identity?

In this respect, Francesco Vitale mentions that Derrida came with the conception of

> "non-discursive" or "prediscursive" writing. Given that arche-writing is the condition of possibility of experience and thus of the elaboration of meaning in general, this writing should build up a concrete articulation of these conditions and in particular of those possibilities of meaning that have been removed by our

tradition through the subordination of writing to speech and the subordination of writing to the linear ideal of phonetico-alphabetic writing. (Vitale 2018b, 50)

According to Vitale, Derrida himself show his extraordinary architectural skills in *Glas,* where he works inventively with the graphical matter of his text written in phonetic writing: he builds a strange common house for Hegel and Genet with two columns of text devoted to their works.

In my view, such an architectural writing of philosophy redirects the readers' logocentric interest to the graphical side of philosophical text, which, suddenly, transforms itself into a calligram. *Glas* is supposed to be not only read as a verbal message, but also seen as a picture where letters of the alphabet become visual material for unique construction of this philosophical work. In *Glas,* Derrida mentions that the signature metaphysically identifies the author with the narrator and guarantees the performative truth of autobiographic texts. Besides the metaphysical conception of identity as total presence of meaning, Derrida suggests his own conception of deferred meaning, which is haunted by the undecidable. In his own words, "The remain(s) is indescribable, or almost so: not by virtue of an empiric approximation, but rigorously undecidable" (Derrida 1986, 2). In Derrida, one's signature is uncompleted, it is a gesture prolonging one inscription with other inscriptions. Every single signature is just one of the multiple versions produced by the same signer. The personal style—understood as genuine representation of a unique soul—is unreachable in its totality. No interpretation of remains—nor the expert's examination—can entirely get it. According to Royle's claim, "As works such as 'Glas' and 'Envois' make clear, one never finally, completely signs something, leaving a mark of nick that would be uniquely and purely one's own" (Royle 2003, 124).

If, despite all observable differences in Derrida's texts from the beginning to the end of his work, early and late Derrida still remains Derrida for us, it is because we suppose that there is something that goes across and unifies all of his works: the author must be responsible for it. As Jay Williams notices, Derrida used the word signature to suggest that its producer has "'to take responsibility' as an author" (Williams 2013, X). Because of this signature, we tend to believe that readers recognize the "Derridean" *style*. Without it, there would be no "Derridean" text. There is no aporia without metaphysics.

From the viewpoint of deconstruction, Western philosophy cannot quit Western metaphysics, which produces pragmatic paradoxes and forces us to build our legal institutions on them. This includes Derrida's own thinking, which is parasitically rooted in Western metaphysics. Derrida performs his own signature for us by iteration of his conceptual traces. This way, he constructs his philosophical identity and enables to recognize his own thinking. Put otherwise, even if Derrida's philosophical signature is fragmentary and disseminated in his texts, varying of the iterated traces still produces Jacques Derrida's signature as a philosophical reference. The originality of the work is both enabled and questioned by usual mediations, which are supposed to allow the author to fulfill her goal. This concerns Derrida, just as for any other author. One cannot be a genius outside the order of metaphysics, which constructs this concept. One can only be a deconstructed genius,[11] which subversively reconstructs the metaphysics.

Derrida's signature functions as the *signer's illegible remainder,* a supplement, which is expected to reappear in the same context, but which will never return graphically identical, because it is ontologically impossible to enter the same context at the same moment of writing. What remains from the event of signing—the moment of handwriting in the previous context—is just ashes of the signer's past presence. The result—a relic, a revenant, a specter—is (onto)logically ungraspable, but—because of our metaphysical expectations—still *quasi-present*. Derrida's ashes, the forgotten thing edged out of memory, partially return to haunt the metaphysical certainties of our "reliable" memory, archive, and logos. As Derrida puts it in *Feu la cendre*, "Ashes are this: what is kept in order to not remain, to let vanish the rest. The person is not missing anymore. She has left ashes, just her name, but illegible. Maybe just a nickname of the so-called signatory" (Derrida 1987a, 19).

Even if it is illegible, we used to expect that handwritten signature naturally nominally substitutes its signer. Nevertheless, as Bennington noticed, "The signature, and this is precisely what distinguishes it from the proper name in general, attempts to catch up again the proper we have seen depropriate itself immediately in the name" (Bennington and Derrida 1999, 150). Therefore, the act of signing should not be reduced to simple manual writing of the signer's own name. The signature functions as *meta-handwriting*, which indicates that "this is the name of the one who writes this way." By means of leaving physical traces, the signer makes herself present in her absence: "In speech, what is called the enunciation marks the presence of the present moment in which I speak. The signature ought to be its equivalent in writing . . . The I-here-now implied in every enunciation and lost in writing is in principle recuperated in the signature appended to the text" (Bennington and Derrida 1999, 150). When the signer leaves a trace of her handwritten signature in some place and time, she locks her name in the place and time of the writing act.

As such, the signature exists only in a semantic gap—despite its declared legal reliability, no handwritten signature can ever reach identity with any other handwritten signature. As Derrida mentioned, the writing cannot reach identity; it only reaches similarity: there is always more meaning in the writing than in the voice, which comes to reduce the possibilities of interpretation and to determine the precise meaning. The writing offers similarity, which is translated by the voice as identity. The writing is an unrepeatable event of instant self-expression, which both prevents and exceeds the standardized meaning produced by the voice. Writing is not totally graspable by the voice. The similarity of individual traces can perpetually approach the metaphysically required identity, but it can never reach it. In this subversive view, I do agree with Derrida's intention to deconstruct this metaphysical concept. In the rhetorical conditions of Western metaphysics, handwritten signature as civic sign is partly based on the rhetoric of relic, or personal trace left by the signer's past presence. Handwritten signature functions as an existential remainder of the signer's past presence, which makes it a legal proof of civic identity.

The law requires identity of living beings and their traces of life.[12] But this requirement is impossible to satisfy: living beings and their traces can only be similar. Their expression is only instantaneous, their supposed origin—the soul of the signer—never transparent. And, still, the transparence is required: the law forces the similarity to play the role of the identity. It is the aporias that Derrida is interested in.

His philosophical work searches for *aporias:* it is not just a reproachful critique. For him, a repressive critique is a too easy and vain goal. Instead, his aim is to awake *mistrust in critique* as such. This mistrust is produced by his ethics of deferred meaning and his semantics of a blind spot, an aporetic negativity. If Derrida formulates something positively on the level of philosophical principles or laws, he formulates them as an aporetic law, as an untouchable generator of *préjugés,* naive expectations of direct accessibility of the law's meaning. According to Derrida's *Before the Law,* such an expectation ignores the aporetic prohibition of direct reach of meaning generated by the law itself. If such an aporia occurs, it is because

> The law interdicts and contradicts itself while placing the man in contradiction with himself: we cannot reach it, and in order to have some *rapport* with the law based on respect, *one must not, one must not* have any rapport with it, *the relationship must be interrupted.* We must *establish a relationship* only with its repre-

sentatives, its examples, its guardians. And these are interrupters just as much as messengers. One must not know who the law is, what it is, where it is, where and how it is presented, where it comes from and from where it speaks. (Derrida 2018, 51–52)

In this respect, I find necessary to mention possible *tensions* in my own arguments, which are not contradictions because they are not simply errors. These tensions are *aporias* inherent to Derrida's deconstruction, to the way he works with double-binds. Derrida himself calls his deconstruction a "dark" way of thinking—a thinking "according to aporia."[13] In *Aporias,* he writes that he is not interested in logical contradiction, but rather in metaphysical conditions of possibility that are impossible to satisfy. He is interested in "aporia, rather than antinomy: the word *antinomy* imposed itself up to a certain point since, in terms of the law (*nomos*), contradictions or antagonisms among equally imperative laws were at stake" (Derrida 2006, 16). If this Derridean "antinomy" deserves rather the name aporia, it is because it is neither an apparent antinomy, nor a dialectizable contradiction in a Hegelian or a Marxist sense, "nor even a 'transcendental illusion in a dialectic of the Kantian type,' but instead an interminable experience. Such an experience must remain such if one wants to think, to make come or to let come any event of decision or of responsibility" (Derrida 2006, 16). Derrida's aporia is no logical antinomy, but an experience of never-ending careful decision, which leads him to a quasi-ethical obligation.

I find reconciliation of some of tensions in my argumentation, which instrumentally follows Derrida's way of thinking, particularly timely considering his recent publication *Life Death* (Derrida 2020). First, Derrida tells us his deconstruction is double; both ontological and pre-ontological. The same goes for the sign of handwritten signature, aporetical trace of life, which can be understood as both representation and meta-representation. Handwritten signature, just like life, the "object of biology and biography" (Derrida 2020, 27), is what has trouble becoming the object of a science, obtaining the "legal status of scientificity" (Derrida 2020, 27). Second, Derrida tells us that one cannot quit logocentrism of Western metaphysics; deconstruction is therefore situated on its margins—neither completely inside nor completely outside. His systematic interpretation of Western metaphysics *as a whole* "stems from the unity of Western metaphysics" (Derrida 2020, 158). Therefore, the autobiographical forces of signature have to "regain the inessential status or place that has always been theirs in the history of metaphysics" (Derrida 2020, 158).

I follow Derrida in his search for these logically paralytical places in Western metaphysics, where it is impossible to logically formulate problems and to suggest their clear solution. Such aporetical places produce an interval between the logically ungraspable writing acts and the easily understandable speech acts. This problem is treated in a more complex way in the next chapter, which focuses on the fact that a handwritten signature is a line traced by hand, which is considered to be the signer's authentic trace. Nevertheless, unlike biometrical traces, a handwritten signature is neither a mechanical imprint nor a physiological sample.

Chapter V
Deconstructing Handwritten Signature II

Handwritten signature is supposed to be an authentic trace of the signer. But, contrary to biometric traces enabling relatively easy and reliable identification of citizens, handwritten signature is neither a physical imprint nor a sample from a citizen's body. It is a written trace, a line of manual writing, which is written again by the signer's own hand each time. For this reason, a handwritten signature is considered to be an authentic trace of the signer's personal style, a singular manner of manual expression, which is also characteristic for original works of art. Yet handwritten signature is not a work of art, but rather a supplement to it, which is expected to enable identification of its author. Although it is expected to be both, handwritten signature is neither a biometric trace nor a work of art.

As I have demonstrated in "Pragmatical Paradox of Signature," this ontologico-semantic curiosity can be better understood from the viewpoint of deconstruction, where the signature is grasped as performative.[1] By means of her handwritten signature, the signer does something; he/she performs some occasional act. She declares her authorship (signing a work of art or a letter), her agreement (signing a petition, a charter, a bank transaction), her commitment (signature of a declaration, a contract), or her physical presence (signing a presence sheet, giving an autograph). This is not done by speaking, but by writing. It seems that it is not enough to pronounce the name; it is necessary to write it. Moreover, it must be written by the citizen's own hand, not by a writing machine or a computer. Why? Is manual writing able to do something that neither speech nor mechanical writing is able to do?

In "Signature Event Context," Derrida formulates his definition of the act of writing as a gesture producing a mark constituting a kind of productive machine, which will continue to function even in the case of future disappearance of the writer. Such writing necessarily continues "to 'act' and to be legible even if what is called the author of the writing no longer answers for what he has written, for what he seems to have signed" (Derrida 1977b, 316). While spoken communication is based on repetition in the presence of the addressee, written communication is based on iteration in her absence: "A writing that was not structurally legible—iterable—beyond the death of the addressee, would not be writing" (Derrida 1977b, 315). Derrida's conception of *generalized writing* does not specifically designate the medium of legal handwritten signature. The condition of iterability in the absolute absence of the addressee structures the mark of writing itself "for no matter what type of writing (pictographic, hieroglyphic, ideographic, phonetic, alphabetic, to use the old categories)" (Derrida 1977b, 315).

Yet the specific case of handwritten signature is included in the conception of generalized writing. Derrida mentions that authentic signature is a special case of double bind. Our metaphysical expectation of authenticity depends on an aporia that obliges the signer to accomplish in each individual act of signing the impossible task of manually reproducing her previous traces. While without attempts to repeat previous traces, there would be no recognizable signature; every attempt at manual repetition brings unexpected variations that inevitably betray the authenticity of signature and make its recognition difficult. As Derrida puts it:

> Effects of signature are the most common thing in the world. But the condition of possibility of those effects is simultaneously, once again, the condition of their impossibility, of the impossibility of their rigorous purity. In order to function, that is, to be readable, a signature must have a repeatable, iterable, imitable form; it must be able to be detached from the present and Singular intention of its production. It is its sameness which, by corrupting its identity and its Singularity, divides its seal. (Derrida 1977b, 20)

Just like any other writing in the Derridean sense, the handwritten signature is iterable, legible, identifiable thanks to the repeated code: "The possibility of repeating, and therefore of identifying, marks is implied in every code, making of it a communicable, transmittable, decipherable grid that is iterable for a third party" (Derrida 1977b, 315). Put otherwise, although identifying one's handwritten signature—that changes its singular form in every single performance of signing—is clearly not as certain as reading a typed text, the condition of its possibility, *iterability*, remains the same.

Because handwritten signature as *writing* is iterable *in absence*, its performance remains semantically ambiguous: one cannot overcome phonocentric and logocentric determination of Western metaphysics to benefit a new graphocentrism. As Derrida himself puts it, "it has never been a question of opposing a graphocentrism to a logocentrism, nor, in general, any center to any other center" (Derrida 1981d, 12). Total transgression of metaphysics is impossible: "every transgressive gesture re-encloses us—precisely by giving us a hold on the closure of metaphysics—within this closure . . . One is never installed within transgression, one never lives elsewhere. Transgression implies that the limit is always at work" (Derrida 1981d, 12). In all transgressions, we deal with the code of binary oppositions, which is necessarily linked to Western metaphysics of total presence and total absence of meaning.

Therefore, it is impossible to be understood in any place beyond metaphysics, in a center that also will be the center of speech or writing. As Butler noted in *Bodies that Matter*, Derrida makes clear that the power of the performative is not the function of an originating will, but is always derivative:

> Performativity is thus not a singular "act," for it is always a reiteration of a norm or set of norms, and to the extent that it acquires an act-like status in the present, it conceals or dissimulates the conventions of which it is a repetition. Moreover, this act is not primarily theatrical; indeed, its apparent theatricality is produced to the extent that its historicity remains dissimulated (and, conversely, its theatricality gains a certain inevitability given the impossibility of a full disclosure of its historicity). (Butler 2011, 31)

On the other hand, as Leslie Hill claims, Derridean performative is always aporetic: "what is expelled as incompatible with the pure enactment of performatives turns out in fact to be the very condition of possibility of performatives occurring at all" (Hill 2007, 31). Derrida believes no context can be ever totally saturated, handled, and grasped: it necessarily contains excesses and gaps. As Hill puts it, by means of iteration, one can reach variation in traces and destinations, but never their identity:

> Signatures only prove authenticity, however, because they are repeatable, i.e., because the signature I put at the bottom of the traveler's check *more or less* exactly replicates my signature at the top. But precisely for that very reason, because there is necessary repetition, the threat of inauthenticity, duplication, or forgery, can never be excluded. Indeed, what this iterability shows is that an authentic signature shares the same conditions of possibility as an inauthentic one, and it is impossible to have the one without the threat or promise of the other. (Hill 2007, 31)

A precarious question arises here: if it is impossible to reach identity by handwriting, how is it possible that it is currently used to identify us? How can one identify someone else by relying on something that keeps on changing? How can one be sure that someone else did not forge the signature on a contract? Does not the writing act oscillate somewhere between the two poles of similarity and dissimilarity? Can it be understood as Austin's performative, which was pronounced in bad faith?

The problem I formulate here is apparently simple and banal. Nevertheless, I find it controversial. I suppose that the handwritten signature—as a physically authentic manual inspiration of the civic name—can be related neither to linguistic theory nor to theory of speech acts. Therefore, I find it necessary to formulate the reasons for its philosophical rethinking. First of all, it is important to say that handwritten signature is a material trace referring to its origin, its author. Its supposed authenticity becomes an important sign proving the past presence of the signer at the place of signing. As a materially founded proof, the handwritten signature can not only be used, but also misused (for instance, if a signature is considered to be forged). If an expert believes that the expressions of the signer's soul are different from the qualities of analyzed handwriting, she can uncover the falsum of this of type of sign. Because of the belief in the signer's natural expression, graphology tries to reconstruct the signer's soul by means of reconstructing the signer's style of handwriting. This presupposition is also shared by the forensic analysts Caligiuri and Mohammed, who distinguish authentic from forged signatures through cinematic analysis of the signer's motoric control (Caligiuri and Mohammed 2012, 50–51). Both kinds of expertise are based on the same metaphysical presupposition that turns the handwritten signature into an authentic performative, which I propose to call the *writing act*.

To show how the speech act differs from the writing act, I start with the definition of *spoken performative* from Austin's position and of *speech act* from Searle's position. To demonstrate the aporia of handwritten signature as a pragmatic paradox, I then look at Derrida's reconsideration of their conceptions and the polemic developed from the following confrontation.

First of all, the pragmatic paradox, understood as a logically true but pragmatically false statement, is not Derrida's discovery. Austin examined this philosophical problem before him, but with different intentions and results. The discovery of the pragmatic paradox is crucial for both, but their reaction to it is divergent: while it makes Austin stop developing his own conception of speech acts, it inspires Derrida to keep constructing his deconstruction. As Raoul Moati mentions in *Derrida/Searle*, for Derrida, the *parasitism of writing* is inevitable: "writing in the empirical sense of the word is thus only one of the modalities of a more global parasitic order" (Moati 2014, 117). While Austin regards it as an obstacle, Derrida welcomes it as a goal that can be repeatedly reached by means of deconstruction. Derrida valorizes the undecidable double bind of the contradictory performative, which performs an impossible intention, and which Austin himself treated as *Infelicity*. I would even say that Derrida keeps deconstructing this impossibility of the declared authorial intention in all of his critical readings of the works of other philosophers (e.g., of Rousseau, but also of Foucault, Lévi-Strauss, de Saussure, etc.). Put otherwise, deconstruction is actually reactivated and nourished by this pragmatic paradox.

Aporia of Authentic Tracing

Derrida presented his deconstruction of signature in "Signature Event Context," which provoked contradictory philosophical feedback. Besides sharp polemic with Searle, Derrida's paper provoked some positive reactions, even so positive that it is understood today as one of the founding texts of politically and ethically oriented philosophy of performativity, which deals with the problematical formation of subjectivity by means of gender norms. This line of contemporary philosophy develops thoughts on the aporetic relation between politics and performativity. Besides late Foucault, it finds its inspiration in Derrida's reading of Austin's theory of the performative.

As Moati recently pointed out, both Derrida and Searle admire and criticize Austin—each of them for different reasons. It is well known that

Searle profoundly hated Derrida's interpretation of Austin and that Derrida turned his rejection into a ridiculous misunderstanding. Even more interestingly, neither of them interpreted Austin correctly. Furthermore, as shown by Moati in *Derrida/Searle*, while Derrida misinterprets Austin, Searle misinterprets both. Thus, Derrida's and Searle's misunderstanding can be explained by their divergent ways of reading Austin's work. In his critical reading of Austin, Derrida missed one point that, surprisingly, should have brought his reading of Austin closer to his own strategy of deconstruction. Searle, who has always presented himself as one of Austin's most engaged followers, missed a key point in Austin's work—the point that should have let him see that Derrida's work is much closer to Austin's conception than Searle's own. Let us examine this curious chain of misinterpretations, starting with a brief recap of Austin's work.

In *How to Do Things with Words,* Austin conceived the *speech act* as a summary of locutionary, illocutionary, and perlocutionary acts.[2] According to Austin, the illocutionary force of speech acts depends on conformity with conventional situations. Social conventions—and their occasional iteration—give speech its performativity. Austin explains the problem of intention in performatives by using the example of false promises. In the particular case of promising, it is appropriate that the person uttering the promise should have a certain intention, for example, to keep their word. Yet the utterance "I promise that . . ." is not false in the sense that even though she states that she does, she does not, or that even though she describes, she misdescribes, or misreports. In fact, she does promise, but the promise given here is in bad faith. This can be called a false move. Therefore, Austin considers some "false" speech acts as Infelicity: there is a pragmatic contradiction (which is not a logical paradox), a *pragmatic double bind* based on the disjunction between what is declared being done and what is actually being done. When something goes wrong, and the act is therefore at least to some extent a failure, the utterance is then not indeed false but in general unhappy. As Austin says in *How to Do Things with Words,* "for this reason we call the doctrine of *the things that can be and go wrong* on the occasion of such utterances, the doctrine of the *Infelicities*" (Austin 1962, 14). Because of his discovery of Infelicities, Austin's iteration becomes characterized by the curious fact that it is a repetition that spreads differences and never lets the same return—it sets new situations and makes it impossible to predict every context. Although Austin never defines the concept of speech act, he offers a preliminary and unfinished classification of speech acts (according to their illocutionary effectiveness). Austin himself emphasized the impossibility of creating a totally satisfying classification without any exceptions.

The first misinterpretation of Austin's work was proposed by Derrida in "Signature Event Context." In his reading of *How to Do Things with Words*, Derrida welcomes Austin's destabilization of the traditional true/false opposition in his analysis of word meanings. But he does not accept Austin's moving from truth value to context value. For Derrida, Austin's performativity, depending on social conventions, does not allow the meaning to leave the context (which guarantees the full presence of meaning). Derrida criticizes Austin's theory of performatives for his communicational intention: communication is limited by context. Therefore, in Austin, a word can only be performed as a voice (logos) repeated in the right context, not as writing (*grammé*) disseminated out of the conventional context. To demonstrate that Austin has not taken account of the graphemic predicates that already structure the locution, Derrida emphasizes that Austin's analysis requires a value of context, and even of a context exhaustively determined. Therefore, according to Derrida's "Signature Event Context," there is no irreducible polysemy, no dissemination escaping the horizon of the unity of meaning in Austin: "the long list of 'infelicities' which in their variety may affect the performative event always comes back to an element in what Austin calls the total context" (Derrida 1977b, 14). According to Derrida, Austin also excludes the possibility of every performative utterance being quoted. He insists on the fact that this possibility remains "abnormal, parasitic, that it constitutes a kind of extenuation or agonized succumbing of language that we should strenuously distance ourselves from and resolutely ignore" (Derrida 1977b, 16). In other words, in Derrida's reading, Austin rejects citation as a *dangerous supplement*, while he should have accepted it as a case of metaphysically inevitable general iterability—without it, there would not even be a successful performative. Therefore, Derrida comes to his "paradoxical but unavoidable conclusion—a successful performative is necessarily an 'impure' performative, to adopt the word advanced later on by Austin when he acknowledges that there is no 'pure' performative" (Derrida 1977b, 17).

The second—even more striking—misinterpretation of Austin's conception appears in the reading of his follower John R. Searle. By the end of *How to Do Things with Words*, Austin has given up on the idea of a theory of performatives as such. He concluded that all utterances are performative in nature, and thus he replaced his failed theory of performatives with the goal of a theory of speech acts in general. Trying to complete Austin's work (and ignoring the fact that Austin intentionally left it unfinished), Searle created his own classification of speech acts. In "Expression and Meaning. Studies in the Theory of Speech Acts," Searle mentions two main purposes of his ambitious reworking of Austin's conception. In his own words, his primary purpose is "to develop a reasoned classification of illocutionary acts into certain basic categories or types. It is to answer the question: How many kinds of illocutionary acts are there?" (Searle 1979, 1). His secondary purpose is "to assess Austin's classification to show in what respects it is adequate and in what respects inadequate" (Searle 1979, 1). This way, Searle prepares the ground for an exhaustive analysis of speech acts, based on his general theories of rules, meanings, and facts.[3] By doing so, Searle proves that he did not pay enough attention to Austin's important point that it is impossible to create a totally satisfying classification of speech acts. Moreover, Searle claims that the literal meaning of a sentence only determines a set of truth conditions (or other sorts of conditions of satisfaction) against a background of assumptions and practices. In "The Background of Meaning," Searle writes that the background is not fixed, but it is by no means in flux either: "since meaning is always a derived form of intentionality, contextual dependency is ineliminable" (Searle 1980, 231). Contrary to Austin, in Searle, responsibility for the Felicity of speech acts shifts from illocution to perlocution, from the speaker to the addressee, who is supposed to recognize the speaker's communicational intention in order to eliminate Infelicity. That is the main reason why Searle strictly refuses Derrida's contesting of the role of context and communication, as well as Derrida's welcoming of the parasitical supplementarity and intertextuality of writing.

Searle published his critical answer to Derrida in "Reiterating Differences." Derrida then responded to Searle's "Limited Inc abc . . ." Their polemic exchange was later published in *Limited Inc*—but without Searle's original critical paper, because he did not consent to its republication. As Gerald Graff recalls, Searle claims that citing means conventional contextual repetition enabling communication by means of speech acts. In Searle, iterability is an authentic, not a parasitical, repetition: one does not quit communication to benefit dissemination, because the iterability of linguistic forms is a necessary condition of the particular forms of intentionality that are characteristic of speech acts (Graff 1988, 27).

In *Derrida/Searle*, Moati pointed out that both Derrida (critically) and Searle (approvingly) present Austin as a philosopher of communication, which was not Austin's ambition. According to Moati, Austin opted for understanding the occasional effects of words that change the situation where they are pronounced. As Moati explained, although Searle considered himself as Austin's most truthful follower and even advocate in this debate, Derrida's own conception is still closer to Austin than Searle's is. In the words of Moati, "what fascinates Derrida in Nietzsche, what he despairs of not finding in Austin, is the thematic *of an intention that is unpredictable in its effects*" (Moati 2014, 61). Yet, writes Moati, it is not so: this topic can be found in Austin, because perlocution drives the speech act outside itself "without the result of the intention being *predictable* beforehand: I can have the intention to insult another without knowing if my act will have the *desired effect* on him" (Moati 2014, 61). It is problematic that Derrida regrets that Austin did not go far enough in his analysis of the cognitively uncapturable force of the performative, and that he only valorized the intentionality of the illocutionary act. According to Moati, "this reproach would be justified if Austin had reduced his theory *to perlocutionary acts alone* and in such a scenario had proposed to ground the perlocutionary teleologically—which would have contradicted Austin's own theory of perlocutionary 'force'" (Moati 2014, 62). But this is not so, because Austin describes the perlocutionary as impossible to be captured by cognition and, simultaneously, makes Felicity of the illocutionary act conditional on its conformity with the realizable conventional procedure in conventional circumstances. The source of reach and effectivity of illocutionary force is not in the will: "It is thus impossible to make the Austinian performative into a concept that insidiously reproduces the problematic of intentional presence, and to consider it a disguised logocentric constative" (Moati 2014, 62). Put otherwise, Austin's distinction of illocutionary and perlocutionary acts allowed him to formulate his theory of Infelicity: it is this discrepancy between illocution (my intention) and perlocution (effect on the other) that generates the Infelicity. Derrida missed this important fact—in his reading of Austin, illocution and perlocution pervade. As Moati explains, Searle's interpretation of Austin is not any better. Although Searle considered himself to be Austin's most truthful follower, Searle's philosophical conception differs from Austin's thinking so much that Austin appears to be even closer to Derrida than to Searle. Austin's and Derrida's conceptions are principally unfinishable: both take into account the pragmatic problem of iteration, which is completely missed by Searle.

Besides the divergent misreadings of Austin, this altercation is interesting because it clarifies Derrida's own philosophical conception of iterability. Derridean iterability is no repetition of the identical; it is rather transgression[4] of such a conception. In the words of Moati:

> For Searle, iteration is a phenomenon that conditions intentionality to the extent that it is through iteration that the rules of language are applicable, and the pragmatic communication of intentions becomes possible. Derrida draws precisely the inverse conclusion; for him, iterability is not fully taken into consideration by Searle, who confuses it with repeatability, with a recursive conception of rules that postulates their identity in repetition. When it is fully accepted, iterability is an opening to the advent [*venue*] of the Other: it does not repeat anything except its own alteration in the *nonidentical* of the new. (Moati 2014, 117)

I find that these objections miss their target because Searle does not understand the role of grafting in deconstructed writing, which is inseparable from deconstruction. From the beginning, Derrida and Searle do not understand each other: each of them speaks about another citation and about another writing.

Disseminated Tracing

I suggest understanding Derrida's writing act as subversively grafted on Austin's speech act. The writing act as a graft simultaneously overcomes and refers to the speech act. Because of the pervasiveness of constatives and performatives, and based on his discovery of the performative Infelicity, Austin declares that it is impossible to construct a total classification of speech acts, and thus, any totally satisfying theory of communication. Derrida missed this fact in Austin, when he took Austin's theory of speech acts for a theory of communication.

Nevertheless, Derrida follows Austin's discovery of Infelicity in his conception of the aporia. Derrida turns Austin's performative Infelicity into performative Necessity: Derrida calls this an act of dissemination (*grammé*) and places it in opposition to the metaphysical requirements from acts of communication (logos). While both the act and the performativity remain, Derrida turns speech Infelicity into writing Necessity. What matters here is not a critique of the theory of speech acts, but its continuation in subversion. Derrida's grafting consists in this continuation, transforming an individual problem into a general metaphysical rule—the problem of performative Infelicity in speech transforms into the problem of performative Necessity in writing. Because of its generalization of Necessity of Infelicity, Derrida's performativity of the writing act is principally dependent, grafted onto Austin's performative Infelicity of the speech act.

Moreover, Derrida's understanding of signature is much broader than the case of handwritten signature that is the subject of this book. In *Signsponge*, Derrida writes that deconstructed signature is a specter of the signer.

> Hence, the signature has to remain and disappear at the same time, remain in order to disappear, or disappear in order to remain. It has to do so, it is lacking, this is what matters. It has to, it fails to, remain by disappearing, it has to have to disappear, it has to have yet to disappear, a simultaneous and double demand, a double and contradictory postulation, a double obligation, a double bind which I have translated as the *double band* of the signature, the double band, the double band(s), hence the double(s) band. (Derrida 1984, 56)

Derrida's signature is an aporetic revenant, a specter of the undecidable identity, which is expected to reappear the same in the same context, but which never returns graphically the same because it is ontologically impossible to join the same context. As Leslie Hill puts it, in the deconstructive dissemination of meaning, the Felicity and the Infelicity of the performative cannot be put in mutual opposition: "the failure of performatives cannot be written off; it must be seen as a consequence of the structure of all performatives, in which case it becomes necessary to rethink the logic commanding so-called successful performatives, in so far as they are necessarily always marked by the possibility of failure, and by the ghostly, virtual prospect of that outcome" (Hill 2007, 30). Therefore, if the possibility of failure exists, then "no performative, even an allegedly successful one, can be deemed wholly to have succeeded. Failure, too, is only ever partial. Felicity and Infelicity cannot be opposed. The one always already inhabits the other. The outside is already inside" (Hill 2007, 30). The inevitable possibility of the Infelicity of each performative consists in the fact that, when an attempt is made to repeat it, the situation and the original context of the performative change. Derrida proposes to grasp this repetition, which makes return of the identical impossible, with his concept of *iterability* that "is not a feature of written language alone, but of *all* language, *both* spoken *and* written in general. For if all signs are by definition repeatable, there are no limits to that movement of repetition. Any sign, in so far as it repeated, can be detached from its context" (Derrida 1977b, 28).

Derrida's following of this postponed meaning leads him to situate his own thinking not beyond, but on the margins of Western metaphysics. I would even say that these margins delimit the only context accepted by Derrida's thinking: the main interest of deconstruction is limited by the total context of Western metaphysics. As such, the signature exists only in a deconstructable original gap,[5] between the metaphysical expectation of authenticity of handwritten traces, which can be also tested on the level of its stylized nature in order to identify the original signer, and to inevitably practically produce the difference in each individual act of manual signing. It is in this gap between the ideally supposed identity and the really present difference, where is situated the Derrida's *différance*, or precarious difference, which is evident only in the writing, not in the voice. Although the civic name of the signer is the same, the authenticity of its inscription is not. Despite its declared juridical sovereignty, no signature will ever reach this level of authenticity. In fact, the similarity of singular traces will always be infinitely approaching identity, trying to get as close as possible but never attaining it. Nevertheless, although in the performative act of legal handwritten signature, the signer herself ideally becomes identical with her civic name, each time the reality is slightly different. Handwritten signature is therefore a generalized unnatural essence of manual writing, or inevitable Infelicity, which is an aporetic condition of possibility of the performativity of writing. Austin's particular Infelicity in language becomes, in Derrida, a generalized aporia in writing, inseparable from Western metaphysical thinking.

Derrida comments on this in his "Force of Law," where he mentions the original *mystical force* that legalizes law. He defines the mystical as the place where "the discourse comes up against its limit: in itself, in its performative power itself" (Derrida 1992, 13). I find that the aporias of the performative of gender and signature are founded in the same movement: by every chosen gesture, choice of clothes, and chosen way of moving or speaking, the individual occasionally performs the formally established gender norms. Every single time, she does it in a slightly different way, which is conditioned by the singular state of mind in that particular event of writing. Contrary to the standardized rhetoric of tests and proofs of recognition rooted in the Western metaphysics of onto-semantic presence, no signer can ever reproduce the exact shape of her specimen signature in her individual signature: every single signing act produces a slightly new shape. Yet every new shape is supposed to be equally characteristic of the signer's soul as the previously written and archived specimen signature. In the sense of this aporetical interval between unpredictable event of signing and legal expectation of recognition, Petra Gehring recalls Derrida's claim on ultimate insolubility of the problem of legal mediation: "Law admits no pure solutions, no good decisions, and in this sense it must admit to being violent just as . . . language—everything in which mediation is somehow at work—is necessarily 'contaminated'" (Gehring 2008, 61).

If I find Derrida particularly helpful for conceptualizing this aporia, it is because he understands the performative in a broader sense than Austin does in his linguistic conception. Derrida even goes as far as considering the pragmatic paradox to be the condition of possibility of the deconstructed writing. Austin separated stating and performing, but Derrida rejoins them: because there is no metaphysics without aporia, *there is a performative dimension of the truth*. Austin's particular pragmatic paradox becomes a generalized pragmatic paradox in Derrida, who takes it for the aporia inseparable from Western metaphysical thinking. As such, the concept of pragmatic paradox could be useful not only in the linguistic, but also in the theatrical or musical sense of performing as playing or interpreting the given role according to the given scenario or libretto. Nevertheless, there is still a difference between this conception of the performative and Derrida's conception of the subversive performative. In the conventional signature act, the signer legitimately becomes identical with her civic name, but every time, she does it slightly differently. This formal difference is simultaneously ideally impossible and really inevitable. The style of handwriting is not just a rhetorical work of self-imitation and self-authentication. Its goal is self-identification. The authenticity of the analyzed signature is usually recognized by two things: first, by its similarity to the signer's previous traces; second, by its originality, which links the signer's personal ability to produce similar traces to the existential trace of that particular inscription. This combination of ideal and real aspects of the examination results in the supposed recognition of authentic and forged signatures. However, the signature that is considered to be authentic fits in the interval between a dissimilar signature written by the true signer, and a strongly similar signature written by a forger.

Although the metaphysical force of law enforces the signer to perform a recognizable repetition of her previous handwritten traces, this requirement can never be fulfilled. Each single reading, translation, or replica generates ontologically inevitable variation and, thus, demonstrates the inevitably different nature of each new act of re-presentation. Derrida does not believe in anything like accurate or precise reading of a text. As Legrand puts it, "also a 'precise' repetition implies the new, *any* repetition *causes* the new and, thus, produces the difference" (Legrand 2003, 254).

The authority of the identity test is based on the difference between speech act and writing act in the sense that, contrary to the speech act, the writing act is linked to the expectation of the politico-ontological identity of the signer, which should be verified by examining the authenticity and similarity of the traces left by her. The civic identity of the signer is also determined by her absence. If one considers that the supposed signer, whose name is legibly written next to the signature, really signed by her own hand, one can proclaim the given signature to be authentic. But the authenticity of this final speech act about the authenticity of the writing act is not tested by experts. In Austin's theory of speech act, there is no "doing" in the sense of forging: his speech act does not have the status of a falsity, but of an Infelicity. Infelicity happens when the speech act is pronounced in bad faith. For Austin, in such a case, the speech act is not performed successfully: one does other things with words than one should. But still, what decides about Felicity or Infelicity is only the speaker's conscience. Austin's Infelicity of the speech act is not inauthenticity of the writing act, which has to be tested by an expert. The result of the authenticity test of the signature's writing act—the signer is innocent/the forger is guilty—is communicated by means of a speech act, which is usually accompanied by a series of further speech acts: identifying the forger, proclaiming her guilty, sentencing her for fraud, and so forth. Writing acts can be tested and the test results can be translated into speech acts that can declare the signer guilty of forgery and even fraud. In this sense, the writing act provokes speech acts, which determine and distribute its further effects.

Nevertheless, if one wanted to solve positively the problem of signature as authentic and unrepeatable performative, which I propose to call the *writing act*, one would have to quit Derrida's aporia. His ethical way of thinking, calling for respect for the deferred meaning, does not bring us to any solution of this problem. Instead of proposing a theory of rigorous interpretation, Derrida emphasizes the impossibility of fulfilling a meaning promised by the performative. It only points to the danger of totalities, which hides in any radical solution of any problem.

Derrida repeatedly claims it is impossible to quit the expectations of Western metaphysics and to overcome the prejudice of meaning in its total presence. Our language is metaphysical, and, as such, it does not allow any other understanding of meaning than the metaphysical one, which is performed in the constructed semantic presence of the law. Derrida's aporia does not have (and cannot have) any solution: it is a melancholic way of thinking in which metaphysical certainties and prejudices are an inevitable trap[6] that cannot be escaped, but are ethically necessary to speak about.

From Derrida's ethics of meaning, it is worth retaining his call for modesty (resisting metaphysical violence) in our metaphysical expectation. I aim to positively formulate the difference between speech act and writing act, using metaphysically acceptable definitions and critical thinking. In such a conception, the handwritten signature is a writing act that makes it possible to pre-conventionally change the form of things in the performing event. In this respect, it does not differ from the speech act, as it was formulated by Austin (not by Searle). But their principal difference[7] consists in the fact that the writing act is a unique performative event of testimony.[8] In this testimony, the signer performs an occasional and unrepeatable trace of manual writing, which is to be interpreted as the signer's expression of her unique and recognizable style of handwriting. Scientific discourses on signature use this aporetic *double conception of authenticity*[9] to achieve a metaphysically accurate conception of authenticity of signature. Thus, signature as performative is double: on the one hand, there is a writing act, which is always an inevitable Infelicity, as Derrida demonstrates; on the other, there is a personal expression of the signer's unique soul in her handwriting, which is always a successful performative, as experts presuppose. In this metaphysical manner, the signature expresses the soul of its signer, as in both the psychological discipline of graphology and the forensic analysis of handwriting.

Therefore, the answer to the previous question is positive: the writing act is characterized by the fact that manual writing does something that language and machine writing do not. Handwriting is able to generate a metaphysical expectation of authenticity; not in the Derridean sense of radical uniqueness and unrepeatability of the traces of writing, but rather in the forensic discourse sense of repeatability of natural style of writing by the signer herself (and no one else). The metaphysical expectation of authenticity of traces of manual writing is rooted in the expert's belief that the signer inevitably naturally expresses her soul in every movement of her hand in the process of handwriting.

From the ethical viewpoint of deconstruction, forensic semiotics would have to resign to its metaphysical expectation, identifying similarity with authenticity of personally stylized traces. Such a deconstructed forensic science would understand similarity as similarity, without forcing it to signify identity. An expert's deconstructed speech acts would proclaim the signer's similarity, not identity. What happens in the practice of manual signing is an iteration of traces, not a repetition of models: in an individual handwritten signature, style cannot be expressed at once, but only generated in time. Style is processual, continuous, and unfinished. A handwritten signature does not uncover any ready-made psychological pattern. On the contrary, the signer's style is continuously composed and completed with every single writing act. In this respect, from Derrida's perspective, the stylized signature is a parasitical performative, which should be understood in the interval between recognition and transgression of the constructed identity.

I find that the legal practice of manual signing, inspired by deconstruction, should take into consideration this gap between the legislative conception of the signer's style as a constantly repeated gesture of identification and her inevitable transgression in every single iterated trace, given by the changing movement of the writing hand. Authenticity of manual writing means unrepeatability of instant hand movement, which is so unique that even the signer herself cannot repeat. She can only imitate it, just like the others can. Every writing act is unrepeatable, not even by the same signer. In this rigorous sense it is a *radically authentic* trace of immediate and occasional manual writing.

Such an *authenticity of traces* of manual writing, or the writing act, considerably differs from the *authenticity of style* of manual writing—or the handwriting—that it is often mistaken for. Contrary to the writing act, which is authentic in the sense of being immediate and unrepeatable by anyone else, handwriting is authentic in the sense of being constantly repeatable by the signer's own hand. This second authenticity differs from the first one by its founding aporia. In order to recognize the signer by her handwriting, it is necessary to grasp the authenticity of manual writing in an aporetic way: on the one hand, as a uniqueness (each signer has a way of handwriting that no other signer can perfectly imitate); on the other hand, as a repetition (each signer has her own way of manual writing, which enables her to constantly generate her own shapes of manual writing). The term "handwriting" is based on the idea of the signer's natural—thus, inevitable and constant—repetition of handwritten forms, generating her recognizable and identifiable personal style. In this view, transformations of the dynamical composition of manual writing occur in each individual signature act, which is not a citable speech act successfully developed in the process of communication, but a *parasitical writing act* iterated in the process of dissemination. In deconstruction, the politics of signature is inevitably parasitical, anticipating the metaphysical order of the law, which materializes in each individual event of the writing act.

Thus, the meaning of handwritten signature can be found in the semantic interval between repeatable, mechanical imprint and unrepeatable, singular authorial work. This gap in total presence of meaning is covered by the legal requirement for civic identification, which generates a double—biometric and artistic—expectation. Handwritten signature is captured in the aporia of metaphysical expectation of both the reproducible identity of quality present in authorial style and the unreproducible similarity of events producing traces. In the next chapter, I focus on the fact that each individual handwritten trace is unrepeatable because of iteration, which helps to constitute the signer's original style, but which simultaneously destroys the originality of her traces.

Chapter VI

Deconstructing Handwritten Signature III

The main problem with handwritten signature is that the expected recognizable style of handwriting is not only produced by a repetitive intentional imitation of one's own previous trace. It is also produced by an accidental iteration of other traces that were not intended to imitate and repeat. Without this metaphysical aporia, the handwritten signature as a civic sign would not be possible. Without signature as stylized trace, there would be no experts in authenticity of handwritten signature, handwriting, and artwork, because one could not have distinguished between the original and the forgery of the author's style. The event of writing cannot be liberated from its aporetic metaphysical determination: the handwritten signature as sign could not exist without this double-binded conception of author's style.

    This metaphysical expectation that manually produced traces can be identically shaped is linked to the metaphysical category of personal identity. From the viewpoint of metaphysics of the law, handwritten trace makes it possible to identify the person who signed—this means that until some degree of resemblance is found, a similar trace has to be seen as an identical trace.[1] Moreover, if experts in graphology and forensic analysis compare several versions of handwritten signature with the specimen signature, they can tell which versions of the former are "not similar enough" and which are "already too identical" to prove the civic identity of their signer. Despite the necessary distinction between civic identity and alterity of the supposed signer, there is no generally admissible degree of similarity between her registered specimen signature and any further version of her manual signing. According to the given discourse, until the conventionally set degree of similarity, similar is considered to be identical.

Can the signer's recognizable style of handwriting generate and guarantee the signer's civic identity? Is handwritten signature an authorial work? Is the author the only person who is able to produce recognizable variations of her handwritten signature? If one's signature is recognizable, does it mean that it is sufficiently similar, because it is identically stylized? Does it mean that it is a *stylized work*, which carries a strictly personal style constantly repeatable by its author, but unrepeatable by anyone else?

And what about the specimen signature? What is its relationship with the signer's style? Is every version of handwritten signing a falsification of the origin of style, the specimen signature? Or is it, on the contrary, its verification?

I suggest searching for answers to these questions by comparing two conceptions of ontological semiotics formulated by Gilles Deleuze and Jacques Derrida. Both thinkers agree that no signer can identically manually repeat her own traces and thus fulfill the expectation of identical repetition, but for different reasons. For Deleuze, the reason is varying of sense, and for Derrida, it is dissemination of meaning. Based on this consideration, I propose reconsidering the possibilities and limits of their understanding of the controversial problem of logical repeatability of ontologically unrepeatable traces.

Derrida's ontological semiotics is quasi-melancholic: its ambition is neither to construct nor to destroy the meaning, but to deconstruct it—to trace and to defer it. Derrida introduces into his thinking a double gesture, which allows him to balance between metaphysical certainty of the total presence of meaning and metaphysical certainty of the total absence of meaning. The movement of deferral brings him to an ambivalent semantic zone of Western metaphysics that was firstly described by Plato. It is Derrida's philosophical zone of pragmatic paradox, the source of deconstructed writing. As Derrida puts it, Plato determines metaphysically present meaning based on a hierarchy of couples of semantically opposed concepts, such as universal and particular, true and false, or masculine and feminine. Elements of these binary oppositions are submitted to an apparently natural hierarchy, which determines one of the elements of the couple as the superior carrier of the totally present meaning. The meaning of the other element is its negation: it is a place of totally absenting meaning of the first element. Observation of these binary oppositions enables Derrida to formulate two complementary characteristics of Platonism: on the one hand, Plato's oppositions are secretly hierarchically organized; on the other, all variations that do not fit into the relation of strict opposition are marginalized.

Derrida indicates that Plato's thoughts about written mediation, which is considered to be relieved from ontological authenticity, are pervaded by a semantico-ontological hierarchy. Plato considers writing to be a humanly imperfect instrument to represent divinely perfect Ideas. Derrida describes Plato's marginalization of writing in his *Pharmacy,* focused on the metaphysical constitution of meaning in Plato's dialogue *Phaedrus*. In it, Plato explains the lack of authenticity of writing by means of an ancient legend about the invention of writing and its problematic legitimization. By means of his reading of *Phaedrus,* Derrida aims to demonstrate that Plato bases his explanation of the ontological insufficiency of writing on a semantically ambivalent use of the Greek word *pharmakon*. In dialogue between the inventor of writing and the monarch-legislator, who holds the supreme power of legitimization, the writing grasped as *pharmakon* semantically oscillates between a useful remedy helping memory and a harmful poison perverting the original meaning of spoken words and destroying the living memory. In Plato's dialogue, the legislator is skeptical: he prefers the spoken word, which, unlike the written one, is not perverted by supplementation and interpretation. As Derrida puts it in "Plato's Pharmacy," the king objects to writing because "under pretext of supplementing memory, writing makes one even more forgetful; far from increasing knowledge, it diminishes it" (Derrida 1981b, 100). Because writing always comes from the outside, it only copies the originally pronounced meaning: the exteriority of writing is the reason for having recourse to treacherous mimetics. Derrida's reading of *Phaedrus* finally demonstrates that the legislator sees writing as an unreliable invention, which is ontologically degraded and always derived from the spoken word—the carrier of the totally present meaning.

Derrida reconsiders the contradictory status of writing in "Signature Event Context," where he pays attention to writing that performs the role of a signature. On the one hand, signature is understood from the position of legal metaphysics as a signer's legal representation. It is a performative disposed to communication, which is functional because it supposes that the signer's graphic expression will be constantly repeatable. On the other hand, the deconstructed signature is a *grammé*, writing, and material side of the semantic process: unrepeatable traces lead only to another traces. In terms of dissemination, handwritten signature can be taken for a *stylized trace*—unrepeatable trace of a repeatable style—whose semantic and legal authority is built on the contradictory requirement to repeat the unrepeatable. Because of its unrepeatability, handwritten signature is neither a performative nor a speech act: it cannot be functionally repeated, because every individual attempt to repeat it exactly by hand produces a new form, a new version of the signature, more or less similar to the previous ones, but never the same. Every signature is a new variation of the specimen signature. In Derrida, there is no original version of the signature: the original signature does not exist. Paradoxically, what is original is the deferral: the repeated meaning is always already deferred. Derrida's quasi-melancholic strategy of deconstruction aims to formulate a theory of neither signification nor interpretation. It tries to grasp the performative dispersion of meanings into other meanings. The sign is grasped here as a representation of representation, a trace deferring its meaning to other traces. Such a trace is metaphysically unsatisfying, ungraspable, unclassifiable: it is a specter, revenant, haunting remain of meaning of the previous traces. Handwritten signature as a trace is an alogical remainder of being, a specter, which comes to haunt the metaphysical certainties: its ontologico-logical meaning is not totally present, never entirely graspable. On the contrary, as David Appelbaum accurately puts it,

> Logical thought, in some sense of the term, that censors and secrets proscribed files, in that very act phantomizes the demon. The ghost's alogical apparition lurks as a potent disinterment of introverted material capable of subverting metaphysical commitment and imperiling intentional consciousness. The rupture may be explosive, seductive, or merely plaintive, but the reaction of philosophy is predictable (predicative). It will repeat the purgative: sharpen definitions, refine distinctions, deploy further argument, or detail dialectics. (Appelbaum 2009, 62)

Derrida understands his *hauntology* as a science of warding off specters, revenants, supplements, parergons—all the meanings that emerge and call for attention despite the fact that they were supposed to remain hidden, well covered, forgotten. As Nicolas Royle puts it, Derridean supplement haunts us by the very fact that we can never grasp all its effects. The only thing that deconstruction can do is to "describe the effects of what leaves its trace without ever itself being either present or absent, and thereby to transform the terrain" (Royle 2003, 50). Deconstruction is a supplement of prejudices generated by Western metaphysics. As a supplement, it acts in its margins: in its relation to logos, it is neither totally present nor totally absent. Derrida's thinking is a specter,[2] which comes to haunt the certitudes of our metaphysical expectations: "Supplement haunts. It is ghostly" (Royle 2003, 50). Its partial presence and partial absence is unbearable, because it is by directed *ethos*, which cannot be simply repressed. Therefore, in *Specters of Marx*, Derrida suggests a new philosophical work with texts that treat revenants not repressively, but accommodatingly, and that enable their "performative interpretation, that is, of an interpretation that transforms the very thing it interprets" (Derrida 1994a, 63). As Williams writes in his preface to *Signature Derrida*, Derrida's performative use of the concept of signature means that one has to "to take responsibility as an author. One must own up to one's words" (Williams 2013, X).

The metaphysical expectations of handwritten signature can be deconstructed as follows. The violence of the law forces every citizen to write her own name correlatively to the specimen signature: one occasionally performed signature must permanently represent the civic identity of the given signer. The deconstructed handwritten signature cannot be used to identify the signer, because no signer can manually repeat[3] her specimen signature to achieve the identical graphic expression. Because in deconstruction, the event of writing is not equal to conventional sign, civic identity cannot be reached by handwritten signature: it cannot be reached in any iterated movement of the hand. As such, the deconstructed specimen signature is radically unrepeatable: contrary to the legal expectation, manual writing cannot be used to verify the signer's civic identity. So how is it possible that the signature usually fulfills this function?

Aporia of Identical Repetition

According to the metaphysical expectation of identity, by repeating a presentation of an unrepeatable event, one can generate a representation of the event as its reliable and repeatable sign. In Derrida's view, the metaphysical concept of identity is expected to ward off the recurrent *différance* in the practice of representation. But *différance* persists in iteration, which disseminates repeated fragments of texts into new contexts and generates their perfidious supplements instead of reliable signs.

Although both Derrida and Deleuze work with the problems of events and signs, their understanding of these concepts is very different. For Deleuze, the main role of signs is to capture vital affects from individual events. Although, as Poché claims, deconstruction "holds on the side of 'yes,' consents to life" (Poché 2007, 55), Derrida's nod to life is mostly a kind of resistance to the violence of Western metaphysics. But "deconstruction does not do only the *act of resistance*, it does also the *act of belief*. It says 'yes' to the justice, which is never identical with the law" (Poché 2007, 55). Such a justice conceived in a melancholic way cannot be established inside any metaphysical order: one can only dream it, imagine it as a promise that is to come, but that will never be fulfilled. Contrary to the metaphysical expectations, justice is not produced by the law; it conditions the law. Therefore, justice is a condition of possibility and not a result of the legal performativity, which continues to promise its arrival. In Derrida, justice and writing are metaphysically ungraspable: they are the spectral, the *quasi-legal*.

In this respect, in his own way, Derrida gets closer to Franz Kafka's literary work, especially to his novel *The Trial*. Derrida's understanding of the Kafkaesque is characterized by his ethics of aporia consisting in the trap of prejudice, of metaphysical expectation that cannot be fulfilled. In Derrida's subversive ethical thinking, the traditional hierarchy in binary opposition of law and justice is reversed: justice is not performance of the law, but an a priori condition of possibility of the law. Because justice is prior to law, it is unreachable by legal representation: justice is a metaphysical expectation of performance of the law, which cannot be fulfilled. According to Derrida, direct access to the law is a prejudice coming from misunderstanding of the legal performativity.

In "Préjugés: Before the Law," Derrida comments on Kafka's allegory of the man before the law: although every citizen is obliged to know the law, his access to the law is denied by legal representatives, insiders of the law, who make their living by deferring its meaning. Their supplementarity is essential: it is impossible to get through it any further. Reaching justice by means of legal representation is a mere prejudice of someone who is external to the legal performativity. The supreme authority and force of the law consist in its promise of justice, which is expected but remains absent.

In "Force of Law," Derrida conceives *justice-to-come* as a promise, which can be fulfilled by the practice of legal representation only as perpetually deferred. Although it is impossible to reach justice by law, law is possible because of this promise given in bad faith. Derrida comes from Kafkaesque legal aporias to ethical memento. Ethic of deconstruction is an un-representational expectation of justice, not a representational moral of the law. Derrida himself situates deconstruction into an aporia—on the margin of every scientifically positive method and practice of representation. In his work, he systematically calls attention to prejudices contained in metaphysical expectation of representation, that is, in demonstrating that the law always betrays life, and vice versa.

Contrary to Derrida, Deleuze's ontological semiotics is positively vital and creative. His philosophy of immanence would like to be an anti-dialectical thinking. In this respect, Deleuze speaks about an irreducible difference, which is in opposition to dialectical opposition. In his eulogy for Deleuze, Derrida emphasizes his agreement with this Deleuzean thesis concerning "a difference 'more profound' than a contradiction (*Difference and Repetition*), a difference in the joyously repeated affirmation ('yes, yes'), a taking into account of the simulacrum" (Derrida 2001b, 193). In order to turn away from the dialectic way of representation, Deleuze considered it necessary to rethink Plato, for whom dialectics is the supreme method that helps thinkers to understand reality. In the *Logic of Sense*, Deleuze finds out that Plato's critique of the sophist as producer of images subverts his own hierarchical ontology of sense. As soon as the simulacrum is grasped by words and integrated into the language, it stops being an ontologically degraded copy: "it harbors a positive power which denies *the original and the copy, the model and the reproduction*" (Deleuze 1990, 262). The impossibility of the method of division so dear to Plato is the price for including the simulacrum in the language, which gives it a positive verbal being, or definition. A scandalous situation occurs: simulacra require their civic rights in Plato's state. Trying to understand the reasons behind this "innocent" subversion of Platonism by Plato himself, Deleuze situates it on the *plane of immanence*: when Plato stops relying on his method of division—between the philosopher as a true candidate and the sophist as a false candidate—he sets off to the unknown. An event of unprecedented dimension occurs: Plato is aware that what he fears and pursues in the person of the sophist is the simulacrum. The appearance and its unstable being subvert the strict ontological hierarchy of the world of Platonism.

But, as Deleuze puts it, Plato is not the only one who meets simulacrum while distinguishing between the model and the copy: every searcher for truth risks experiencing a similar event. She moves in the plane of immanence: the truth she finds there is the truth of a singular experienced event, or a singular affect linked with her own *becoming-other*.[4] Plato's and Deleuze's ontologies differ radically: instead of rethinking the truth of Plato's perpetual being, Deleuze is interested in the sense of transforming being, of becoming. His critique of Platonism is motivated by the effort to shift toward the conception of immanence without any opposite—Deleuze's immanence does not have anything apart from itself. As such, immanence does not need transcendence, defined as the outside of the world we live in. Therefore, he proposes a philosophy that creates concepts based on the processual transformation of a *multiplicity of becoming*, and not on a presupposition of an unchangeable *identity of being*. According to Deleuze, philosophical thinking is not motivated by any perpetual truth, but rather by a varying sense, involved in a process of formation that remains unfinished. Philosophers are supposed to create new concepts in encounter with something suddenly lived, but previously undescribed. This encounter can help us to express the *pure events* that, as Pearson puts it, " 'ground' language in the sense that they enjoy a singular, impersonal, and pre-individual existence inside the language which expresses them. In other words, events enjoy an independence of expression in relation to their actual incarnation in bodies and states of affairs" (Pearson 1999, 122).

Based on his reading of Nietzsche and Spinoza, in *Difference and Repetition* Deleuze explains that a singular expression can be only repeated by producing a new variation: identity between the previous and the following expression can never be reached. "Repetition" is a singular expression of the past event, an *eternal return* of the difference. Such a production of sense happens in the name of something excessive that causes a metamorphosis without end. This excess is the pure event that puts in motion everything that happens in the plane of immanence. Therefore, a being involved in a process of metamorphosis always has an unfinished identity. As Zourabichvili notices, such an immanent conception of "the event puts the idea of history into crisis. That which happens, insofar as it happens and breaks with the past, does not belong to history and cannot be explained by it" (Zourabichvili 2012, 53).

If we return to the problematics of signature, we should grasp it as a stylized work. In Deleuze, style is a singular creative continuity, which is characteristic for semantic systems in permanent imbalance. Style varies, evolves: it is a pure variability. Creation is an affective production of signs, which react to ontologically prior events,[5] and which form ideas. In Deleuze's conception of immanence, an idea is someone's creative product: it does not exist beforehand; it is produced in the process of becoming in the plane of immanence. As he puts it in *Proust and Signs*, it is actually in this process of becoming or metamorphosis that the affect is born: ontological signs are born from affects. Proust finds his past being in signs composed of his past affects—by means of these signs, he can recall them from his memory in the form of blocs of percepts, to reconstruct his affective relation with the past being. In his own words, "an essence is always a birth of the world, but style is that continuous and refracted birth, that birth regained in substances adequate to essences, that birth which has become the metamorphosis of objects. Style is not the man, style is essence itself" (Deleuze 2000, 48). In Deleuze's conception of immanent artistic creation, essence is individualizing; it "is in itself difference" (Deleuze 2000, 48).

From Deleuze's viewpoint, the event of signature can be grasped as a production and a stylized sign of the signer's affect. The graphic style is created by varying the signs of affects. Because varying is not repetition of the same, the style of signature does not always generate the same affect. Therefore, the stylized graphic expression can only perform a creative *becoming-signer*, not the signer's civic identity. As Daniel W. Smith puts it, "for Deleuze, Being is difference, and time is repetition" (Smith 2003b, 51). In the Deleuzean conception of immanence, the style—produced in time, as a repetition—performatively creates new Being, as a difference. Comparison of these two ontological semiotics shows the possibilities and limits of these two different ways of poststructuralist thinking: one keeps representation, the other rejects it. Derrida's negative ontology of supplementarity considerably differs from Deleuze's positive ontology of becoming, adds Smith: "Derrida explicitly aligns himself with the trajectory of transcendence, while Deleuze consistently follows the trajectory of immanence" (Smith 2003b, 47). While Derrida tries to deconstruct Western metaphysics, Deleuze tries to construct it in his own manner.

In Deleuze, to stop rejecting the falseness of appearance means to accept the simulacrum and to resign to its opposite—the representation.[6] In contrast, for Derrida, the thing that subverted Platonism was not the thing that subverted representation. In his view, Plato rethought both sides of representation at once: the simulation and the truth, the original and the forged copy, the poisonous and the healing effect of the *pharmakon*. Plato simultaneously constructs and deconstructs his metaphysics. He can neither get rid of representation nor fatally subvert its universe: he can only misrecognize it in his own practices of recognition. Contrary to Deleuze, Derrida does not believe it is possible to reach any pure, undialectical immanence or creation. As Evans warned, "Derrida believes neither in the pure positivity of the sign nor in communication, for him simply 'rational decoding' for, as he says in late work, in it is maintained an inherent 'secret,' something that remains in any communication beyond its intelligible content" (Evans 2014, 20). Derrida's understanding of representation subverts the expected hierarchy of binary oppositions: he can see the principle of its functioning in admitted substitution of one being by another and, at the same time, in admitted simulation of their semantic identity.

But, as Derrida explains in *Positions*, his deconstruction does not stop at the stage of the overthrow of oppositions, because such an overthrow would leave unchanged the oppositional structure of metaphysics. More precisely, Derrida's work with the concept of *aporia* reveals an interval between the binary oppositions. To better mark this interval, Derrida introduced several conceptual simulacra with undecidable properties, which can no longer be included within binary oppositions, but which, however, inhabit philosophical opposition, resisting and disorganizing it, without ever constituting a third term:

> the *pharmakon* is neither remedy nor poison, neither good nor evil, neither the inside nor the outside, neither speech nor writing; the *supplement* is neither a plus nor a minus, neither an outside nor the complement of an inside, neither accident nor essence, etc.; the *hymen* is neither confusion nor distinction (neither identity nor difference, neither consummation nor virginity, neither the veil nor unveiling, neither the inside nor the outside). (Derrida 1981d, 42)

As he clarifies in *Positions*,

> I try to keep myself at the *limit* of philosophical discourse. I say limit and not death, for I do not at all believe in what today is so easily called the death of philosophy (nor, moreover, in the simple death of whatever—the book, man, or god, especially since, as we all know, what is dead wields a very specific power). Thus, the limit on the basis of which philosophy became possible, defined itself as the *episteme*, functioning within a system of fundamental constraints, conceptual oppositions outside of which philosophy becomes impracticable. (Derrida 1981d, 6)

In his readings, he operates this double gesture, double play that establishes a "simultaneously faithful and violent circulation between the inside and the outside" (Derrida 1981d, 6) of Western philosophy.

I find Derrida's conception of *aporia* both philosophically productive and systematically neglected in Derridean studies. The concept is crucial: it helps us to think in intervals, and not in oppositions. In this sense, the oppositional structure of traditional metaphysics is deconstructed. Derrida's sensitivity to limit zones, margins, intervals, and aporias is particularly important regarding my methodological approach, which is based on my revision of Peirce's metaphysical categories that condition his ontologically rooted logical system of signs. To be sure, not all semiotic conceptions are ontologically oriented. De Saussure's conception of sign, for example, avoids any ontological claims—no real object is involved in his conception of sign. Peirce, on the contrary, builds a complex semiotic ontology, including real object as an important part of his conception of sign. Because Derrida's work is first of all the deconstruction of any form of ontology, it is helpful in building aporetical distance from Peirce's ontologically oriented semiotics. By taking an instrumental approach to both of these philosophical conceptions, I formulate a triple metaphysical aporia, which builds a triple metaphysical expectation of handwritten signature as a sign, as a representation.

In Derrida's aporetical approach to both ontology and semiotics, the legal handwritten signature appears to be a precarious trace: it must be traced in a recognizable way, which is enforced by the legal demand to manually repeat the form of one of its previous versions. The law supposes that handwritten repetition of the once registered picture guarantees that even if a name is illegibly written, the trace will be recognized and identified as someone's authentic signature: the signer and her signature are supposed to be essentially and authentically similar. In legal studies and similar disciplines, such as forensic analysis or criminology, the determination of degrees of similarity becomes the attribution of the given signature to one pole of a binary opposition: either the signature is considered to be authentic and proves the identity of the signer, or it is considered forged and does not prove anything. In legal practice, stating the similarity became stating the identity: the approximative turned into the identical. In this respect, Derrida warns that the law presents metaphorical similarity as legal identity: meaning must be totally present. This could explain the fact that the signer tries to be as pictorially consistent as possible: the continuity of her civic identity depends on the recognizability of her unique style. Even this is not enough to fulfill the legal demand: civic identity cannot be fully attained by means of handwritten signature.

Handwritten signature is a trace of past presence and as such returns to our presence from the past. As Derrida notices in *Les yeux de la langue*, handwriting produces a revenant, which "comes to us, returns to us and speaks to us *after* the death of its signatory. Something in it resonates the voice of a ghost" (Derrida 2012a, 15). In *Surtout, pas de journalistes!* he experiences a similar situation when a sound "recording of voice re-produces a production. The 'image' of voice is here an image of life production and not an object of spectacle. In this sense, it is no longer an image, but a re-production of the same thing, the same production. It always strikes me, when I hear the voice of someone who is dead, what I am not when I see a photograph or a picture of someone who is dead" (Derrida 2016, 42). For Derrida, whether handwritten or technical, recording is a repeated presentation, re-presentation of the passing past being, which is captured in a recorded perpetual, returning "image that erases itself as an image, a re-presentation, which is put as a pure presentation. The life itself can be archived and spectralized in its self-affection" (Derrida 2016, 43). In Derrida, the returning trace of the past being is its revenant, or its specter. Deconstructed signatures are specters of the signers, who do not have and—as specters—cannot have any civic identity.

Is it possible—despite all of the objections raised by deconstruction—to explain the fact that the handwritten signature remains a legitimate sign, which is expected to enable recognition of the signer? How can the signature as sign still assume this ambition? What—despite all individual variations and modifications—remains so similar that we tend to approximate and to consider every single signature by the same signer to be the same? Put otherwise, what is a signature and what is a style?

To answer this question, I begin by comparing Derrida's and Deleuze's work with literature. Derrida himself tries to deconstruct the rigidity of difference between philosophy and literature. Every writing—both philosophical and poetic—bears in itself metaphysical violence of the law, the order, the code. Because neither philosophy nor literature can be relieved from metaphysical construction of language, both can reach subversive play by approaching each other: philosophy can adopt an autobiographical view and literature can adopt vigilance against metaphysical violence built in the words in use. Contrary to Derrida, Deleuze understands philosophy and literature as two distinguished domains of human creativity. While he understands philosophy as an assemblage of concepts, literature is for him a creative assemblage of percepts and affects. In both cases, Deleuze's creative arrangement of signs is made out of chaos—it gives semantic consistency to events happening in the plane of immanence. This comparison helps to understand the difference in their conceptual preferences—while Deleuze prefers the concept of style, Derrida opts for the concept of signature. Derrida understands writer's signature as a result of performative iteration due to return of displaced specters; Deleuze defines artist's style as a result of productive creation caused by encounter with unique event.

Contrary to my understanding of signer's style as an iterated play with visual material of handwritten letters, and to forensic and graphological definitions of signer's style as a reliably recognizable personal pattern in handwriting, Derrida himself uses the concept of *style* to indicate a working strategy. He also uses the concept of *signature* as linked to biographical and autobiographical characteristics of one's strategy in writing. In this sense, he even formulates it as a new imperative for philosophical writing, which "must today undergo—is today in the process of undergoing—a complete reevaluation.

> A philosopher's biography can no longer today be considered either as an empirical accident that leaves the philosopher's name and signature simply outside the system that then lends itself to a simply immanent philosophical reading and thereby makes it possible to write the lives of philosophers in the ornamental, traditional style that you well know, or as psycho biographies that give an account of the genesis of the system on the basis of empirical mechanisms . . . A new problematic of the biographical in general and of the biography of philosophers in particular must mobilize more than one new resource, including, at the very least, a new problematic of the proper name and the signature of the philosopher. (Derrida 2020, 26)

To illustrate Derrida's use of the concept of *signature*, I propose to have a closer look at his *Signesponge* where he mentions *signature* as a continuous iteration of a certain set of distinctive signs by which one can recognize the author. Ponge's literary signature organizes his own dissemination of signs, which are absorbed by other signs. Following the idiom of his own name—Ponge or "sponge"—his "spongy" signature becomes both dissolved and monumental in his work. According to Derrida, this personal manner of using words generates a literary idiom of writing, which does not guarantee any reasonable, reliable, and solid civil identity of the author, but rather imposes an autobiographic "signature without border, thrown overboard" (Derrida 1984, 124). This performative literary signature is produced by compulsive return: "but according to the law, a small part of the text, (the) *signature,* takes hold of the text, which it covers to the point that it also makes the text into a small part of itself, and therefore overflows it" (Derrida 1984, 122).

Contrary to Ponge's artistic literary signature, legal handwritten signature does not perform an unusual use of words, but their unusual plastic form: handwritten signature is a singular picture of the given word of a name. The picture of name, which is invented, needs to be distinguished from the word of name, which is given beforehand. As Derrida principally does not distinguish between plastic and literary texts, his deconstruction does not principally distinguish semantics of pictures from semantics of words.[7] This *textual homogenization*, which is proper to Derrida's deconstruction, does not help to principally distinguish pictures from words. I find this distinction particularly important in the case of handwritten signature, which can be understood as a picture of a word, a picture of the signer's name. The precarious nature of legal handwritten signature, discussed in this book, comes strictly from its pictorial aspect, not from its verbal aspect.

For this reason, Deleuze is more suitable than Derrida for describing differences between spoken words and visualized pictures. This can be proved by Deleuze's opinion formulated in his book *Foucault* that pictures and words are different things, that visibilities are not enunciations, and that to visualize does not mean to enunciate: "it is in vain that we say what we see; what we see never resides in what we say" (Deleuze 2006, 66). Although Deleuze himself does not speak about handwritten signature in this respect, I find that if one wants to come to a positive definition of the stylization, one has to come from his understanding of style, which turns words into pictures.[8] While in literature, style tries to become music by means of speaking (here, speaking turns into music), in handwritten signature, style tries to become picture by means of writing: signature is a drawing of the author's name (here, writing turns into picture). With every new trace a new affect appears in the signer's handwriting and transforms the style of her previous traces. In this respect, the style is a changing set of all the author's affects and creative variations: in every repetition, the signer becomes her new self-portrait. The signer's style is a sign of her continuous affective becoming: *becoming-form, becoming-shape, becoming-line*.

A signature is not one single accurate self-portrait of the signer's identity, but rather one of the many versions of her self-portraits: the multiplicity of the signer's self produces a multiplicity of self-portraits. Therefore, no signature will ever be exactly repeated by the signer's hand—every singular affect that the signer experiences in the moment of signing forms the trace he leaves. Every time the signer signs, one of her affects signs for her. In *What is Philosophy?* Deleuze and Guattari describe their effort to produce philosophical portraits of other philosophers, while they admit that every portrait changes the traditional understanding of the given philosopher's distinctive traits. As they put it, "the history of philosophy is comparable to the art of the portrait. It is not a matter of 'making lifelike,' that is, of repeating what a philosopher said but rather of producing resemblance by separating out both the plane of immanence he instituted and the new concepts he created. These are mental, noetic, and machinic portraits" (Deleuze and Guattari 1994, 55). Such a portrait is also the handwritten signature: every single version of the signature produces a singular portrait of the multiplicity of the signer's self. Signing is an infinite work on the signer's own affective self-portrait, on assembling her pack of affects. Self-portrait never visualizes the author's perpetual identity but is one of the changeable affects of her multiplicity.

Iterated Repetition

Besides this essential semantic openness, for Deleuze, it is still important to maintain semantic consistency by means of repetition. Although he admits varying, he is aware of the fact that he cannot keep only the difference. Otherwise, claims James Williams, the style would perish: "repetition is a process that underlies all identities. Free will is, therefore, an illusion" (Williams 2005, 84). What is kept and recalled in variations from the event of signature is the signer's recognizable style, which is generated in two phases: first, the language is submitted to an original treatment producing a "foreign language" inside the mother language; second, this treatment is intentionally pushed until the limit dividing language and music. As Gregg Lambert notices in "The Philosopher and the Writer: A Question of Style," Deleuzean style is alongside, adjacent, and contiguous: it expresses the unity of a multiplicity of fragments, tissues, and parts: "its function is to unify a multiplicity of viewpoints, even at the level of the sentence, without thereby submitting this unity to a closed totality" (Lambert 2003, 125). At the same time,

> style must also be defined as the unifying trait that is produced after the work, at its end—one might say as the gesture of a final brushstroke or word—but which nevertheless continues to exist alongside the work. The fact that this unity continues to exist "alongside the work," contingently related, possibly undergoing further permutations, is what makes style an object of criticism.

Each critic seeks to grasp the unity of a work (of a given author) by discovering the most stylistic element that defines the work's genetic structure and its essential idea. (Lambert 2003, 125)

Similarly, Deleuze and Guattari write in *A Thousand Plateaus* about *refrain* as a rhythmically repeated sign, which marks a territory with its numerous returning variations. In this rhythmic territorial assemblage, it is possible to recognize both musical and plastic style. Graffiti tag makers on city buildings, for example, are used to appropriate a territory by marking it repeatedly.[9] Graffiti are plastically stylized nicknames of their producers that bring back the composed form in a new variation, which is still recognizable by the members of the given graffiti community. Every signer's tag—her territorial signature—carries a recognizable rhythmic assemblage: as Deleuze and Guattari put it, "it is the difference that is rhythmic, not the repetition, which nevertheless produces it: productive repetition has nothing to do with reproductive meter" (Deleuze and Guattari 2005, 314). It is only possible to speak about forging a signature if one presupposes rhythm and repetition in stylization—even for illegal graffiti tags. Although the style is grasped as a creative repetition with constant new variations, it remains conservative. Otherwise, it would not be recognizable.[10]

In the cultural environment and conventional alphabetic writing of Western metaphysics, the handwritten signature is a curious semantic phenomenon. On the one hand, the signature produces pictures and texts at the same time: the one means the other. In signature, text and picture pervade: in the gesture of handwriting, the imitable style of the picture (abstract picture of the name of the author) becomes equal to the conventional meaning of the text (civic name of the author). On the other hand, it is supposed that every single signature carries in itself a singular plastic style composed by its author, the signing citizen. The metaphysical presupposition of singularity of the author's style leads to efforts to identify the signer by her plastic expression: it is supposed that every signer has a strictly individual—recognizable and inimitable—style of tracing her name. The combined emphasis on the singularity of personal style and on the authenticity of handwritten traces, understood as a double presupposition for a successful civic identification, is characteristic for the Western semantic tradition, where the author's stylized signature is taken for a very important and reliable sign. But how should one maintain a plastically consistent, recognizable style of manually written signature? What is the plastic constant, which composes the author's style of handwriting? How is it possible that the metaphysical trust in style remains—despite the real impossibility of attaining identical copy by manual reproduction?

In the Western cultural tradition, the specimen signature is grasped as a singular self-portrait, a portrait of the signer's name. Every time it is handwritten, its plastic form is singular and will never be exactly repeated in manual reproduction. The author of the style, just like the imitator of the style, wishes to repeat, but can only vary—thus, repeatedly falsify—the specimen signature. Nevertheless, from the legal point of view, it is no falsification: it is supposed that a specimen signature and every other signature written by the same signer's hand have a common authentic style, which lasts in time and interconnects all of the author's expressions. The author of the specimen signature is understood here as generator of a strictly personal style, which is directly projected onto every further signature written by the author's hand. The idea of personal style guarantees the relation of identity between the signer's authorship and citizenship. According to the metaphysical presupposition of recognition of the signer's identity, any other signer can only imitate the singular author's style: no imitator's manually written signature will ever attain identity with the original specimen signature, the first expression of the author's personal style. According to the shared metaphysical expectation, only the author herself, the only generator and holder of her personal style of writing, can achieve the state of identity with all of her individual signatures.

Therefore, two important concepts of Western metaphysics—style and author—cannot exist separately. Signature exists only because we believe in style; style exists because we believe in author. If we had lost our belief in authorship, style would have collapsed, and the legal meaning of signature would have perished. Derrida sees this possibility clearly, but does not believe that it could ever happen in the world of transcendental thinking. Deleuze, in contrast, describes a world of immanence, where it has already happened.

From this viewpoint, Deleuze's affective semiotics of event is very distant from Derrida's vigilant semiotic mistrust, that is, his aporetic *militant melancholy*.[11] In Deleuze, the style cannot be created and established at once, because it is a work in a process of permanent formation. Style is produced in time by repeated use of chosen elements, which constantly vary during the repetition. Only their performative repetition enables the mutuality of these elements to be recognized as part of a certain style. Yet the elements of the specimen signature cannot be repeated totally identically. They need to be continually varied to constantly create—and to maintain—the authorial style. Thus, as the style evolves in time, it inevitably transforms itself: this is Deleuzean multiplicity, the *pack of affects* that lives its creative becoming in each signature act, in each performative event. As Jean-Clet Martin puts it in *Variations*, Deleuze's event is "contact or contrast, which hits and penetrates various ways of evolution and heterogenous lines in an a-chronological, a-historical time" (Martin 1993, 176).

Put otherwise, the signer becomes original only successively, in the process of her *becoming-style*. If the signer becomes more and more stylized, it is because she wants to be recognized by others and to become an original for them. In this perspective, paradoxically, becoming-style means becoming-original. In Deleuze's conception of creative process, the signer's original does not become original by returning to any original sign. It happens by keeping the machine of unconscious going on, by maintaining continuity with the previous signs, by producing their varied versions. In Deleuze's vital semiotics, the handwritten signature is a "machinal" picture of the signer's name, a self-portrait composed of a consistent assemblage of lines, which should be repeated in all of its numerous written variations. This *refrain* works not only aesthetically, but also strategically: by its regular repetition, it gives the work a vital rhythm as the authority of a locally respected ritual, a territorial rule. Deleuze helps us to conceive of the repeating gesture as necessary for every work, no matter how popular or professional it is wished or supposed to be. Each compulsively repeated pattern establishes its locally functional refrain, which evolves mechanically, returning a given form in a given rhythm, in order to formally designate the inside and the borders of a particular image of thought, that is, the locally shared pattern of a recognizable territory.

Handwritten signature is a particular semiotic affair of the Western cultural sphere, where a conventional set of alphabetical letters or arbitrary visual signs are used for manual writing. Like Egyptian hieroglyphs that perform pictures and texts simultaneously, the one cannot exist without the other; the one means the other and vice versa. In the case of handwritten signature, text and picture pervade: a repeatable style of picture (recognizable picture of the author's name) corresponds to conventional meaning of the text (civic name of the signer who is the author of her style). At the same time, it is supposed that every signature is holder of a singular graphic style of its author. Its falsification can be uncovered and punished, as is the case for forgeries of authorial works of art in the Western cultural tradition. Metaphysical presupposition of the singularity of authorial style of writing leads to efforts to identify the signer by her inevitably individual graphic *expression*[12]: it is supposed that each signer has her own style of manual drawing and writing, which generates essential differences from the handwriting of any other signer. Western mediation politics, which takes the personally stylized signature for a very important and reliable sign of civic identity, is based on a double presupposition: it combines the prejudice of originality of personal style with the prejudice of authenticity of handwritten traces.

How can one keep the style of handwritten signature graphically consistent—recognizable and repeatable? What is the graphic content of the signer's personal style? How is it possible that the metaphysical trust in personal style still lasts—despite the evident impossibility to reach identical copy by means of manual reproduction?

In the Western cultural tradition, the specimen signature is grasped as a singular work of art, a self-portrait of the signer's civic name, which is produced out of her handwriting. Therefore, just like any handmade work of art, the handwritten signature has a shape that can never be exactly repeated by manual reproduction. Even if the author of her style, just like an imitator of her style, tries to attain identity with the previous trace, she can only achieve a new variation of that trace. Thus, each time the signer tries to confirm her civic identity by handwritten signature, she falsifies her specimen signature. From a legal viewpoint, the specimen signature is not a singular and unrepeatable work of art, but a pattern for an aporetic personal industrial design, which is created and registered only once, and then simply identically reproduced by hand. This is linked to the expectation that every copy done by the author's own hand should be stylized in the same way. It is supposed that the specimen signature and each further signature written by the same signer's hand expresses the same authentic style, which remains unchanged and interconnects all of the author's expressions. The author of the specimen signature is taken here for the founder of her own style of handwriting, which is supposed to be repeatedly naturally expressed in every further signature written by the author's own hand. The legal understanding is that the style of handwriting is proof of its signer's civic identity and guarantees verification of her authorship. According to this discursive expectation, no other signer is able to identically reproduce the unique author's style: no handwritten signature, written by someone imitating the style of some other signer's specimen signature, will ever achieve this identicalness. In this understanding, the specimen signature is the first institutionally registered expression of the signer's style, which can be identically reproduced only by its author, and by no one else. Only the author herself, who is both producer and holder of her own personal style, can achieve identity between her specimen signature and every successive individual signature.

Finally, the metaphysical expectation of the possibility of civic identification by means of handwritten signature is based on the presupposition that every citizen can be recognized and identified by her manual repetition of her specimen signature. Derrida described this presupposition as a metaphysical aporia of the signature. This consists in the contradictory legal obligation to repeat the unrepeatable, which inevitably produces a forgery for the purpose of obligatory verification. The expectation of identity as natural identical repetition, where the similarity between the signer's soul and specimen of her handwriting evolves into the authenticity of all traces written by the signer's hand, again evolves into the identity of personal style of handwriting, which enables permanent self-reproduction of the signer. Adding the expectation of authenticity to the expectation of similarity makes it possible to postulate the signer's identity, which is based on the expectation of identity between her specimen and subsequent signatures. This is no longer a matter of the limits of discursively acceptable similarity—it is directly about identity. Deconstruction of the metaphor's semantic violence examines the rhetoric of similarity, which became a rhetoric of identity.

In a way, Derrida's practice of deconstructive writing is a realization of Deleuze's theory of affective style. His concept is an autobiographic signature rooted in the materiality of writing—the text's *texture*—and produces an immediate effect of difference. When the subversive event of becoming-original occurs, Deleuze's affective stylization of portraits seems to be close to Derrida's aporia of the always already deferred meaning. Its goal is not a reliable return to the supposedly original trace, but a perpetual approaching of it by performing new traces. Contrary to Deleuze, Derrida does not believe that the very goal of philosophy is to create new concepts.[13] Derrida's philosophical melancholia, which lacks Deleuze's vitalism, appears also in his view of the signature as a sign anticipating its author's death, the end of her unique world. In *The Work of Mourning*, Derrida claims that

> a signature not only signs but speaks to us always of death. Before anything else, even before the name, a signature bespeaks the possible death of the one who bears the name; it offers assurances of this beyond the death that it recalls just as soon, the death that is promised, given, or received, the death that thus always comes before coming—and so, alas, comes always before its time. There where to expect it always means not to be expecting it. (Derrida 2001b, 136)

In Derrida, signature's meaning is always deferred. It is either a specter of past existence, or a promise of future existence, but it never appears in a state of total semantic presence enabling a reliable expression of the signer's soul or identification of the signer as a citizen. We can only trace her in her new performatives. The origin of style is always deferred: one can approach it only by following similar—approximatively identical—traces. Surprisingly, deconstructed origin of style should be found not only in the iterated past, in the revenant, but also in the promised future, in the *arrivant*, in an expectation that will never be fulfilled. In "Derrida's Memory, War and the Politics of Ethics," Maja Zehfuss emphasizes Derrida's claim that "to speak of memory is also to speak of the future, of that which is totally unexpected. . . . Memory, therefore, has the potential to underline the aporia, the uncertainty with which we are confronted when we face ethico-political questions, and the failure of knowledge, especially because knowledge of 'the past' relies on an impossible conception of linear time" (Zehfuss 2007, 108). From the perspective of deconstruction, only in this aporetic way can one be stylized, or recognizable, for the other.

Derrida's way of writing[14] is performative also because it uses verbal constructions, which are both descriptive and concentrated on rethinking the concepts shifting the text from representation to performance. One could even say that, by his performative way of writing, Derrida practically fulfills Deleuze's claim that philosophical truths remain arbitrary and abstract if they are not rooted in events that force the reader to think, and that generate the need for what is produced in the act of thinking. Put otherwise, Derrida performs Deleuze's theory of affective style, but he refuses to formulate positively any theory of style, as Deleuze does it. In this respect, Lambert notices that Derridean "nonstyle, therefore, can be defined as virtual, suspended between the tensors of the 'to come' and the 'not yet,' scattered and fragmentary. On the other hand, Deleuze also defines style as essentially economical: 'Style is the economy of language'" (Lambert 2012, 148). Derrida's own practice of writing grasps the style as an aporia of recognition: the style cannot be established at once, because it is formed successively, by repetition of selected elements that inevitably vary in their iteration. Contrary to Deleuze, who considers their recurrent varying as a chance to recognize the consistency and mutuality of their assemblage, which is supposed to form a pack of affects and to mark a territory of percepts, Derrida does not believe in such a genuine creativity. For him, deconstructed style is not a recognizable form of vital expression, as it is in Deleuze: it is rather an *arrivant* that will never completely arrive, a promise that will never be totally fulfilled. Like his justice, Derridean style is partly present and partly absent: it is the ghost of every trace, of every performative event. As a whole, the style remains unfinished, permanently postponed from past to future traces, to those that are still to come. The only thing that finally terminates the compulsory continuation of iteration in life and makes one's personal style total, totally graspable, and finished is the end of one's life. Only ending life can end this iteration and turn it into an easily recognizable and closed representation, a style purified from events and from the unexpected.

Handwritten signature should represent the signer's singular style of handwriting. In order to compose and establish her recognizable style, the signer must inevitably try her best to repeat her previous gestures, or even her original gesture. Imitation is continuous, not original: there is no original pattern. Every individual signature is simultaneously a pattern and an expression—a type and a token—for all further individual signatures written by the given signer. That is the aporia of signature as an expression of style: because every trace is unrepeatable, iteration, which is necessary for constitution of the signer's original personal style, destroys originality of her traces. While each original trace loses its originality in repetition, no original style can be created without continuous effort to repeat the traces, while all of them are original. The signer's personal style is born in the effort to repeat, which disseminates slight differences from the originally registered trace. If the signature is written by hand every time in a singular way, it is because it is only one of the infinite versions of the specimen signature, a version that will never be identical to any other version. While the signer tries to reproduce the previous expression of herself and to bring the performed signature closer to her legal identity, the previous and current signatures will never be identical in shape. By means of handwritten signature, I will never succeed in being identified sufficiently: no attempt will ever re-render the previous—or even the original specimen—signature. The inevitable difference between the originally registered and every succeeding trace haunts the signer each time she is asked to sign, sometimes even to re-sign, in order to perform a shape of signature that is as similar as possible to the specimen signature. Although from a logical point of view, identity cannot be graded, identification by signature is based on grading. From a certain discursively determined degree of similarity of traces, the high grade of similarity legitimately becomes identity.

In the next chapter, I approach this problem through Derrida's understanding of the authority of representation, which allows me to grasp handwritten signature as an aporetic sign of civic identification. Using his reading of Rousseau, I show that, contrary to the signer's civic obligation to sign identically, because of the remaining difference between the logical universality of law and ontological singularity of life, no signer can ever satisfy the metaphysical obligation to repeat her previous traces in the event of signing.

Chapter VII

Event of Manual Signing

On Repeating of the Unrepeatable

My previous reading of Derrida's works helped me to show that every expert's recognition of the natural and authentic trace that a handwritten signature is supposed to constitute is necessarily situated in the interval between sufficient and insufficient resemblance of produced traces. It is only in this aporetic range of similarities that the signer's civic identity can be recognized. To generate her recognizable personal style of handwriting, the signer must constantly try to imitate the shape of her specimen signature. Nevertheless, as I wish to conclude, the result of this imitation is neither natural resemblance between signature and signer's soul nor authentic presence of the signer's soul or identical repetition of the signer's previous traces, but rather dissemination of similarities that will never achieve the civic identity required by the law.

Although this consideration is mostly inspired by Derrida's works on the aporetic margins of Western metaphysics, it is necessary to reveal several possible methodological difficulties with Derrida's own tactic of reading and writing, which he declares is neither an analysis nor a method. Derrida's philosophical work does not directly help to formulate any positive determination of communication, because his "deconstruction is explanation of the impossible, experience of the impossible" (Derrida 2011, 113). His aim is not to conceive any critical, vital, or scientifically positive theory of ontological representations. Rather, he opts for a *quasi-ethical memento*, indicating both rhetorical conditions of possibility and empirical conditions of impossibility of all kinds of semiotics trying to turn observed being into reliable signs of the observed being.

In *Life Death* (2020), Derrida recalls his earlier commentary on contemporary biologists' suggestions to speak metaphorically of writing in relation to the processes of information within the living cell. His point was to show that this appeal to a non-phonetic writing in genetics should "incite an entire deconstruction of the logocentric machine" (Derrida 2020, 23). Instead, biologists did not problematize what they meant by this graphics of life, "this non-phonetic writing that they claim to be 'without writing' and that they are so ready to reinvest with all the values linked to logos" (Derrida 2020, 23). Regretting this lack of understanding of non-phonetic writing in biology, Derrida proposes his onto-*graphical* or bio-*graphical* conception of writing, his deconstructive account on "graphics of life" that both exceeds and includes phonetic inscription. This bio-*graphical* approach to signs, proposed by Derrida, understands writing as "not only the physical gestures of literal pictographic or ideographic inscription, but also the totality of what makes it possible; and also, beyond the signifying face, the signified face itself" (Derrida 1997, 9). In this sense,

> we say "writing" for all that gives rise to an inscription in general, whether it is literal or not and even if what it distributes in space is alien to the order of the voice: cinematography, choreography, of course, but also pictorial, musical, sculptural writing. One might also speak of athletic writing, and with even greater certainty of military or political writing in view of the techniques that govern those domains today. (Derrida 1997, 9)

Such a political writing can be also the legally used handwritten signature that is both a formally unique trace of life and a supposedly reliable sign of civil identification. In this double deconstructive sense, I propose to grasp the sign of legal signature as Derridean grammé, graphics of life, which is at the same time inevitably exposed to logos, to metaphysical expectations.

This goal of instrumental use of Derrida's deconstruction is, however, difficult to fulfill. Because Derrida's deconstruction is neither a method nor an analysis, it cannot be simply applied. Every application of a method strengthens the metaphysical violence of hierarchized binary oppositions that deconstruction intentionally questions. As Royle puts it, "Deconstruction involves an overturning of this hierarchy and a reinscription or transformation of the basis on which the opposition functioned in the first place" (Royle

2000, 5). If Derrida's haunto*logy* is no method*ology*, it is not simply usable without any objections. For my own examination of signature, deconstruction is applicable only if the limits of such an application are clearly indicated. For this, two of them are particularly important.

The first limit of Derrida's deconstruction is his textual homogenization of media/technology: Derrida does not distinguish picture from writing. In Derrida, there is nothing outside the text; everything is inside the text. The text contains everything. This indiscernibility is a homogenization proper to deconstruction: Derrida's concept of the writing concerns not only computer, machine, and handwriting, but also other works such as picture, music, accent, building, or dance. In Derrida's conception, writing is performed as an instant expression, which is expected to be read by others: it anticipates every reading or interpretation produced by the voice. Contrary to Deleuze's semiotic classification of images in the cinematic medium, Derrida's semantic conception does not make it possible to discuss media differences between a painted picture and a written text, or various types of rhetoric linked to technologically various kinds of pictures and to various kinds of writing.

In *Of Grammatology*, Derrida explains that if he refers at some point to a transcendentality that he elsewhere puts into question, it is to escape falling back into "naive objectivism." He believes that there is a "beyond of transcendental criticism" (Derrida 1997, 61) that does recognize the necessity of a pathway. However, "that pathway must leave a track in the text. Without that track, abandoned to the simple content of its conclusions, the ultra-transcendental text will so closely resemble the precritical text as to be indistinguishable from it" (Derrida 1997, 61).

This is also the case of Derrida's relation to phenomenology, which remains ambiguous. As he puts it, "a thought of the trace can no more break with a transcendental phenomenology than be reduced to it" (Derrida 1997, 62). On the one hand, Derrida's concept of *arche-trace* helps him formulate the conditions of possibility of the phenomenological retention of consciousness and therefore of all possible empirical writings. On the other hand, as he emphasizes, even this concept "must comply with both that necessity and that erasure. It is in fact contradictory and not acceptable within the logic of identity" (Derrida 1997, 61). Understood in this double way, Derrida's concept of *arche-writing* draws attention to the pictorial nature of written words. It is therefore useful for understanding handwriting, which simultaneously produces a phonetic and a pictorial inscription of words.

Contrary to Derrida, who understands *arche-writing* transcendentally and *writing* meta-historically, the politically legitimized Western cultural history and paleography generate their own knowledge of Antiquity, as a period of progressive cultural evolution from the picture to the pictogram and, afterward, to "true"[1] (or phonetic) writing. Paleographer Jean claims in *Writing* that in Near Eastern monotheisms, especially in the Koran and the Bible, where phonetic writing is understood as the holy representation of divine words, "the very word 'writing' takes on religious connotations" (Jean 1992, 56). Not only because of the phonetization of writing, but also because Judaism and Islam forbid pictorial illustrations of holy texts, exuberant floral and systematic geometric ornaments are produced to compensate for the double elimination of the pictorial from writing. "Sacred" phonetic writing introduced a strange repression of imagination, which was unknown in cultures using pictograms.

Deconstruction avoids this historical classification for two reasons: because of Derrida's mistrust in historiography and his intentionally flowing work with the concepts of *grammé* or writing. Derrida's subversive conception of writing is grafted on the traditional Western conception of phonetic writing, but it already means something else. Derrida criticizes the thinkers who find the origin of meaning in voice, or *phoné*—and who consider phonetic writing as secondary to the voice—for their phonocentrism. Derrida turns this phonocentrism upside down: deconstructed writing is not a supplementary conventional representation of spoken language, but its marginal zone, which precedes and envelops the voice. Therefore, Derrida and the phonocentrists do not speak about the same writing. Derrida's definition of writing is much broader than their definition of phonetic writing, and even broader than their definition of voice. In his subversive conceptual turn, the writing (*grammé*) becomes primary and the voice (*phoné*) secondary: Derrida's writing is a disseminated side of mediation imposed by the life itself that can be iterated, which precedes and envelops the precise repeatability of the voice required by the law.

Derrida's concept of signature is related to his autobiographical understanding of writing, but it does not mean only handwritten signature. The sign and medium of handwritten signature is not Derrida's primary interest, but he comments on the remains of manual signing among other personal traces with "singular identity" (Lahey Dronsfield 2013, 171) left in philosophy, literature, and the spatial and visual arts. As Lahey Dronsfield puts it, "For Derrida it is irreducibly a matter of experience, the event of the singular artwork cannot exist independently of my experience of it, it is in the experience of the work that the condition of its identity is to be found. The experience inscribes a trace structure, which is the condition of a certain return and repetition" (Lahey Dronsfield 2013, 171).

My own concept of handwritten signature is inspired by Derrida's deconstruction of writing, which means that I propose to understand it in a double way: as a semiotically violent product of Western metaphysics reducing life to law by the act of signing, and as a trace of life that envelops and disseminates the law in the event of signing. Because of its aporetic foundation, the sign of handwritten signature is expected to be both unrepeatable (singular, momentary, born instantly, in the event of writing) and repeatable (constant, conventional, recognizable, and identifiable). As a legally reliable sign of civic identity, handwritten signature is determined by the legal obligation to sign correlatively to the specimen signature, which means to sign "from memory" by repeating previous movements of the writing hand. However, because the signer is a living being and not a copy machine, this legal demand remains technically impossible to satisfy. The signer can only iterate her previous traces, with all the risks of unexpected differences that the event of signing can bring.

In this respect, handwritten signature generates Derrida's *différance*, a *neographism* that brings neither total identity nor total difference. Borrowing Derrida's vocabulary, I would say that handwritten signature works as *différance*. Just like the neographism *différance*, the handwritten signature is pronounced identically with the signer's name and written differently from the signer's name. It is manually written in a constantly and instantly changing way: each time, handwritten signature adopts one of an infinity of instantly formed shapes. This instantly changing form of writing is read by the voice, which violently reduces its variations into one single—unchanging, fixed, stable—meaning of identity. By force of the law, differences of written form are turned into voiced identity of content; the instantly varying picture of a civic name is reduced to the attributed civic name; the trace of life becomes the sign of law.

The second limit of deconstruction I consider important to mention is Derrida's homogenization of local particularities. Derrida respects neither epistemological nor discursive limits of interpretation. For this reason, Derrida's work is not compatible with discursive semiotics. As he considers the context to be without limits, he does not work with the concept of discourse that imposes limits on the reasonable interpretation of texts. The only limits that determine the deconstructed text and context are the limits of metaphysical thinking.

It may be surprising that Derrida, who refused correct interpretation and openly declared the principial ambiguity of his theoretical position, was criticized for his misinterpretation or incorrect interpretation. For example, J. Claude Evans, who severely critiqued Derrida's philosophy in *Strategy of Deconstruction*, tried to present the deconstructive reading as a misinterpretation in contrast with his own rigorous reading. Evans supposes Derrida is a critic, who does not read and analyze correctly, but it is Evans himself who does not correctly read Derrida's work. Deconstruction does not do any critique or analysis. Evans misses the fact that Derrida searches for traces of metaphysical violence in the texts he reads and creatively turns these into new connections. Derrida himself finds in "Une certaine possibilité impossible de dire l'événement" that interpretation is no correct or pertinent explanation. Interpretation is also a translation and a transformation: "while it pretends to introduce, to demonstrate, and to explain, it produces, in a way, it is already performative" (Derrida 2001a, 90). Every single handwritten signature interprets or performs—thus, produces in a new way—the signer's name. Moreover, Derrida does not speak about phonetic writing in the Greek philosophical tradition and Jewish theological tradition,[2] but about *arche-writing*, which exceeds both Socrates's voice and Kant's critique.

Derrida's deconstruction cannot generate any scientifically positive semiotics, because it tries to reconcile empiricism with logicism without willing to unite them. As Lawlor says in *Derrida and Husserl*, Derrida neither reduces the ideal to the real, nor absorbs the real into the ideal: "while recognizing the essential solidarity between logic and sensation, Derrida's dialectic does not succumb to empiricism. . . . while recognizing the essential distinction between logic and sensation, Derrida's dialectic does not succumb to logicism" (Lawlor 2002a, 48). Instead of succumbing to one of these poles, Derrida's dialectic simultaneously maintains "a distinction and solidarity between the real and the ideal" (Lawlor 2002a, 48).

This distinction leads some critical readers to see deconstruction as insufficiently rigorous, terminologically vague, methodologically contradictory, and even unacceptable philosophical work. They warn that although Derrida does not speak about a method, but rather about a tactic or strategy, the intention of his work still involves a metaphysical scientific ambition. As David Wood mentions in "Différance and the Problem of Strategy," deconstruction was designed as a philosophical prevention or vaccination:

> Derrida's general strategy is surely this: to infiltrate *différance* into the syntax of foundationalist and generative thinking with

a view to depriving it of its attraction. (One might compare the release of sterile male mosquitoes as an anti-malarial measure.) But once we realize that this *is* the strategy, it is possible to ask whether this substitutive infiltration is acceptable. Derrida may say that of course it is not acceptable—that it is a transgression. (Wood 1988, 64)

For this reason, writes Wood, deconstruction is necessarily contradictory: "Derrida either uses transcendental forms of arguments in explaining the term *différance*, in which case he undermines his whole project, or he does not, in which case the force of all he says about *différance* (and its intelligibility) evaporates" (Wood 1988, 65). According to Wood, Derrida's most important discovery remains his questioning of the sense of any transgression: "his lesson, or the lesson we draw from him, is not *merely* that, as he says, there is no sense in doing without metaphysical concepts in trying to overcome metaphysics, but that there is no prospect whatever of *eliminating* metaphysical concepts and strategies" (Wood 1988, 68). The result is a radical melancholy coming from a real helplessness in the face of the inevitable semantic violence of Western metaphysics. Therefore, "philosophy on the move is the only possible transgression of metaphysics. There is no Other Place to go" (Wood 1988, 69).

In order to get out of this aporetical trap of deconstruction, which Gregg Lambert beautifully described by means of Bartleby's formula "I'd rather not to" (Lambert 2012, 134–37), I propose to partially rehabilitate the concept of discourse that deconstruction avoids. To balance the aforementioned limits of deconstruction, I emphasize the role of discursive limits in the interpretation of handwritten signature as a sign. Therefore, in the next sections of this chapter, I focus on two complementary determinations that transform the event of signing into a recognizable signature: the discursive trap of interpretation and the metaphysical trap of representation.

Event Trapped in Interpretation

The aim of Derrida's philosophical project, named deconstruction, was often understood as an attempt to conceive a new philosophical methodology. However, Derrida himself refused such a definition of his work. He claimed that his deconstruction is a kind of thinking that is rather playful than methodological: he introduces his tactic of a double game with language, which enables him to balance in the marginal zone of philosophy, where it is possible to both remain in and step out of metaphysical determination of meaning. Deconstruction examines these marginal zones of language by means of its neographisms, which resemble, but are not, well-known and defined concepts. Contrary to well-established philosophical concepts, the meaning of his neographisms is never fully present, because these neographisms do not have any legitimate place in the official language. With these tactical movements—both for and against the law of language—Derrida tries to subversively rebuild the metaphysics of total presence of meaning that he understands as an important generator of semantic violence. In Derrida, the language forces us to understand the meaning in the intentions of its own unjust construction, which is predetermined hierarchy of binary oppositions in Western conceptual thinking. One of the goals of deconstruction is to introduce the possibility of justice into these conceptual oppositions by systematically subverting their hierarchically determined positions. This cannot be done by either language or the law.

I can see the problem with such a tactic of deconstruction in the fact that Derrida is not always as playful as he claims to be in his description of deconstruction. The early Derrida is a strict, rigorous reader. His melancholic fight for justice is performed not only by his effort to be precise in reading, but also by a great courage that accompanies his questioning of the metaphysically violent nature of methodologies in other thinkers' texts. In this respect, Derrida declares and realizes two different, mutually exclusive, intentions. He revolts against the Western metaphysics of presence by his inventive work with concepts, but confirms this metaphysics in his precise reading. Thus, the question is: does Derrida's tactic have the ambition to get to something other than the metaphysical truth? Is anything like that possible?

Rodolphe Gasché expresses his conviction that this contradictory situation is saved by Derrida's claim that deconstruction aims at a double gesture, which is always both constructive and destructive in its relation with the representation, the repeatedly present meaning. In his commentary on deconstruction, written in *The Tain of the Mirror*, Gasché proposed to call Derrida's double tactic *quasi-transcendentalism*: a kind of transcendental or critical philosophy that goes further than the traditional metaphysical philosophy of reflection. In this respect, I agree with Kates's claim that Gasché reads Derrida against Rorty, who criticized the philosophy of reflection from his pragmatist position in *Philosophy and the Mirror of Nature*. But Gasché's reading, oriented against Rorty, also works against Derrida, who produces neither any new systematic methodology nor any new kind of transcendental critique. If Derrida's critical arguments come from transcendental philosophy, deconstruction cannot be the other side of metaphysics, as Gasché supposes. According to Kates, "Derrida, by his own testimony, engages with the unthought of philosophy, but this ultimately in order to carry on thought and its responsibility, not abandon it altogether" (Kates 2005, 6).

Although Rorty claims there is always a pragmatist irony in Derrida's 'transcendentalist' thoughts, he admits Derrida's concern with metaphysical conditions of possibility is far from his own conception of pragmatism. As Rorty puts it, "what pragmatists find most foreign in Derrida is his suspicion of empiricism, and naturalism—his assumption that these are forms of metaphysics, rather than replacements for metaphysics. To put it another way: they cannot understand why Derrida wants to sound *transcendental*, why he persists in taking the project of finding conditions of possibility seriously" (Rorty 2005, 16). In this respect, in his paper "Is Derrida a Transcendental Philosopher?" Rorty wonders how to understand Derrida correctly: "How does one go about deciding whether to read Derrida my way or Gasché's way? How does one decide whether he is really a much-misunderstood transcendental 'philosopher of reflection,' a latter-day Hegel, or really a much-misunderstood nominalist, a sort of French Wittgenstein? Not easily. Derrida makes noises of both sorts" (Rorty 1996, 243). Rorty is especially bothered by the fact that Derrida uses the word "rigorous," which is in contradiction with his own pragmatist conception of interpretation. Nevertheless, Rorty himself proposes a rigorous evaluation of Derrida's work when he writes: "Derrida himself, I have to admit, used to use words like 'rigorous' a lot. There is a lot in his early work which chimes with Gasché's interpretation. But as he moves along from the early criticisms of Husserl through *Glas* to texts like the 'Envois' section of *The Post Card*, the tone has changed" (Rorty 1996, 243). As he clarifies, "I should like to think of Derrida as moving away from the academic, 'standard rules of philosophy' manner of his early work to a manner more like the latter Wittgenstein's. Indeed, I should like to see his early work as something of a false start, in the same way that *Being and Time* seems to me, in the light of Heidegger's later work, to have been a false start, and as Wittgenstein thought his *Tractatus* had been a false start" (Rorty 1996, 243). As we can see, Rorty repeats the methodological problem that Umberto Eco had found in Rorty's own work.

How does Derrida himself respond to these commentaries? Again, in a double way: he partly accepts both Gasché's methodological quasi-transcendentalism and Rorty's productive pragmatism,[3] but he turns away from philosophy to experimental literature as to an ethical "asylum" of his philosophically contradictory dissemination. Derrida himself did not resign to mediators of philosophical production of meaning. He even refers to this fact in his cautious reaction, when he rejects both Gasché's attempt to turn deconstruction into a solid analytical method and Rorty's attempt to turn deconstruction into a creative pragmatic drift. As Leslie Hill puts it, if Derrida emphasizes that deconstruction is characterized by a certain resignation to positivist methods of analysis and interpretation, it is because "there were no authoritative norms, values, rules, or procedures that might reliably be deployed in reading, other than the imperative demand of justice, but which, in the name of justice itself, was irreducible to any prescriptive methodology" (Hill 2010, 321).

Nevertheless, Derrida is surely aware that, outside Western metaphysics, one can be neither philosophically accurate nor inaccurate, and not even critical. Thus, he rejects the possibility of defining deconstruction strictly from the inner position of philosophy.[4] His continuous attempt to blend philosophy with experimental biographical literature could be understood as an attempt to deconstruct himself as both a philosopher and a writer, the one who writes philosophy. As he puts it in *The Animal, Therefore I Am*, "Nothing risks becoming more poisonous than an autobiography, poisonous for oneself in the first place, auto-infectious for the presumed signatory who is so auto-affected" (Derrida 2008b, 47). This self-questioning biographic suffering, which makes him his own revenant, is necessary for Derrida, because he finds it fruitful material for his later work. His own writing is no longer mostly strictly penetrating; it becomes more and more biographic. Thus, Derrida's late philosophical writing enables him to sign not representatively, but blindly. In *Memories of the Blind*, he asks:

> What happens when one writes without seeing? A hand of the blind ventures forth alone or disconnected, in a poorly delimited space; it feels its way, it gropes, it caresses as much as it inscribes, trusting in the memory of signs and supplementing sight. . . . The image of the movement of these letters, of what this finger-eye inscribes, is thus sketched out within me. (Derrida 1993, 3)

In this self-portraying way, Derrida blindly composes his philosophical signature, the signer's style of handwriting, where he makes present again—re-presents—his past presence.

I propose to deconstruct Derrida's tactic of deconstruction, but in another way, which makes it possible to keep Derrida's deconstruction inside philosophy. Similarly to Eco in his theory of conventional realism and discursively given limits of interpretation, I am convinced that it is possible to formulate an interpretation that can not only propose an acceptable way of reading, but also recognize the precision and the imprecision of other interpretations. This can be attained only if the reader emphasizes her own position of interpretation, compares it with other expert voices, and places her fragmentary and relative representation in the corresponding discourse.

In his own practice of interpretation, Derrida proceeds just like the thinkers he criticizes. Although Derrida disclaims it, his deconstruction is a certain systematic procedure in philosophical work, a kind of a subversive methodology. Moreover, his neographisms are modified philosophical concepts, which have their definitions and rules of self-construction. Without these, they would make no sense. For example, Derrida keeps the word "text" for the purpose of his conceptual parasitism: he grafts a new meaning onto an old reference. After Derrida's deconstructive grafting of a new element into the current definition, the concept of text can mean a body, an institution, a dance, a book, an architecture, a photography, or a handwritten signature. The goal of these conceptual neographisms is not to establish a reign of nonsense, but to conceive of situations where sense and nonsense cannot be reliably separated, in order to revolt against injustices fatally built inside the language. In the name of justice, Derrida occasionally subverts the traditional hierarchical relation between the degrading and the degraded in the binary oppositions of language and systematically produces newly shaped concepts, which enriches his philosophical language and occasionally moves its limits. But this does not make him leave metaphysics: his own philosophical "fight for the rights of the degraded" is played inside metaphysics. Finally, Derrida could never leave metaphysics, because he has built his thinking on polemics. These polemics were based on a critical thinking that cannot be other than metaphysical. In his polemics, he fiercely defends the total presence of meaning he speaks about—and not only in his own texts, but also in the texts by other authors that he reads.

While Derrida deconstructs the metaphysical force of conceptual schematism[5] underlying the text he reads, Eco's reading tries to keep and respect the discursively approved coherence of the work. Although Derrida does not explicitly work with this discursive determination, in his own philosophical practice he tries to respect this coherence. Otherwise, he would not be considered rigorous in his interpretation. For this reason, I suppose that Derrida's reading presupposes both quasi-transcendental and quasi-deferred meaning, which can be also deferred to various discourses.

Let us illustrate this claim by the deconstructable discourses of graphology and forensic analysis. The precarious case of handwritten signature is interpreted by experts of these two disciplines within the range of their discursive limits. Graphology has several discursive limits on its knowledge of handwritten signatures. Contrary to phonology, which examines aberrances from the accurate pronunciation, graphology examines aberrances from the prescribed forms of orthography. Every literate citizen learns this formally accurate way of writing at primary school. Both disciplines examine individual variations and produce typologies of speakers and writers. These sciences presuppose that as the distance from the generally given norm increases, individual pronunciation becomes less understandable and handwriting less legible. To get the communicational practice of citizens closer to the generally prescribed norm, individual aberrations from the norm are typologically described, classified, and "cured." But, in the case of handwritten signature, which does not imitate any generally prescribed shape of writing, the situation of graphology gets complicated. Every handwritten signature is strictly personal: it iterates the individual formal solution of the specimen signature, conceived by the signer herself. A handwritten signature has no generally prescribed specimen signature to imitate. Although a specimen signature has its value of precedent for all further signatures by the given signer, it is a norm for that one signer and for no one else. This aporia subverts the typological ambition of graphology. In this respect, handwritten signature is for legible handwriting what signing is for comprehensible pronunciation: handwriting abuts with drawing and pronunciation abuts with signing. The same is valid for scientific discourses: while phonology abuts with theory of music, graphology abuts with theory of design. This is the marginal zone, which links linguistics and aesthetics.

Let us move to the discourse of forensic analysis. If we combine Eco's analysis of discursive limits of interpretation of copies and forgeries with Derrida's metaphysical aporia of identical expression, we can realize that every single handwritten signature is an *aporetic forgery* of the first or original signature, which is the reiterated specimen signature. Because no signer will ever achieve the required total consistency of all her manual expressions, the handwritten signature of the same signer will never be sufficiently recognizable; it will never be totally identical. In deconstruction, the signature is based on the aporia of a metaphysically inevitable and—practically vain—effort to attain the required identity ontologically, in life. The practice of legal civic identification is based on the expert's empirical observation of the signer's signature, which is legitimated by the metaphysical expectation relying on the prejudice of total presence of logical meaning in being, in life. Contrary to this legal practice, Derrida's deconstruction considers handwritten signature to be an expression neither of the signer's soul, nor of the registered specimen signature: instead of a constant repetition of expression of the previous signature, handwritten signature changes its shape in every act of handwriting. Because of the inevitable transformability of handwritten shapes, the signer can only desire[6] to be as formally consistent as possible in her handwriting, and hope that, every time, she will be correctly identified by the experts of forensic discourse. This undecidability between the repeatable work of craft and the unrepeatable work of art—just like the constant suspicion of forensic experts that handwritten signatures can be forged and the principal possibility of forging them—is based on the metaphysical aporia of the force of law, which requires a legal interpretation of handwritten signature as a sign of civic identification.

Finally, let us look at our complex expectations of handwritten signature *as a sign*. How could deconstruction be helpful? Contrary to both realist and nominalist ontological semiotics, I find that Derrida's distrustful deconstruction has two philosophical advantages.

First of all, as Derrida noticed, handwritten signature as sign cannot be analyzed either linguistically or logically, because signature is not just a written word. Deconstruction makes writing conceivable simultaneously as a conventional inscription of a name and as its prelinguistic picture. Because logical parameters cannot be applied to handwriting, deconstruction perceives signature in terms of probability, not of dichotomy of truth and falsehood. Contrary to what graphological and forensic experts suppose, the material pictorial component of handwritten signature, which is the very object of scientific expertise here, can be considered as more or less similar to the imaginary essence of the signer's immaterial soul, but it will never be identical with it. For these reasons, deconstruction tries to rethink the metaphysical determination of handwritten signature as a sign subversively—not positively, as Peirce and other realists used to do.

Second, by putting the discursive limits of meaning aside, Derrida's thinking allows us to grasp the metaphysical expectation as a prejudice that is shared by both forensic and graphology discourses of handwritten signature. In this respect, it is fruitful that deconstruction focuses on the whole Western metaphysics as the only acceptable context. For this reason, it is an advantage that Derrida does not work with discursive limits of meaning—as is strongly emphasized by conventional realists—and does not do this positively, as Eco and other nominalists used to do.

In this double way, Derrida's deconstruction subversively overcomes semiotics by focusing on the metaphysical expectations that organize the legal mediation politics of handwritten signature, as inevitable and unsolvable aporias of this empirical sign of civic identification.

I base my own philosophical conception of handwritten signature, inspired both by Derrida's deconstruction and by Eco's semiotics, on shared discursive and metaphysical expectations. I reached this new understanding of signature in two steps.

First, from the position of Eco's semiotics of conventional realism, I have described two kinds of discursive expectations linked to different experts' knowledge of handwritten signature in graphology and in forensic analysis. Later, from the position of Derrida's philosophical conception of aporias, I have deconstructed the common set of metaphysical expectations in graphological and forensic knowledges of handwritten signature. Derrida helped me to point out the shared aporias, while Eco helped me to demonstrate the conventional limits of such sharing. Put otherwise, if the signer's recognition is determined by an expert's deconstructable metaphysical prejudices in general, it is also determined by discursive limits framing the perceptual judgment of the expert in a given field. While in graphology, the handwritten signature is understood as a replica of the signer's soul, in forensic analysis, understanding of it oscillates between an artistic partial replica and a crafted duplicate. This oscillation is due to the fact that the personal style of handwriting is an ensemble of all of the signer's individual writing expressions. Not all of her qualities are concentrated in either her individual signatures or the selection of them that is usually offered to forensic experts.

The proposed correlation of Eco's conventional realism of discursive expectations and of Derrida's quasi-ethics of deconstruction of metaphysical expectations enables me to articulate the ethically vigilant melancholy of the deconstructed metaphysical dimension of the legal mediation politics with the politically effective conventional positivity of the reliable sign of signature. In my reading of Eco, I have presented his "perceptual judgment" as a conventional way to recognize and identify signs. In Eco's late conception of recognition, partly inspired by Peirce's ontological realism and partly by Foucault's normative conception of discourse, metaphysical expectation of similarity and authenticity prevents and conditions the metaphysical expectation of identity. The expert's recognition is already limited by the discourse of her specialization: in Eco's conventional realism, every expert sees and recognizes something else. This way, an ontologically unrepeatable event of manual signing becomes a logically repeatable sign of civic identification.

Eco's semiotics allows to understand how signs established by aporias turn into signs established by experts' metaphysical and discursive beliefs. Once the handwritten signature is turned into a sign based on shared metaphysical and discursive beliefs, it becomes a work of craft, which can be forged. To avoid this suspicion, the signer tries to keep her self-representation by handwritten signature as formally consistent as possible. Even if each individual trace left by the signer generates many variations of the previously registered signature form, once it is considered to be similar enough, it can metonymically confirm the expectation of identity of all her traces, of the fragment and the whole. Although this metaphysical lust for identity will never be sated in the signer's gestures of handwriting, we keep on believing that it can. Moreover, we tend to believe that it is sated every day, in every single act of manual signing. Without this metaphysical belief, *préjugé*, there would be no civic sign of handwritten signature.

What does deconstruction say to such metaphysical expectations? In order to impeach the contradictory force of law that sets the impossible task and enforces obedience in this respect, Derrida proposes to rethink the source of authority of the law. As he mentions in "Force of Law," the origin of this authority can rely only on itself: that is its mystical limit. But this does not mean that the authority of the law is wrong in the sense that it is illegal. At the moment of its foundation, the law is neither legal nor illegal. It overcomes the opposition between the founded and unfounded, every foundationalism and anti-foundationalism. But, once it is legalized and gains an unpolemical authority, the situation changes. Contrary to justice, which is absent in the legal construction, the law is fully present in the legal construction and forces us to accept its meanings. The logocentrism of legislation has its own margin, or supplement, which is justice. In the next section, I propose to clarify this aporetic supplementarity of writing, drawing on Jean-Jacques Rousseau's work with the concept of representation.

Event Trapped in Representation

Rousseau, the writer and philosopher, is known for his destructive critical tone. In his *Essay on the Origin of Languages*, Rousseau reproaches philosophers for estranging themselves from the truthfulness of the direct speech and deliberately taking refuge in the writing and its insidious—artificial, additional, supplementary—qualities of communication (Rousseau 1998, 297–98). Rousseau complains that philosophers write their philosophy only for themselves. He tries to do the opposite: in *The Discourse on the Sciences and Arts*, he tries to write philosophy that will be accessible to everyone, not just to philosophers (Rousseau 2002, 48–50). Bernard Groethuysen mentions in *J.-J. Rousseau* that this effort is contradictory. If Rousseau wants to write philosophy, he cannot be separated from it. After all, he is no "savage coming from a dream land to criticize the existing order" (Groethuysen 1949, 260). According to Groethuysen, this contradiction is characteristic for Rousseau's whole destructive philosophical project. He simultaneously builds and destroys what has been already built: "the whole of Rousseau's thinking can be resumed into oppositions: opposition against his century, opposition against everything obtained from civilization; he even appears to be the greatest destructivist" (Groethuysen 1949, 389). Groethuysen admits that Rousseau's negations are not absolute, but paradoxical, because they allow various contradictory expectations to coexist while totally disclaiming none of them.

In *Of Grammatology* and "The Linguistic Circle of Geneva," Derrida gives a similar opinion of Rousseau's contradictory "self-destructive" philosophic ambition. Derrida claims that Rousseau's ambition is metaphysically based on a metaphor, which links the metaphorical meaning of an original and natural writing to the literal meaning of an additional and artificial inscription. In this respect, the history of philosophy is a history of this metaphor, which pervades all modifications of metaphysical thoughts of God, nature, and law. As he opposes the subliming voice and the declining writing, Rousseau postulates opposition between nature and supplementarity. This way, claims Derrida in *Of Grammatology*, "Rousseau repeats the Platonic gesture by referring to another model of presence: self-presence in the senses, in the sensible cogito, which simultaneously carries in itself the inscription of divine law" (Derrida 1997, 17). Rousseau's writing "in the common sense is the dead letter, it is the carrier of death, [it] exhausts life, [it is] representative, fallen, secondary, instituted" (Derrida 1997, 17). On the other hand, Rousseau's writing in the metaphoric sense is venerated as "natural, divine, and living" (Derrida 1997, 17).

To understand Derrida's interpretation of Rousseau, it is important to understand what he means by supplementarity. Derrida sees Rousseau as conceiving of the radical utopia of absent mediation when he "dreams" about the situation of pure origin. From Derrida's point of view, this project cannot be fulfilled, because the process of representation and of its supplementation goes on permanently. Derrida's subversive reading calls attention to the fact that "contamination of thinking by writing, original contamination of the origin of thinking betrays Rousseau's dream of purity and origin without additive and without supplement" (Goldschmit 2003, 49). The logic of supplementarity leads him toward the problem of origin of the supplement that he would like to erase. The writing haunts him: Rousseau tries to turn it to the outside by avoiding it, and by covering it. But by the same gesture, he excludes the material, differential, falsifying, parasitical dimension of each writer, including himself. The result is an aporia and a pragmatic paradox: Rousseau develops the deficiency that he tries to let disappear. In this respect, Derrida's philosophical project is "double and ambivalent: supplement and writing threaten the truth, but they also represent its occasion and its historical possibility. Supplement of writing is inseparable from the possibility of lie *and* truth. There is no speech without writing, origin without supplements, being without appearance and without simulacra" (Goldschmit 2003, 51). This supplementary function of imagination, which makes Rousseau feel perplexed,[7] is what Derrida takes for the ultimate semantic, communicational, and cultural inevitability.

Derrida reevaluates Rousseau's destructive potential when he refuses Rousseau's thoughts on the need to eliminate the semantic supplements. He considers that Rousseau's distinction between fully present and deferred meaning was an important philosophical step emancipating philosophy from metaphysical positivism, partially initiated by Descartes. At the same time, he claims that Rousseau's critical understanding of supplement was not consistent, because it omitted the second aspect of the practice of representation, namely the inevitable nature of supplementarity. One cannot quit the metaphysics of presence just by seeking to critically destroy the semantic *prison* of supplementarity, as Rousseau proposed it.

Derrida observes that Rousseau's relationship with writing is contradictory: by making the writing marginal, he tries to erase the representation, which is actually what enables the emergence of the philosophy. Rousseau fears the ambivalent human principle of representation and rejects it, because it does not allow thinking and communication to be immediate. Derrida proposes to philosophically rehabilitate writing and to redefine representation as a *supplement of supplement*, or a permanently deferred meaning. In this respect, he warns that Rousseau is afraid of supplements as dangerous, morally bad things: Rousseau considers writing, masturbation, culture, and history to be dangerous human inventions, which are inserted into thinking as apparently neutral and innocent. Rousseau understands the danger of supplements as indirectly proportional to their ontological insufficiency: the supplement is "just" the thing, which is added to the already totally present meaning and to the ontologically autonomous being. In Rousseau, writing as supplement is not nothing, but it is the thing's outside: it is added to the full presence of the voice as its outside.

Thus, one cannot be emancipated from the metaphysical constitution of meaning; neither by accepting it as a human necessity, which consists in a permanent fight for the sense of representation, nor by radically rejecting this fight. For Derrida, Rousseau remains a contradictory metaphysician: although he is aware that no meaning exists beyond the human production of the representation of representation, he still gives priority to the divinely perfect truth before the humanly imperfect representation, which cannot stop deferring the meaning. Contrary to Rousseau, Derrida does not recognize the authority of the original. For him, origin is just a supplement of supplement and a product of permanent deferral of meaning.

Concerning the destruction of meaning, Derrida insists on his aporetic requirement to conceive of the supplement as the original deferral of meaning. He tries to show that presence, being, and the origin of meaning are never clear and pure. They are always already opened, cut, parasitized, and loaded by what was supposed to remain external and strange to them: an appearing matter, or a supplement of the idea. For Derrida, this contradiction is a metaphysical necessity that has had an important impact on Western thinking. Rousseau's concept of supplement is a haunting ghost: it causes emanation of what Rousseau tries to let disappear for the benefit of the supposed truth. As he believes, this truth is accessible by means of a return to naturalness and immediacy. Derrida conceives of signature supplementarily, as a trace prolonging meaning toward other traces.

Let us admit that the individual trace of handwritten signature is a disseminated representation of representation: the registered specimen signature *represents another representation*, which is the signer's civic name, which represents the writing citizen herself. If we admit this, we should also admit that the meaning of such a postponed sign is open to occasional performativity and leads to dispersion of the metaphysical origin of meaning, the foundation of ontology, and semantics of the total presence of meaning.

But I would like to emphasize that the philosophical position from which Derrida formulates this onto*logy* without origin is not outside Western metaphysics. Derrida repeatedly stated that it is vain to denunciate the order in the order, the metaphysics in the metaphysics, and continue to use the metaphysical instruments of the same metaphysics (concepts and definitions, examples and methods, argumentations and solutions). According to Derrida, such a strategy would not allow us to quit metaphysics at all, because all of the destructive discourses turn in circles. If the sign is indispensable to Derrida's deconstruction, it is because it enables communication. Nevertheless, when understood as writing, communication is not a way of carrying or transporting meaning. In Derrida, the semantic horizon that determines the concept of *communication* (what belongs to community, what is common, shared) is the deconstructed notion of *dissemination* (dispersion of the common meaning).

Let us try to link Derrida's thought on this to the legal sign of handwritten signature. Because in Western metaphysics the signature is considered to be a product of a unique personal style disseminated in occasional traces of authentic handwriting, it is also expected to be a reliable sign of civic identity. But these metaphysical expectations contain a trap: in both graphological and forensic examinations, the handwritten signature is simultaneously seen as a repeatable imprint and an authentic expression of the unique signer's soul. Nevertheless, in signature, the expression is authentic because it is manual, not mechanical: handwritten signature is not a stamp and does not produce mechanically repeated or repeatable imprints. It cannot be both a manual expression of the occasional state of mind of the signer and a mechanically repeatable, always recognizable imprint of the unique signer's soul. The event of signing is aporetic: without falling into contradiction, one cannot expect the handwritten signature to be simultaneously an unrepeatable manual expression and a repeatable mechanical imprint. To rethink the psychological and legal authority of this personal, authentic, and repeatable sign, I suggest seeing the act of signing by hand as an aporetic semiotic event.

In my own approach to signature as event, inspired by Derrida, the issue is not the traditional ontology, which corresponds to the problem of communication performed by means of signs disposing of total presence of meaning. The issue is rather a subverted ontology, which corresponds to the problem of dissemination performed through constantly deferred meaning. This position of aporetically subverted ontology makes it possible to conceive the *unstable meaning* of any event. Instead of determining the meaning of event, in "Une certaine possibilité impossible de dire l'événement," Derrida prefers to speak about event as a rise of supplements, where "producing events is covertly exchanged for speaking of events" (Derrida 2001a, 91).

Nevertheless, the return to the state of natural communication, which Rousseau dreams of, cannot be realized by refusing the principle of representation. By rejecting it, Rousseau came to litigation with his own philosophical practice: similarly to Plato's allegory of cave, Rousseau speaks about himself as a prisoner in the world of representation, which is a world full of reflections, shadows of things, and signs of signs. Jean Starobinski indicated that Rousseau has a problematic relationship with mediation; Rousseau tries to attain the state of immediate communication deprived of any mediation, translation, or interpretation. For Rousseau, writes Starobinski in *Jean-Jacques Rousseau: Transparency and Obstruction*, speech is the analytic sign of thought, and writing is in turn the analytic sign of speech:

> The art of writing is therefore a doubly mediated representation of thought. Nothing could be further from the privileged state of immediate communication, which Julie hoped to enjoy in the afterlife. We are caught up in viscous instrumental action, whereas the ideal would be to be understood without having to *make oneself understood*. Marvelous writer that he is, Rousseau is constantly protesting against the art of writing. (Starobinski 1988, 141)

On the one hand, reliable signs give sense immediately, directly, and transparently. However, as Starobinski mentions, Rousseau is aware that this "transparency" of signs is practically impossible: "He feels constantly obliged to reestablish the truth, to reconstruct an accurate image of himself, to prove that words that have slipped from his pen do not represent him as he really is, and to challenge the validity of evidence that he himself has to put into the hands of his judges. Ultimately he claims the privilege of being understood and accepted without being obliged to speak" (Starobinski 1988, 143). But, as he adds, Rousseau "can claim this privilege only by writing and speaking about it: he needs the mediation of language to say that he does not want such mediation. Until the silent felicity of immediacy has been achieved, all one can do is deplore the absence of immediacy by *means* of words whose purpose is to state the desire for the death of words" (Starobinski 1988, 143).

Derrida considers Rousseau's prison of the sign as a *prison of supplementarity*. Rousseau understands writing as a dangerous supplement: he worries about its artificial, inauthentic, unnatural character. As Derrida writes in *Of Grammatology*, Rousseau minds about supplementarity, which, in his eyes, is the basis of the "perversion" (Derrida 1997, 147), the "monstrosity" (Derrida 1997, 41) of every mediation: writing is a representative supplement of the speech, but also its mediator and translator. Writing is a technology of communication, a medium, and a mediator: when we write, we do not express ourselves immediately, but *mediately*: by means of writing.

In Derrida's reading, Rousseau fears supplementarity[8] because it inevitably destroys the original meaning, which becomes destabilized, decomposed, and dismantled into its individual components. Rousseau finds it necessary to fight against supplementarity, because he is afraid of questioning his own metaphysical demands. He regrets that the supplement ignores both the demand of total presence and the demand for originality of the meaning he produces. Rousseau's supplement, which escapes this double metaphysical guarantee of truthfulness, is a threat to morality, valorizing both the principle of authenticity and the principle of identity. As Derrida writes in *Of Grammatology*, Rousseau's supplement is a representation of nature, which is neither inside nature nor outside it. Such a representation is dangerous because it overturns nature and "modifies it in its interior, denatures it and obliges it to be separated from itself. Nature denaturing itself, being separated from itself, naturally gathering its outside into its inside, is catastrophe, a natural event that overthrows nature, or monstrosity, a natural deviation within nature. The function assumed in Rousseau's discourse by the catastrophe (as we shall see), is here delegated to monstrousness" (Derrida 1997, 211–12).

Thus, Starobinski's and Derrida's readings of Rousseau differ considerably. For Starobinski, Rousseau's obstinate fight for the renewal of communication was vain, because he constantly refused to admit that human communication is natural only when it is mediated.[9] For Derrida, Rousseau is a double philosophical agent, who simultaneously constructs and destroys Western metaphysics by means of his own ambiguous texts. While according to Starobinski, Rousseau locks himself in the prison of representation, according to Derrida, he is aware of his own communicational freedom, which allows even his own practice of representation. While he writes, he liberates himself. And Rousseau writes, abundantly and with passion. He is a writer, a philosopher, and a writing thinker. In other words, he is a *man of writing*. Nevertheless, from Derrida's viewpoint, one cannot say that Rousseau writes, because he longs for the supplementary prison of his own writing. He writes to liberate himself. His "prison" of the graphics of supplementarity is one of the inevitable aporetic conditions of human communication, the very source of its nature.

For this reason, Derrida accepts Rousseau's philosophical practice in its ambivalence. On the one hand, Derrida refers to the unfeasible character of Rousseau's philosophical project. On the other hand, he explains the necessity of his aporetic way of thinking. In Derrida's reading, Rousseau constantly liberates himself from the prison into which he has locked himself. Like any metaphysical thinker who is aware of the aporetic nature of her own practice of writing, Rousseau simultaneously constructs and destroys the metaphysical prison around him. This supplementarity that makes Rousseau hesitate and worry, is, in Derrida's thinking, the most powerful semantic necessity. It is the work of iteration and dissemination of traces.

The aporia of handwritten signature as iterated trace—the pragmatic paradox of graphic repetition, which is simultaneously required and impossible to satisfy—is played out inside Western metaphysics. Its outside is total madness and total absence of justice. Without metaphysical expectations, there would be no signature as sign. Moreover, signature is not any manual trace: it is a trace of a stylized form. It is style that raises the question of authenticity of signature as a condition of recognition. What is a style in handwriting; what is a style in drawing? Is it a personal way of tracing a line? When are the iterated manual traces sufficiently graphically constant to allow me to be sure that I can recognize the personal style of the signer? Why do we believe that one can identify an author by her style? Searching for answers to these questions bring me to the second aspect of Derrida's semantic thinking, the hauntology of style.

Let us admit that the handwritten signature is a conventional trace that should be occasionally manually reproduced on various documents in order to represent the signer's presence. If this is possible, it is because there is something in handwritten signature that returns. This revenant, which is expected to help one recognize the signer, is her handwriting; the individual and recognizable style of her manual writing. Signature's revenant never returns in the same form: every time someone signs a document, she produces a specter of her specimen signature. As Marder puts it in *The Event of the Thing*, the work of self-reference as reproduction of oneself produces new forms of the self as a certain kind of "structuring self-erasure" (Marder 2011, 31). All the individual signatures of a person, in which we try to recognize her specimen signature, are her specters coming to haunt her metaphysical certitudes. This spectrality reveals the impossible metaphysical task of each act of signing: the necessity of keeping the handwriting formally constant, thus repeatable by the same signer, and simultaneously authentic, thus unrepeatable by any other signer.

What does it mean that the handwritten signature must be authentically repeatable? Does it mean that it must be formally similar enough? And what does it mean to be similar enough? To fit into the interval of discursively acceptable resemblance? To be slightly different—neither mechanically identical, nor too different?

To answer these questions, let us turn once again to Derrida's reading of Rousseau. In *Of Grammatology*, Derrida mentions that Rousseau is afraid of the violence and artificiality of the written word, or writing, which tends to replace spontaneity and naturality of the spoken word, or speech. Rousseau considers that speaking is naturally close to the natural way of thinking, but writing is artificially added to the spoken word as its unnatural representation. As he believes that the cultural practice of writing distorts and corrupts human nature, "writing would thus have the exteriority that one attributes to utensils; to what is even an imperfect tool and a dangerous, almost maleficent, technique" (Derrida 1997, 34). As Derrida puts it, for Rousseau, such a deviation that links immediate speech to its visual representation is a recourse that is "not only 'bizarre,' but dangerous. It is the addition of a technique, a sort of artificial and artful ruse to make speech present when it is actually absent. It is a violence done to the natural destiny of the language" (Derrida 1997, 144). As such, the written word is dangerous because of its tricky effort to defer and replace the immediate and original meaning of the spoken word. Because Rousseau believes that writing has no right to this *trick,* he suggests keeping it in a hierarchically subordinated and dependent position. Liberating writing from its dependence on speech would not keep speech safe: it could threaten the metaphysically natural order of things and lead to its dangerous subversion.

Desiring to preserve and maintain the natural hierarchy of metaphysical order of things and of their meanings, Rousseau discovers a liar disguised as an authority. He denunciates the ambivalence of writing, which he understands as a supplementary practice having two mutually influencing roles. The sign is always a supplement of the original meaning of the object it represents. Unlike the complement, the supplement is an exterior addition. In *Of Grammatology*, Derrida notices that "as substitute, it is not simply added to the positivity of a presence, it produces no relief, its place is assigned in the structure by the mark of an emptiness. Somewhere, something can be filled up of itself, can accomplish itself, only by allowing itself to be filled through sign and proxy. The sign is always the supplement of the thing itself" (Derrida 1997, 145). Moreover, in Rousseau, the exteriority of supplementary practice has moral consequences: "the negativity of evil will always have the form of supplementarity. Evil is exterior to nature, to what is by nature innocent and good. It supervenes upon nature" (Derrida 1997, 145). Derrida notices that Rousseau's worries come mostly from his own characterization of supplement as a strange element external to the natural metaphysical order of things. But Rousseau is not the only one who is worried by this problem: it haunts every thinker who considers that the original meaning is always the correct and the good one. Thus, the supposedly evil nature of the supplement is given by its exteriority to supposedly good, true, and correct reasoning. Moreover, Derrida writes in *Of Grammatology*, "Rousseau is not alone in being caught in the graphic of supplementarity. All meaning and therefore all discourse is caught there, particularly and by a singular turn, the discourse of the metaphysics within which Rousseau's concepts move" (Derrida 1997, 246). It is impossible to emancipate oneself from writing from the inside of philosophical discourse.

Derrida tries to use his subversive reading of Western philosophy to indicate that nothing is semantically transparent: meaning is produced and shared neither naturally nor immediately, but by means of a certain *convention of mediation*. In Derrida, representation is a construction, which simultaneously enables communication and defers the original meaning. Under such conditions of series of representation, meaning is neither totally present nor totally absent. Therefore, Derrida speaks about the origin of meaning as already deferred—not as existing, and not as non-existing. In this view, we are all Rousseau's collogues in the alogical prison of materiality, similarity, and representation. In this semantic prison, meaning is constantly deferred by means of graphics of supplementarity.

Derrida's philosophy can be characterized by a *double gesture*, which questions the basic operations of Western metaphysics without resorting to a destructive critique. Derrida does not search for a way out of metaphysics: as soon as he points out a metaphysical schema in the text he reads, he lets it go on. As he is aware that every critique of metaphysics uses metaphysical concepts, he deliberately keeps the movement of critical thinking inside his melancholic, vicious circle. Derrida subversively profits from the metaphysical principles that organize the whole philosophical discourse to show that Rousseau conceives of a utopia of a direct access to natural meaning and criticizes writing as a dangerous supplement, which turns us away from it. If Derrida suggests accepting the fact of supplementarity as a communicational necessity, and if he suggests systematically following the postponed meaning, escaping in infinite series of representation of representation, he calls for a philosophical vigilance and mobilization against all totalitarian expressions inside philosophy as such. Tracing the deferred meaning is a movement of thinking that brings deconstruction to the margins of Western metaphysics. These margins are the very place where the *event of iteration* occurs.

The Event of Iteration

The goal of the handwritten signature is to express the unique soul of the signer in the matter of writing. In order to compose a style, the signer needs to try to repeat her previous establishing gesture of signing, which once produced the specimen signature. That is the aporia of handwritten signature as style: because every manual trace is unique, it cannot be exactly repeated by hand. Manual work is not mechanical: it cannot produce identical copies; it can only produce iterated differences. No identity of traces can be attained by iteration. Iteration is not mechanical repetition: while repetition eliminates uniqueness, iteration respects it. No trace of style can be simultaneously unique and repeatable. Every handwritten signature is written differently, because it is just one of the versions imitating the shape of the specimen signature; no version will ever be identical with other versions. Whenever one tries to reproduce oneself graphically by means of one's signature, one never does it sufficiently: none of one's attempts to sign will ever make the exact form of the specimen signature return. The inevitable drift from the original trace betrays the signer: every time she is asked to (re-)sign by hand, the specter of the registered specimen signature haunts her, but never really appears.

The handwritten signature is no work of art; it is rather a supplement to a work of art that guarantees the authenticity of the manual work. Without this aporia of manually repeatable manual traces, the signature could not exist as a sign. The semantics of signature depends on the aporia that requires fulfillment of the impossible task of exact manual reproducibility. That is the aporetic trap of every performative theory wishing to liberate the event of manual writing from its metaphysical determination: handwritten signature as sign does not exist beyond metaphysical expectation of the unifying style, which transversally crosses all the individual writing acts. Handwritten signature is not any unrepeatable trace performed by hand. A signature must be the carrier of author's style, which functions as one of the respected metaphysical categories: without the expectation of the author's unique and consistent style of work, there would be no experts in handwriting and in art.

The conception of *manual writing as tracing* can explain the reappearing inevitable difference depending on unique events: it prevents the signer from exactly reproducing herself in her manual traces, even if they are traces of her own style. Every recognizable personal style is born from self-repetition and self-imitation. The continuous work of self-imitation makes the signer recognizable: systematic iteration of her previous traces produces the style of her actual traces. The more the signer tries to imitate her previously manually written traces, the more she "resembles" herself; the more consistently she becomes her own style. Contrary to Peirce's affirmative ontological metaphysics, Derrida's deconstructed metaphysics allows us to point out that by means of the deconstructed style—composed of the iteration of individual existential traces—one can reach similarity or probability, but never identity or truth.

Therefore, I can see philosophical advantages of deconstruction in formulating the semiotic question from an ethical viewpoint. Signature as sign can be based on one of the two "former directions" in modern semiotics: neither on the dyadic and rhetorical arbitrary conception of sign in structuralism, nor on triadic and logico-realist conception of sign in Peirceanism. A semiotics of signature that is not naive would be based on deconstruction of these ethically unsatisfying semiotic directions. In contrast, Derrida's deconstruction proposes a *meta-semiotics*: an ethical call for permanent semantic vigilance. In deconstructed semiotics, signature becomes a partial representation of representation; its meaning is formed performatively. Derrida tries to use metaphysical principles, which institute and organize each philosophical discourse, to show that there is no direct access to original meaning. In his conception, writing is not a dangerous supplementary practice, which betrays the signer by tearing her away from the origin of meaning. On the contrary, the supplement remains the only way of approaching the origin. If Derrida suggests accepting the fact of supplementarity as the very communicational necessity, he calls for philosophical caution and mobilization against totalities in our metaphysical thinking.

Derrida claims in *Points* . . . that the proper motif is to be found in the singularity "of the 'style,' of the 'phantasmatic,' of the idiom in general" (Derrida 2004, 52). One's style—understood as the author's singular "idiom"—is inaccessible in its totality. Every attempt to grasp the style in its totality is doomed "to a kind of failure for structural reasons, especially if one attempted to link the signature to the name, and even more so to the father's name or the patronymic recognized by one's civil status" (Derrida 2004, 52–53). As Derrida puts it,

> Even if I could, up to a certain point, elaborate such a question elsewhere, put it in the form of general propositions, something would remain inaccessible to me, inaccessible in any case to these approaches, eluding any becoming for itself—and that

would be, precisely, "my" idiom. The fact that this singularity is always for the other does not mean that the latter accedes to something like its truth . . . the idiom is not an essence, merely a process, the effect of a process of expropriation that "produces" only perspectives, readings without truth, differences, intersections of affect, a whole history whose very possibility has to be disinscribed or reinscribed. These limits are valid not only for the relation of someone to his/her idiom, bur for any idiom or any signature. (Derrida 2004, 52–53)

Following Derrida, who paid attention to the aporetic nature of generalized writing and signature in several of his works, Peggy Kamuf focused on deconstruction of the signature, particularly in *Signature Pieces*. She opened this discussion because she regretted that the topic of signature was usually ignored, avoided, and filled with prejudices shaping the past and the present discourse on the writer in her writing. According to Kamuf, the main reason for neglecting research into this problem is that signature itself lacks a reliable definition: it is "an always divisible limit within the difference between writer and work, 'life' and 'letters.' Signature articulates the one within the other, the one *in* the other? It both divides and joins. It is this double-jointedness of signatures that will be lost to any discourse that continues to posit an essential exteriority of subjects to the texts they sign" (Kamuf 1988, viii). Everyday performative practices are organized by legal mediation politics, which tries to cover the precarity of writing acts by means of various conventions

> in a more or less reliable manner, operations of identification, attestation, verification, attribution of responsibility, and so forth. Indeed, many social institutions thoroughly depend, in one way or another, on the reliable functioning of signatures, and whole areas of law can be said to be concerned almost exclusively with the rights and duties guaranteed by signatures (e.g., contract, property, and copyright law). The legal signature signals that, usually on a certain date and according to certain formalities, the subject named was present and assented to, accepted, affirmed some accord with another party. (Kamuf 1988, viii)

If the signature is supposed to function reliably, a guarantee of originality, of authenticity, and of recognition of individual signatures must be determined. When the writer signs, she does not only write her civic name because she could do anything else: "you affix your name as a particular mark. The singularity of the autograph, however, cannot be absolute; on the contrary, verifiability or authentication relies on its reproducibility by 'the subject named'" (Kamuf 1988, ix). If the writer intentionally produced a very different and dissembling mark each time she signed, if there were not two similar signature acts, then it would not be possible to say whether it was she who signed. After some time, the writer could forget completely that she has ever made some particular mark (Kamuf 1988, ix). To prevent this, the performative act of handwritten signature is linked to a particular metaphysical expectation: "the grounding assumption is that the 'subject named' is not only self-identical with itself in the moment of signing but as well remains recognizably the same over time. By a seeming paradox, then, the singularity of the signature's mark depends on its limitation within recognizable parameters of reproducibility or iterability, which is to say of *generalizability*" (Kamuf 1988, ix). The generalized signature, therefore, is

> always detachable from the singular instance it supposedly designates. It can always be and in fact already has been detached from the signatory and expropriated by a field of general substitution. This is to remark that, within such a field of general substitution and exchange, "the subject named" is always finally a general subject, classified in a large but nevertheless limited number of ways. The particularization of this general subject through the functioning of signature is thus also always countersigned by the system of interchangeable likeness, the system of the same, in which singularity is but a necessary *concept*. (Kamuf 1988, ix)

From her formulation of these general presuppositions, linked with the role of handwritten signature, Kamuf moves toward her own examination of the metaphorical signature related to literary works, which she understands as a recognizable style of writing. Her analysis does not focus on writing in the sense of handwriting, but rather in the sense of literary style. In *Signature Pieces*, Kamuf resumes the four aporias of such a literary signature in the following way: "First, the act of signing cannot authenticate itself because it depends necessarily on the possibility of its repeatability and thus on the possibility of an inauthentic double: copy, simulacrum, forgery, imitation, false attributions, distortions, and so forth" (Kamuf 1988, 119). Therefore, according to Kamuf, "a signature cannot determine the limits of its own validity, and there is, theoretically at least, no first or final occurrence of a signature. This is to say that a signature never occurs as a pure event, without precedent, and without copy. Its possibility arises only from its limitation on pure singularity" (Kamuf 1988, 119). The second aporia is that a signature disarticulates the relation of property it appears to name (Kamuf 1988, 119). The third aporia is that even in the case of a pseudonym, a signature functions within the regime of copyright: the anonymity of the signer is only dissimulated (Kamuf 1988, 119–20). The fourth aporia of signature is that although the signature survives its signatory and conserves her name, it is disseminated, dispersed in multiple traces, without the possibility of unitary identification (Kamuf 1988, 120).

I consider Kamuf's most important contribution to the deconstruction of signature to be her reference to the fact that every writer produces many of her own signatures, not just one. The signature is a disseminated multiplicity. It is multiplied from the very beginning of writing, from the origin that was untraceable. The signature is an infinite dissemination of itself. My own conception of deconstructed signature differs in one essential aspect from Peggy Kamuf's approach: while Kamuf treats the problem of signature as a literary style and does not treat the problematic materiality of written letters in work with words, I focus on the problem of handwriting in the sense of plastic work with the material side of words. Handwritten signature is a plastic, not a literary, composition.

In the case of the handwritten signature, which is expected to be a reliable tool to identify citizens, it is necessary to rethink the political dimension of deconstruction. Derrida tackles the aporia of the metaphysical requirement to repeat the unrepeatable in his "Force of Law." As he puts it, his deconstruction is an aporetic domain of thinking situated in the semantic interval between law and justice. On the one hand, justice, which has no deconstructable structure, is the condition of possibility of deconstruction itself. On the other hand, the structure of the origin of law, which should be deconstructed, is the possibility of doing the deconstruction itself. Derrida situates his deconstruction in the interval separating the inability to deconstruct justice from the ability to deconstruct law: "it turns out that *droit* claims to exercise itself in the name of the justice and that justice is required to establish itself in the name of a law that must be 'enforced.' Deconstruction always finds itself between these two poles" (Derrida 1992, 22).

Like the never totally present justice, Derrida's deconstruction generates a quasi-ethical memento of deferred meaning. This memento is characterized by being permanently to come, without willing to definitively arrive. If one wanted to rethink this political ambition of Derrida's thinking, one would have to reconsider the fact that his deconstruction is ahistorical and amethodological, refusing methodological and historical sorting of events as a guarantee of their accurate interpretation. In *Jacques Derrida: Co-Responding Voix You*, Cixous very accurately observed that

> Jacques Derrida will have always been *arche*-political, *acted* and *acting*, and therefore *acting reflexively* and, with time, more and more broadly, forcefully, insisting, testifying, warning, even while thematizing and ramifying the networks of everything there is to think otherwise about the coming times. If one had to say "two words," as he would say, on the subject of Politics of Deconstruction, of Deconstruction as Politics, it would of course be *à venir*, to come. This *à venir* to which he will have joined, is an unforgettable way, the word, the idea, the dream of democracy . . . it will no longer be possible to think democracy otherwise than through this phrase: Democracy *to come*. And not Democracy *coming*. It is not, as he takes care to repeat, a matter of messianic anticipation, not of messianism but of messianicity, of a promise, of a horizon that regulates law. It is necessary that Democracy *remain to come*. It is necessary to think it and to think of it with a thought that will *always and still* remain beyond what is realizable. (Cixous 2009, 43)

Thus, Derrida simultaneously proposes and cannot propose any realizable political action. Derrida does not want to prescribe what one should or should not do. He merely points out the ethical risks of any interpretative or performative act. Because deconstruction produces an ethical memento, a promise that remains permanently to come, it cannot establish and make totally present any order—such a founding gesture would make the very goal of deconstruction vanish. Therefore, Derrida is more an ethical than a political thinker: all of his political thinking is quasi-ethical. In this respect, his deconstruction is not ready for any methodological use or application. One cannot rely on it as on a solid scientific method to solve concrete problems in the political explanation of individual events.

In order to rethink the aporetic authority of law, Derrida proposes to deconstruct the aporia, which forces us to repeat the unrepeatable, and which is the basis of the signature as a personal sign. Signature legally establishes the relation of identity between the civic name and shape of the traces of manual writing. Because its written shape is different each time, handwritten signature makes identification of the signer practically and empirically impossible. Every law that forces citizens to sign correlatively to their specimen signatures generates a pragmatic paradox: despite the legal requirement to remain recognizable by producing accurate traces, the written form of the signature inevitably changes in every single attempt to perform the manual repetition accurately. Contrary to what it is legally required, no signer can either manually repeat the form of her specimen signature or guarantee that she will perform in each single signature the supposed essential attributes of her previous writing. Her past traces are never equal to her future traces. The required act and the performed act, the semantic universality, identity, and ontological singularity, repeatable ideality of the law and unrepeatable reality of the event, stand here in opposition to each other.

Performative mobilization of writing[10] in deconstruction can be illustrated by the example of Derrida's approach to signature as event when he partly leaves ontology linked to signification and its total presence of meaning. As Derrida puts it in "Plato's Pharmacy," his understanding of generalized writing as characteristic dissemination of traces quits the binary opposition between truth and lie. Deconstruction is a subversive way of reading texts—it does not aim to read the logos, but to read the *grammé*. Derrida finds specific potency of writing in "its capacity to communicate thoughts to addressees who are absent" (Glendinning 2001, 116). Derridean writing "emerges as a technical device when the desire or need arises to extend the field of communication to addressees who are present but out of range of the natural voice" (Glendinning 2001, 116).

What Derrida reads is a metaphysically constructed texture of the text. Derrida notices a similar problem in *Histoire du mensonge*, where he mentions that each legal change of the archive's setting inaugurates a new regime of redistribution of truth and lie. If one accepts the truth of another archive, one starts believing in another truth and another order, in another God. Each truth has its believers and its historical (temporarily valid) archive. There is no truth without its archive of rhetorically persuasive evidences. Following Saint Augustine's and Nietzsche's thoughts, Derrida claims that not telling the truth in good faith is no lie, but just an—ethically neutral—error. Contrary to the error, the lie intentionally harms: "To lie means wanting to mislead the other person, sometimes even by saying the truth. One can say the untruth without lying, but one can also say the truth in order to mislead, thus to lie. Although one is wrong, one does not lie, if one believes in what she says, if the belief is added" (Derrida 2012b, 15). Truth is saint, error is human, lie is evil. But Derrida's philosophical goal is not a mere distinction between the things that are and are not worth believing in. He is also concerned with determining the kind of faith in which such a message is communicated. The distinction between truth and lie starts with this faith: both good and bad faith select their own believers and build their own archives. A case of lack of belief in the possibility of attaining identity by manual repetition is a case of archive fever (as Derrida calls the Freudian death drive).

According to Derrida, this archive fever is generated by the *aporia of repetition*: there would be no truth without idealized repetition, but materialized repetition is the movement of untruth. The inevitable materiality of traces causes that the required total presence of meaning vanishes: it disseminates and multiplies by mimesis and simulacra. As Derrida puts it in *Positions*, "The true and the untrue are both species of repetition. And there is no repetition possible without graphics of supplementarity, which supplies, for the lack of a full unity, another unit that comes to relieve it, being enough the same and enough other so that it can replace by addition" (Derrida 1981d, 168). Derrida's grasping of the *grammé as supplementarity*, which is both present and absent, makes the *différance* emerge, the supplementary difference that "renders *itself*, as well as the metaphysical text, readable/legible as a *scribble*," as Ormiston (1988, 44) writes in "The Economy of Duplicity: Différance."

Deconstructed writing loses its phonological legibility and logocentric effectivity. Here, it is important to mention the deconstructive practice of grafting, where Derrida operates a shift in definition of the metaphysical concept of writing. In "Signature Event Context," Derrida states that "it seems necessary to retain, provisionally and strategically, the old name" (Derrida 1977b, 21). If it is possible to communicate by means of writing, it is because this *paleonymy* is maintained. As Derrida puts it, "To leave to this new concept the old name of writing is tantamount to maintaining the structure of the *graft*, the transition and indispensable adherence to an effective *intervention* in the constituted historical field. It is to give to everything at stake in the operations of deconstruction the chance and the force, the power of *communication*" (Derrida 1977b, 21). Philosophy, including Derrida's deconstruction, cannot survive outside metaphysics. It is impossible to totally emancipate from metaphysics. If deconstruction wants to remain resistant to logocentrism, it has to accept the role of parasite. Old concepts of Western metaphysics can be neither eradicated nor replaced by new ones. The only thing that can be done with them is to graft, to parasitize their well-established metaphysical meaning.

Rodolphe Gasché called attention to Derrida's emphasis on performativity in his late work. Gasché sees its main characteristics in its occasional interest with some individual events and in its openness to the unexpectable, unprogrammable, and incalculable, which permanently remains in a state of deferral, of a being to come. As Gasché puts it in *Of Minimal Things*, "the performative nature of deconstruction evident from *Glas* on—performative, however, unlike the speech act defined by its opposition to the constative—increasingly makes Derrida's later works responses, active engagements, processes of negotiation" (Gasché 1999, 11).

Derrida's late interest in performativity is productively developed by Avital Ronell, who demonstrates the ontological problem of the impossibility of repeating events by explaining the aporetic verifying function of testing. If we attribute the ability to verify the quality of an object (or subject) to a test, we conceive of the test as a model situation. We suppose that we can grasp the representative reaction and determine the representative quality of the examined. We expect that we are able to use a test to generate an event, which will be the same as any further event where the tested object (or subject) will behave identically. But, ontologically speaking, this cannot be done, because no event will ever be repeated and the supposed quality of the tested will never be expressed identically. For these reasons, Ronell demonstrates that ontology demands identification to legitimize the practice of testing, but that no test can fully satisfy this demand. In *The Test Drive*, Ronell states that "truth cannot be dogmatically asserted but must each time be ascertained, produce its own justification, 'undergo the test of its own truth'; Ontologically demoted, truth becomes secondary to itself, for only the test has the right to decide and approve the truth that must first submit itself. *Logos*, the concept, owes its authority to a still higher authority: that of the test" (Ronell 2005, 25). Just like the law, the test is parasitic on individual events. It pumps its own materiality from those events.

The authority of the order of transformation turns materiality into ideality. Nevertheless, this ideality nourishes and constructs itself from the materiality. Judith Butler demonstrates this problem in *Dispossession: The Performative in the Political*, written together with Athena Athanasiou. Butler considers performative political gestures as a constant politico-semantic work of the individual that keeps constructing her gender by all of her performative acts in everyday life. Butler refers to the aporia of metaphysical construction of *gender binarism,* where gender does not exist without a performative gesture. But, although we used to speak about gender as about something preexisting, gender is not just expressed as a preexisting model of a normal social behavior; it is also iterated and varied in every single performative act of every individual. Put otherwise, the performative action of a citizen of male or female sex is no expression of a preexisting gender norm—it is rather its perpetual reconstruction. This gender self-construction is independent of a given person's sex and the "normal" sexuality in the given historical period. Either more creative or more conservative, gender self-construction is a lifetime performative project of every single citizen. Finally, everyone does gender differently: everyone chooses different ways to perform a "woman," a "man," or neither, but rather an individual queer figure.

Metaphysical expectation of a constant repetition of the shape of traces legitimizes the requirement for identification. In the view of metaphysics of law, a handwritten trace enables us to identify the person who lets it—here, a similar trace can signify an identical trace. If forensic analysts compare several versions of one's signature with one's specimen signature, they have to determine which versions are "still similar enough" and which are "already too different" to confirm the civic identity of the signer. In my opinion, this is also valid for the discursive limit of similarity, which is conventionally determined by the experts themselves. From the perspective of deconstruction, one can say that in the metaphysics of graphological and forensic discourse, until a conventionally set limit, the similar is interpreted as the identical. In the interpretation of handwritten signature, identity and similarity mutually pervade. Each time, even if one reads the signature identically (interpretation in the mode of logos generates identity), one sees it written differently (interpretation in the mode of *grammé* generates similarity). This double mode of reading the writing of signature becomes problematic when its individual trace is supposed to be repeated, and when this repetition is supposed to lead the analysis not to similarity of traces, but to identification of the signer.

I now propose to answer the questions that have introduced this complex inquiry. The law legitimates scientific discourses that metaphysically force us to think that the sign of handwritten signature is a key personal expression, which enables us to uncover the hidden psychologico-strategical essence of the signer's soul.

Nevertheless, as we have seen, the knowledge of experts in handwriting analysis is not unified. If the experts expect that the manually written signature leads to two different ways of understanding of the signer, it is because two different sorts of discursive expectations coexist. While the discourse of graphology produces psychological knowledge of the signer's soul, the inborn source of natural qualities, the discourse of forensic analysis generates criminological knowledge of the signer's style, the evolving strategy of self-expression. The shared discursive expectations of the matrix of the supposed signer's essential personal expression is different in each expertise.

As I have shown in previous chapters, both discourses share the same set of metaphysical expectations of the matrix, the transcendental core of manual expressions. Contrary to the discursive expectations that can use different methods to examine the communicated message disseminated in the same medium, the metaphysical expectations are linked to the medium of communication itself. Because both kinds of expertise in handwritten signature focus on the same manually produced medium, both discourses share the same metaphysical prejudices about manual work.

More precisely, the experts in both disciplines expect that handwritten signature can confirm the signer's personal essence: true qualities, authentic presence, and civic identity. These metaphysical expectations are respectively linked to our prejudices of similarity (rhetorically exchanged for equivalence) between the signer's soul and manual traces, authenticity (rhetorically exchanged for presence) of the signer's soul in manual traces, and repeatability (rhetorically exchanged for identity) of the signer's expression in manual traces.

Following Derrida's work, I have claimed that metaphysical expectations are conditioned by transcendental prejudices determining our language, our concepts, our descriptions, our reasoning, and our legitimate discourses. In scientific expertise, the event of signature is no longer an event of trace. Once a manual trace is grasped by an expert's conceptual and methodological instruments, it is turned into the expression of essence: by force of metaphysical expectations, the signer's manual trace turns into a sign of identification. When one of the signer's traces is conceived of as the true expression of her essence, the signer's singular life is transformed into a general law. The deconstructed sign of handwritten signature is not critically opposed to such a rhetorical transformation operated by Western metaphysics. It is rather understood as an aporetic necessity; handwritten signature is accepted as a sign of the signer's essential expression, but also seen as an incomplete, fragmentary, momentary expression of her expected essence.

Postscript

The intention of my work was to deconstruct two kinds of expectations, to reveal them as two sources of legitimate prejudices that structure scholarly analysis of handwritten signatures. I found that Derrida's thinking is not equally usable for reflection on both metaphysical and discursive expectations: while it is suitable for reflection on scholarship as such, it is not suitable for positivist analysis of particular scholarly discourses. The same split applies when it comes to positivist distinction of different media. As Derrida's deconstruction is no positivist theory of technologically specific media, it can only help to reflect on metaphysical conditions of possibility of mediation and representation.

Deconstruction thus cannot be used to investigate the discursive expectations of signature that determine current legal mediation politics. I became aware of this problem thanks to Derrida's work on the metaphysical suppositions of historiography and archive work, and I have chosen to demonstrate this point by reference to his polemics with Michel Foucault. In Foucault's later work, there is a methodological shift toward the ethical position of a non-rhetorical search for truth, or parrhesia, which is closer to the quasi-ethical demands of deconstruction. Nevertheless, because I believe that no particular legal mediation politics can be determined without distinguishing between particular scholarly discourses, I introduce my study by revealing the discursive expectations that shape the two currently coexisting discourses of signature: graphology and forensic analysis.

Discursive analysis reveals the common suppositions underlying the metaphysical expectations common to both discourses. Unlike discursive analysis, deconstruction can help us determine the metaphysical expectations of handwritten signature, because it subverts the metaphysical certainties of scholarly work with empirical data. Because all discourses are determined by metaphysics, analyzing different discourses does not help us deconstruct metaphysics itself. From its metaphysically marginal position, deconstruction subverts metaphysical certainties, but does not erase, correct, or criticize them. Deconstruction is neither destruction nor reconstruction of these certainties; it brings no revolution. It is partly motivated by the opposite of revolution: melancholy. Derrida is aware that no critique of metaphysics can either improve or eliminate it. Metaphysics cannot be simply criticized. It can only be deconstructed—presented in terms of pragmatic paradoxes or aporias. Therefore, in the subsequent course of my study, I focused primarily on aporias.

Even though neither philosophy nor semiotics has paid systematic attention to the metaphysical problem of the common use of handwritten signature as a legally reliable sign of civic identification, several historians and anthropologists have presented theoretical contributions to this topic. Elements of the problem have also been analyzed by legal theorists, primarily in relation to the contemporary turn to digital signature. Legally oriented theorists drew my attention to the interesting point that although there is no legal definition of handwritten signature, it has irreplaceable legal functions. This means two things. On the one hand, it is not clear what precisely a handwritten signature is and why experts expect so much from it. On the other hand, it is perfectly clear what roles handwritten signatures are supposed to play in psychological and legal communication. The discourses enforce their demands and oblige signers to try their best to adhere to them. As I found this problem philosophically inspiring, I examined it more closely. Unlike the aforementioned approaches, my investigation focused on deconstructing philosophical aspects of our current communication practices with legal handwritten signature. I wondered what experts expect from signature as sign given that they credit it with such important psychological and legal functions.

In my own research, I was particularly occupied with this logocentric metaphysical expectations of "handwritten-ness," which is supposed to give legal signatures their personal, authentic, non-interchangeable pictorial qualities. In order to minimize uncertainty in this respect, the authenticity of handwritten signatures on juridically important documents is certified by a notary. In the case of handwritten signatures written without a notary's testimony, recognition of originality or forgery is entrusted to the legal discipline of forensic handwriting analysis, which partly shares its knowledge with graphology, or the psychologically oriented analysis of handwriting. Both disciplines expect that it is possible to discern the identity of the signer by analyzing the way the signature is written. The difference between them lies in the way they understand the identity of the signer. While graphology determines the psychological qualities of the signer, forensic analysis assesses whether the signature is genuine or forged. In this respect, forensic analysis does not overcome the main ambitions of graphology.

These shared metaphysical expectations of handwritten signature became the main subject of my research, inspired by Derrida's deconstruction. I focused on three metaphysical expectations, which determine the triple ambition of experts: to recognize the psychological qualities of the signer; to prove the authentic presence of the signer; and to confirm the civic identity of the signer. I wondered how these expectations organize contemporary legal mediation politics based on legal uses and interpretation of handwritten signatures in forensic and psychological practices. The aim of my work was to deconstruct the handwritten signature as a medium in McLuhan's technological sense by describing the triple metaphysical aporias generated by the very specific media message of a handwritten signature. First, through ontological aporia, in the expert's interpretation of a signature, pictures of words become words, and resemblance becomes identity. Second, through semantic aporia, in the expert's interpretation of a signature, a writing act that can be iterated becomes a repeatable speech act, and authenticity becomes identity. Third, through pragmatic aporia, in the expert's interpretation of a signature, an expressive trace becomes a personal idiom, and style becomes identity. A deconstructive approach revealed that the signer theoretically must—but, at the same time, practically cannot—achieve her civic identity by writing her signature. By signing, she occasionally performs a trace, which is understood as an aporetic event of her soul rather than its natural expression or authentic presence. Because deconstruction subverts all three of the metaphysical prejudices of graphological and forensic experts, it inevitably leads to aporias.

But because aporias do not allow us to positively grasp the communicative ambitions of expert interpretation that shape current legal mediation politics, I proposed complementing Derrida's deconstruction with Eco's semiotics of conventional realism. My reading of Eco's semiotics of forgeries helped me explain how the expert's recognition operates within the conventional limits of scholarly interpretation. Eco's discursively oriented semiotics allowed to reveal the handwritten signature as a conventional sign understood differently in two different discourses. Derrida's deconstruction does not allow us to understand such double discursive knowledge. By combining Derrida's deconstructive vigilance and Eco's theory of discursively limited interpretation, I was finally able to formulate a deconstructed semiotic conception of complex expectations of handwritten signature as a civic sign, which generates a conventional belief in the possibility of identifying the personal style of handwriting from an authentic trace of the signer's natural expression. According to this complex expectation, the signer acts as a citizen, who constantly repeats her previous hand movements that inevitably naturally and authentically express the individual qualities of her soul.

It should be clarified that legal signature as a sign of civic identification can currently have two different media forms: handwritten and digital. Although these two media generate different signs and different metaphysical expectations, they are both legitimate in contemporary society. Let us take a closer look at these two technologically different signs.

The handwritten signature—the object of analysis in graphology and forensic analysis—is a conventional picture of a signer's own civic name, which is supposed to be replicated by the signer's own hand each time she is asked to do so. But the handwritten signature is not just any picture of a signer's name: it is her manual work, an authentic copy of a preexisting handwritten trace that was previously registered as a specimen signature. Because this trace is written by the signer's own hand, it is expected that it will have the recognizable shape of her unique style of handwriting. Experts in handwriting suppose that the signer can be identified through empirical observation of repeated formal homologies. Graphology and forensic analysis share the same metaphysical suppositions, because they deal with the same medium of the handwritten signature.

Unlike a handwritten signature, a digital signature is able to achieve identity in the sense of mathematical equivalence or logical truth. There is an important difference between belief in the naturalness of a soul's expression and the authenticity of a handwritten trace, which conditions verification of a signer's identity in the case of a handwritten signature, and belief in the identity of computer code, which conditions verification of a signer's identity in the case of a digital signature. The discourse of cryptography deals with the digital signature, which refers to an algorithmically generated composition of numbers. This type of signature contains encrypted computer code. Unlike forensic analysis of handwriting, the verification of a digital signature's authenticity is not based on an expert's empirical observation of similarities, but on computer processing of an encrypted mathematical formula.

Because a digital signature is not made by hand, but generated by a computer program, the emergence of digital cryptography brought with it not only a discursive change, but also a change of medium. The legitimization of the digital signature not only brings about the transformation of discursive expectations of the signature as a sign; it also transforms metaphysical expectations of the signature as a medium. The new digital medium eliminates the empirical dimension of handwriting with its supposed naturalness of style and authenticity of trace. Consequently, the results of cryptography achieve a mathematical identity and logical truthfulness that neither graphology nor forensic analysis is capable of. A hierarchy has thus been established between these discourses in terms of the credibility of their scholarly results. In the context of contemporary mediation politics, there is growing belief in the reliability of individual analytical discourses, ranging from graphology through forensic analysis to cryptography. The expert's verification moves from empirical research on authentic manual traces toward standardized calculation of randomly distributed numbers.

The discourses of graphology and forensic analysis deal with handwritten signature, while the discourse of cryptography deals with digital signature. These two technologically different signatures are two different media. Because the preference for technologically different media is linked to different metaphysical expectations, this new media turn is being accompanied by a change of metaphysical expectations of signature.

In the following reflections, I focused exclusively on scholarly discourses dealing with the old medium of the handwritten signature. I concentrated on the metaphysical expectations that are shared by the discourses of graphology and forensic analysis. Both of these disciplines are organized by the metaphysical violence of empirical research, which obliges them to understand resemblance as identity and to believe that unification of particular shapes leads to a natural and authentic expression of reality itself. Because of their common metaphysical belief, both sciences systematically turn ontological resemblance and authenticity into logical identity. In their conception, empirically observed qualities of the analyzed signatures correspond to predetermined metaphysical categories.

My discursively oriented reading of graphological and forensic texts allowed me to determine the contemporary discursive expectations of handwritten signature, which I understood as legal prejudices. I intended to show that two discourses of the handwritten signature coexist in contemporary legal mediation politics, which are linked to two different discursive expectations. My reading of selected scholarly texts representing the two discourses of signature helped me to compare the scholarly ambitions of these discourses:

graphology expects that by analyzing her signature, it is possible to recognize the psychological qualities of the signer; forensic analysis expects that by doing this, it is possible to verify the authentic presence of the signer.

In its analysis of handwritten signature, graphology searches for the resemblance between the signer's soul and her signature, which is taken as a recognizable picture of her soul. Graphologists believe that the particular handwritten form of letters hides essential information about the signer's self-conception: a handwritten signature reveals the ego of the signer, her own picture of herself, and her idea of her own social value. It also displays the way she wishes to be seen by others. Like graphology, forensic analysis of handwriting involves observing, comparing, and classifying handwritten traces. Unlike graphology, forensic analysis primarily focuses on the authenticity of a signer's manually written trace, which means there is a discursively given interval between excessive identity (which is a sign of forgery by mechanical copying) and excessive difference (which is a sign of forgery by imperfect manual imitation). Usually the authenticity is verified by comparing the signature with other samples of handwriting previously produced by the supposed signer. Her characteristic graphic expression is forensically understood as her personal style of handwriting, which is unique to that signer. Forensic experts believe that this pattern of handwriting is so characteristic of the signer that no one else can repeat it accurately. Every other signer inevitably and constantly repeats in her forged signature her own pattern of handwriting, which inevitably shines through her imitation. Thus, imitation becomes transparent to the expert's eye, which can discern the unauthentic pattern behind it. The supposition that the imitation of a handwritten signature by any other signer will necessarily be imperfect legitimates the distinction between authentic and forged signatures.

I now return to the metaphysical determination of the two discourses. The psychological discipline of graphology compares the qualities of handwriting with the qualities of the signer's soul—with her psyche. Its discursive expectation is given by the supposition that the resemblance between the varying shape of handwriting and the signer's soul achieves identity. Unlike graphology, forensic analysis compares the formal qualities of one signature with those of another. Its discursive expectation is given by the supposition that the resemblance between varying shapes of particular signatures can be explained as an expression of the same pattern, as their identity. Both discourses achieve the supposed identity by empirical observation: graphology compares psychological with graphic qualities; forensic analysis compares graphic qualities with other graphic qualities, which are determined by psychological qualities. Both disciplines share the same set of metaphysical expectations, namely of natural resemblance, authenticity, and, consequently, identity. In both discourses, the graphic qualities of handwriting are understood as a recognizable expression of the signer's soul. The same medium of the handwritten signature leads both analytical disciplines to the same set of metaphysical aporias.

In order to follow Derrida's reflection on the violence of the Western metaphysics, in my subsequent argument I intentionally left aside consideration of signature in terms of discursively relevant meaning. Inspired by Derrida's deconstruction, I wished to show that although graphology and forensic analysis differ in their discursive expectations of handwritten signature, both disciplines do share the same metaphysical expectations. They both understand the common object of their analysis—the handwritten signature—as a specific medium, which generates specific metaphysical expectations. According to these expectations, a handwritten signature allows experts to recognize the signer's natural qualities, to guarantee the signer's authentic presence, and to verify the signer's civic identity.

Deconstruction of the three metaphysical expectations of signature brought me to compare my conception of media semiotics with Peirce's semiotics of ontological realism, which introduced the metaphysical categories of Firstness, Secondness, and Thirdness. Unfortunately, Derrida's own reading of Peirce in *Of Grammatology* did not prove very helpful for my research, because Derrida neither tried to deconstruct these categories nor saw the ethical trap in Peirce's metaphysical work. My intention was to reveal these triple deconstructable metaphysical expectations as triple aporias of the impossible metaphysical task of achieving resemblance, authenticity, and identity in the sign of the handwritten signature.

First, the aporia of natural resemblance—the Peircean category of Firstness—resides in the fact that the style of handwriting vanishes in mechanical reproduction; it can exist only in imperfect imitation and iteration of previous traces. Psychological and forensic experts expect that a signer will sign naturally, which means in a way that is compatible with her unique soul and inimitable by any other signer. Their common metaphysical expectations enable two different things. On the one hand, they allow graphologists to recognize the natural qualities of the signer in her signature. On the other hand, they legitimate the forensic distinction between authentic and forged signatures. Nevertheless, as I showed by reference to Derrida's reading of Émile Benveniste, the handwritten signature remains a metaphor of the signer's soul, which occasionally adopts the role of the copula. Because of this metaphysical demand, both scholarly disciplines dealing with handwritten signature systematically turn similarity into identity.

Second, the aporia of authentic tracing—the Peircean category of Secondness—resides in the belief of psychological and forensic experts that a handwritten signature allows them to verify a signer's physical presence in the place and time her signature was produced. This expectation is grounded in the belief in the handwritten trace as a meaningful remainder of the previous authentic physical contact between the writing tool in the signer's hand and the signed document. Because every signer can only authentically sign her own name by her own hand, the original signature can be distinguished from a forgery. Nevertheless, from a deconstructive perspective, the signature can be seen as a trace of style that does not achieve identity and truth, but only resemblance and probability. As I seeked to clarify by means of Derrida's polemics against John Searle, Austin's theory of performativity is usable for Derrida's conception of the parasitical iterability of writing. But I found it necessary to modify Austin's theory: a handwritten signature should not be taken as a speech act, but as a writing act, which can be distinguished from metaphysically expressive speech acts by its excessive materiality. Being recognizable by means of the authentic handwritten trace means being as graphically consistent as possible: each particular signer's trace certifies the total presence of the graphic consistency of all her traces. As such, it means identity of samples and style, of fragments and whole.[1] Because of this metaphysical demand, the legal mediation politics of scholarly disciplines analyzing handwritten signature systematically turns authenticity to identity.

Third, the aporia of identical repetition—the Peircean category of Thirdness—resides in the expectation of psychological and forensic experts that a handwritten signature allows them to verify the legal identity of the signer: the signer signs identically to her style of handwriting, not identically to her specimen signature or any other of her previous traces. The identity of the signer is situated in the discursively acceptable range of similarity, in the interval between insufficient difference between repeated shapes of handwriting (formal identity of signatures is seen as a sign of mechanical forgery) and excessive difference (formal dissimilarity of signatures is seen as a sign of manual forgery). Based on Derrida's commentary on Gilles Deleuze titled *I'm Going to Have to Wander All Alone*, I seeked to clarify his deconstruction of Deleuze's concepts of expression, difference, and repetition. These concepts could explain the manual work of signing as a formally consistent composition of recognizable signs: the signer signs in her own creative style. Nevertheless, this identity is processual and multiple. In this respect, the specimen signature is not the original and founding sign of handwriting. It is just one of the traces that collectively create the handwriting. Only a permanent—and discursively acceptable—variation of elements contained in the specimen signature can be regarded as able to constantly create and keep present the signer's style.

In order to bring some philosophical positivity to these aporias, I proposed to complement deconstruction with an approach inspired by media semiotics: my approach is based on both discursive expectations inspired by Eco's semiotics of conventional realism, and on metaphysical expectations inspired by the aporetic quasi-ethics of deconstruction. Why did I reintroduce semiotics in this third and final phase of my argument? Why did I find it necessary to complement deconstruction? It is mostly because deconstruction does not allow any scientifically or philosophically positive understanding of the problems of medium, sign, or style. Its subversive position cannot form the basis for any positive definition of the handwritten signature as a sign determined by legal mediation politics. From a deconstructive approach, one cannot reflect on the discursively privileged interpretation of the handwritten signature. Because Derrida subverts the positivity of both semiotics and discursive analysis, his approach is helpful for considering metaphysical prejudices, but not when it comes to analysis of the specific modes of communication based on them.

By contrast with deconstruction, my conception of the handwritten signature as a sign of civic identification introduced the concept of metaphysical expectation, which I understand as the interpretive demands linked to the specific material foundation of the sign. In my conception, a handwritten signature is a sign determined by a particular medium, which generates specific metaphysical expectations but does not generate unified discursive expectations, as illustrated by the differing expectations of graphology and forensic analysis.

Deconstructed media semiotics, which I suggested, articulates discursive expectations and metaphysical expectations of handwritten signature as two determinants of contemporary legal mediation politics. On the one hand, to describe the differing discursive expectations of graphology and forensic analysis, the proposed media semiotics is theoretically underpinned by Foucault's and Eco's conceptions of discursively acceptable interpretations. The contemporary coexistence of these two discourses structures the legal mediation politics of the handwritten signature, which is supposed to function as a reliable sign of civic identification. On the other hand, my deconstruction-inspired conception of media semiotics enables a new, ethically focused perspective. It calls for philosophical reflection on the inevitable violence of the metaphysical dimension of every mediation politics. Because this violence cannot be reflected on either by structuralism or by Peirce's realistic or Eco's discursive semiotics, for ethical reasons I believe it is inevitable to complete the media semiotics of signature with deconstruction. Deconstruction focuses on aporias as an ethical blind spot of all semiotic ambitions. Thus, the goal of my reflections was to formulate a new reading of deconstruction, which could aid understanding of the metaphysical prejudices of experts dealing with the legal impossibility of grasping events, or life itself. As Derrida notes, philosophy cannot abandon the Western metaphysics, which produces pragmatic paradoxes and forces us to build our definitions of events on them. He thus reveals the inevitable unrealizability of all philosophical and scholarly projects—they are generalized performative failures. This is the source of the quasi-melancholy of deconstruction; it is the reason why it focuses on the fact that the signature is not a signer, the text is not an author, and the map is not a land. No event can be repeated; no one can approach the event of signature closely enough to let us speak of constant formal continuity of traces, or even their recognizable style, which could legitimate the metaphysical ambition of identification and the nominal definition of the author. Although the signer tries as hard as she can, she will never repeat the shape of the specimen signature identically. She generates formally different versions each time, which resemble her specimen signature more or less closely. Despite this fact, signatures are considered to be the expert's reliable instruments of identification.

In deconstruction, all these metaphysical expectations can be conceived as logocentric prejudices, whereby constantly varying handwriting is understood as a constant and typical expression of the signer's soul, which is empirically identifiable and classifiable in the predetermined typology of souls. Such reflection inevitably leads to the aporia of the impossible legal obligation to prove civic identity using a handwritten signature. Contrary to positivist scientific discourses and methods, the goal of deconstruction is not to generate facts from empirical data, but rather to rethink the metaphysical prejudices that make us believe in the knowledge conditionned by them.

For the deconstructionist, the handwritten signature is an aporetic trace of style, a stylized self-portrait of the signer, which does not allow three things. First, it does not allow one to discern the signer (because one cannot change resemblance into definition; similar is not identical). Second, it does not allow authenticity to be proved (because the trace of the signature is not authentic and auratic in Benjamin's sense, but rather disseminated and supplementary in Derrida's sense). Third, it does not allow a signer to be identified as a citizen (because signatures vary, the specimen signature will never be identically repeated). The deconstructed metaphysical expectations ultimately reveal the handwritten signature to be a phantom of (legal or psychological) identity that is merely believed to have been achieved. The deconstructed handwritten signature, understood in its disseminated graphic changeability, makes any identification impossible. If, despite this, the handwritten signature still functions as a natural and authentic sign of identification, it generates an unsolvable aporia.

From this quasi-ethical position, which is sensible to the metaphysical violence of the full presence of meaning of the object in its representation, Derrida cannot positively distinguish specific media. Deconstructive efforts are not directed to attaining a positive understanding of the common scholarly ambition of graphology and forensic analysis, which deal with the same medium. As Vernon W. Cisney puts it, Derrida's philosophical strategy holds the power of the negative: his trace "is produced as a presence, only in a qualified sense, as the *presence of an absence*, the experience of a fundamental lack" (Cisney 2018, 156). Therefore, after deconstructing the metaphysical expectations of naturalness, authenticity, and identity shared by graphology and forensic analysis, I proposed to draw on media semiotics to counterbalance the negativity of the aporia conceived by deconstruction.

Nevertheless, despite complementing it in this way, I do not abandon deconstruction in favor of semiotics. I consider Derrida's strategic melancholy to be philosophically indispensable because it can be neither corrupted nor saved by the suggestion of any new positive methodology. Precisely in this respect, Derrida's insistence that deconstruction is not a scholarly methodology can be understood as a strategy emphasizing an inventive subversive practice of philosophical writing on event and testimony. This strategy allows Derrida to develop the material side of this practice at the expense of developing metaphysically pure conceptual thinking, uncontaminated by any intervention of the materiality of signs. As he observes, deconstruction cannot be limited to neutralizing binary oppositions of metaphysical concepts. On the basis of these aporetic conditions, deconstruction constructs its own means of intervention in the field of hierarchized oppositions of metaphysical concepts. This field includes such binary oppositions associated with handwriting analysis as genuine/forged signature, natural/artificial expression. and authentic/fake trace.

The metaphysical dimension of legal mediation politics cannot be addressed without deconstruction. As Butler notices in her interview with Athanasiou in *Dispossession: The Performative in the Political*, "we are left with a double sense of things: the truth of the law will remain forever inaccessible, but also that the truth of the law can only be anticipated within life itself, and that the closure of life is the end of that anticipation. The law is produced and elaborated every time it is invoked in the scene of its anticipation. At the same time, even as the law is produced time and again, it never finally materializes in any full or definitive way" (Athanasiou and Butler 2013, 129). The law not only gives the changeable forms of life a unified order and the required identity. It also parasitically exploits life; it draws its materiality from life. Deconstruction, which questions the metaphysical conditions of possibility for the hierarchic construction of binary oppositions, is motivated by a drive to reveal aporias. It is interested in material similarities, which are taken to be secondary to ideal identity.

The reading of Derrida's works that I propose invites us to notice that the apparently obvious metaphysical hierarchy between the law and the life is not reliable. Without the ideality of law, a handwritten signature would not be a recognizable sign; without the materiality of life, the handwritten signature would not exist at all. Without *grammé*, logos would remain enclosed in itself; *grammé* offers logos the possibility to escape itself. In the terms of Derrida's subversion, the probability of *grammé* precedes the truth of logos. Ontological iteration intersects with logical repetition.

Finally, according to the metaphysics of law, it is legitimate to expect that a handwritten trace will allow us to identify the signer because the trace carries her unique qualities. The signer is supposed to be naturally, authentically, and constantly present in each of her signatures. Following this metaphysical belief, each particular handwritten signature can be understood as identical with the previously registered specimen signature. And yet, although the signer tries to manually reproduce her previous graphic expression to certify her civic identity by means of her signature, her previous signature and her actual signature will never be the same. The handwritten signature as writing remains an event, an ungraspable fragment of life, which intersects with the logocentrism of law. The supposed unique style of handwriting, which is determined by natural expression of the signer's soul and which becomes material by means of the signer's authentic manual trace, does not generate the civic identity of the signer, but a material supplement of the ideal identity, which issues from the impossible metaphysical obligation to repeat the unrepeatable.

Notes

Introduction

1. By contrast with Kant, who proceeds to the moral question of identity in his aesthetic reflections on the sublime, Lyotard's conception of the sublime proceeds to the ethical question of alterity. As Rodolphe Gasché observes, in this respect "Derrida, no doubt, shares Lyotard's concerns. As far as ethics is concerned, he too has been interested in mapping out the minimal structures of ethicity. His inquiries into the notions of aporia, the impossible, or undecidability, are aimed at elaborating on the conditions under which alone it is possible to speak, rigorously, of decision, rather than merely an execution of pre-programmed, or pre-calculated reactions. Derrida's concern with aporia thus would seem to indicate a strong interest in the political" (Gasché 2007, 120–21). But Derrida, like Lyotard, is more interested in the ethical or proto-ethical conditions of possibility for human action (Gasché 2007).

Chapter 1

1. According to Persifor Frazer, Berthillon's system of measurements differentiates between and classifies living beings so "that one can go almost immediately to the case in which the previous record of an unrecognized but suspected recidivist or old offender will be found" (Frazer 1909, 321).

2. In *Criminal Man,* Lombroso indicates that "totaling 407, the signatures I have collected fall mainly into two clearly defined groups. Only the signatures of semi-illiterate criminals, who include some of our most famous brigands, retain a childish character and are not easy to categorize" (Lombroso 2006, 111).

3. According to Lombroso, "The first group is made up of signatures of murderers, highway robbers, and brigands, who generally elongate their letters, adding curves to the upper and lower extensions. In many of the signatures, the cross of the 't' is very clear or elongated, as also found in the script of soldiers and

other particularly energetic people; in a few other cases the letters have acute angles and flourishes. The signatures of this first group are further distinguished by their extraordinary curlicues and arabesques" (Lombroso 2006, 111).

4. Lombroso claims that the second group of signatures, belonging mostly to thieves, "is distinct from that of highway robbers and lacks emphatic verticals. In general, the letters are soft and ill-formed, and the signatures are clear and easy to read. This kind of writing is similar to that of women and indeed to normal handwriting. In addition to these characteristics and a slight tremble, the handwriting of a certain type of thief—such as Cartouche—has a sort of hook and curvature to practically every letter, which reminds us of the particular configuration of their fingers; similar hooks and curves are also found in the writing of other thieves" (Lombroso 2006, 113).

5. Galton claims that "The possibility of improving the race of a nation depends on the power of increasing the productivity of the best stock. This is far more important than that of repressing the productivity of the worst. They both raise the average, the latter by reducing the undesirables, the former by increasing those who will become the lights of the nation" (Galton 1909, 24).

6. This ethical thread can be related to misuse of the concepts of monsters in political rhetoric. Referring to Derrida's work on spectrality, Ystehede mentions in "Demonizing Being" that "The invocation of monsters in political and scientific discourse is a very powerful mode of organizing thought—of which Lombroso's criminal anthropology may be, if not the sole, then one of the best examples" (Ystehede 2013, 90).

7. Vilém Flusser's phenomenological media theory is inspired by his own conceptual triad: traditional picture, linear written text, and technical picture. Flusser examined the dominating media of communication that determined human perception at different stages of cultural evolution. In his book *Does Writing Have a Future?* (Flusser 2011), he examines historical moments of appearance and disappearance of phonological writing in Western culture, claiming that the invention of the alphabet was motivated by both iconoclast desire to dispose of pictures and narrative desire to produce a linear discourse. As a result, the circular mythical interpretation of pictures was replaced by a progressive causal interpretation brought by the linear and non-resembling alphabetic writing.

8. In one of his twenty pieces of advice given in *Design Elements*, Samara writes that "Type is type only when it's friendly. It should go without saying that type that cannot be read has no purpose, but, unfortunately, it bears repeating. Yes, typography should be expressive, visually inventive, and conceptually resonant. It must still transmit information. Choose typefaces that aid legibility, watch out for weird color contrasts, set text in a size that your grandmother can read, and you should be good to go" (Samara 2014, 20).

9. This is confirmed by Richard Poulin in *The Language of Graphic Design*, who claims that, first of all, every creatively designed font should be legible:

"Typography is also a unique principle in a graphic designer's vocabulary because it has dual functions. It can function on its purest level as a graphic element such as point, form, shape, and texture in a visual composition. However, its primary function is verbal and visual. It is to be read" (Poulin 2011, 247).

10. Jason Tselentis notices in *Type: Form and Function* that "Many of the terms used in the typography lexicon are the same as those used for anatomy and physiology. These terms have been built up over hundreds of years, and can change depending on the culture and language, and letterforms. Some of the more common terms that a designer should understand include x-height, counter, serif style, and stress" (Tselentis 2011, 26).

11. Gavin Ambrose and Paul Harris write in *Design Thinking* that "Different typefaces have different personalities to the extent that they can be said to actually have 'faces' that tell stories and convey feelings other than the words they present. Some typefaces appear serious, some are upright and conservative, while others are fun, adventurous and youthful, for example" (Ambrose and Harris 2010, 118).

12. As Bill Gardner writes in *Logo Lounge 8*, professional designers "are in the midst of creating the future for others. They are hired because they have the uncanny ability to tell a very specific, very effective story using few to no words at all. Because they have the aptitude to summon meaning from a line. Because they can craft an image that brings relevance and direction to a product that has lost its way. Because they can forecast what the public will be yearning for tomorrow and not yesterday" (Gardner and Hellmann 2014, 7).

13. As Huber and Headrick put it in *Handwriting Identification*, "The relevancy of documents in civic and criminal litigation is largely dependent on their authorship or origin. Numerous ways have evolved to attest to the truthfulness of a writing. Before the origin of the signature, the application of a wax seal served to authenticate the document. The wax seal bonded the ends of a ribbon of fabric which fed through a slit in the paper and was embossed with a personal motif. Later, signatures served the purpose, but additionally, the legal process has tended to require the signatures of witnesses to the signing" (Huber and Haedrick 1999, 21).

14. Walter Benjamin claims in "The Work of Art in the Age of Mechanical Reproduction" that the traditional value of a work of art consists in its "aura," uniqueness, or authenticity, which "is the essence of all that is transmissible from its beginning, ranging from its substantive duration to its testimony to the history which it has experienced" (Benjamin 2007, 221). This value of authenticity is necessarily shaken in the era of mechanical reproducibility, because "even the most perfect reproduction of a work of art is lacking in one element: its presence in time and space, its unique existence at the place where it happens to be" (Benjamin 2007, 220). In Benjamin, reproducibility excludes authenticity: handwritten signature is considered to be authentic when it manually reproduces the specimen signature. The signature has its aura and legal authority only if done by the same signer. If someone copies someone else's specimen signature, the result is a forgery—as is the case for a

traditional auratic work of art. Like traditional manual works of art, a handwritten signature must be done by the signer's own hand, but, just like new mechanical copies of a work of art, a handwritten signature is supposed to be reproduced and coexist in a plurality of copies. So Benjamin's conception of the authenticity of a work of art cannot be discretely applied to a forensic understanding of authenticity.

15. Walsham notices that "What one society or religious tradition designates and venerates as a relic is liable to be dismissed by another as distasteful and dirty bodily waste or the useless detritus of daily existence" (Walsham 2010, 14).

16. Peirce's semiotics is based on his triad of metaphysical categories: Firstness, Secondness, and Thirdness. Firstness is a possibility of quality, which is unattainable by senses, but necessary for material existence of the ideal quality. Firstness founds Secondness, material expression of the ideal quality, which is already perceivable by senses. Secondness founds Thirdness, which is the law or rule of expression of the given quality. Peirce creates fixed hierarchic relations within the triad: there is no rule (Thirdness) without existence (Secondness) and no existence without quality (Firstness).

17. In the metaphysical category of Firstness, Peirce distinguishes the first trichotomy of signs: "qualisignum" (Firstness of Firstness), "sinsignum" (Secondness of Firstness), and "legisignum" (Thirdness of Firstness). In the metaphysical category of Secondness, Peirce distinguishes the second trichotomy of signs: icon (Firstness of Secondness), index (Secondness of Secondness), and symbol (Thirdness of Secondness). In the metaphysical category of Thirdness, Peirce distinguishes the third trichotomy of signs: "rema" (Firstness Thirdness), "dicisignum" (Secondness of Thirdness), and argument (Thirdness of Thirdness). In my own conception of handwritten signature as sign, I cannot avoid reduction of Peirce's complex semiotics to his second trichotomy. Because the first trichotomy is unreachable by senses, and the third trichotomy deals with general rules, not with any particular existing signs, only the second trichotomy is relevant to my own thinking on signature. Peirce's conception of semiotics is a partial inspiration, not the only one philosophical line I want to follow. Therefore, I prefer to focus on philosophical problems that I find interesting in his very voluminous, complex, and unfinished work. My ambition is not to re-create from the fragments of his work one coherent and meaningful interpretation, but to allow these fragments to move and become productive in new, previously unformulated philosophical regards.

18. Short noticed in *Peirce's Theory of Signs* that Peirce's Thirdness generates the sign of symbol as a general rule. Contrary to the arbitrary convention in structuralism, Peirce's symbol is ontological law. As its final interpretant is logical, some thinkers tend to grasp Peirce's symbol as the most complex or complete sign, which contains icon and index. Nevertheless, Short says, "degeneration" of icon and index in relation to symbol does not mean their inferiority, because each type of sign has its irreplaceable role in Peirce's metaphysical trichotomies (Short 2007, 225–31).

19. In Eco's view, Peirce's semiotics formulates the idea of an unlimited process of semiosis that starts with every attempt to determine the Interpretant, which is

supposed to guarantee the sign's validity. The Interpretant must be grasped by another sign, which already has another Interpretant, grasped by another sign, and so forth. As Eco puts it in *The Limits of Interpretation*, "semiosis is unlimited and, through the series of interpretants, explains itself by itself, but there are at least two cases in which semiosis is confronted with something external to it" (Eco 1994, 46). In *Kant and the Platypus*, Eco declares how Peircean terminological framework inspired him: "A Dynamical Object drives us to produce a *representamen,* in a quasi-mind this produces an Immediate Object, which in turn is translatable into a potentially infinite series of interpretants and sometimes, through the habit formed in the course of the interpretative process, we come back to the Dynamical Object, and we make something of it" (Eco 2000, 14).

20. In *Critique of Pure Reason*, Kant characterizes the schema as a product of imagination a priori, which interconnects the image with the concept. While the image is any product of empirical imagination, the transcendental schema "stands in homogeneity with the category on the one hand and the appearance on the other and makes possible the application of the former to the latter. This mediating representation must be pure (without anything empirical) and yet intellectual on the one hand and sensible on the other" (Kant 1998, 272). In Kant's transcendental conception of metaphysics, the schematism in the human mind generates an a priori connection between the image of empirical imagination and the concept of pure understanding, making it possible to classify the observed reality.

21. Although Eco claims in *Kant and the Platypus* that he tries to get closer to Peirce, in his own theory, he moves even further from Peirce than Kant is. Kant writes about the metaphysical construction of knowledge in a universal subject's mind, and Peirce writes about the metaphysical nature of knowledge in an ahistorical (universal) subject's mind, but Eco writes about the metaphysical construction of knowledge in a historically situated (relative) subject's mind, which means a discursively normalized subject, as Foucault described it.

Chapter II

1. According to Sassoon, "An individual sample of handwriting reflects the writer's training, character and environment. Collectively, the handwriting of a population of any period is a reflection of educational thinking, but overall it is influenced and ultimately molded by economic need, social habits and contemporary taste" (Sassoon 2007, 9).

2. In his interview with Kearney, Derrida mentions that "Logocentric philosophy is a specifically Western answer to a much more urgent need, existing in the Far East and in other cultures, which is the phonocentric need: privilege of the voice before the writing. The priority of spoken language before writing, or silent speech, comes from the fact that, when they pronounce words, the speaker

and the listener should be present at the same time; they should be the same pure and immediate presence" (Derrida and Kearney 2012, 17). This phonocentric need "expresses the ideal of prefect presence, immediate possession of sense. Writing is, on the contrary, considered to be subversive in the sense that it produces distance in space and time between the author and the audience; writing presupposes absence of the author. Therefore, one can be never totally sure what is signified in the written text; writing can have more various senses instead of one unifying sense. But, this phonocentric need didn't evolve into logocentric metaphysics in other than European culture. Systematic logocentrism is only a European phenomenon" (Derrida and Kearney 2012, 17).

3. In his eulogy for Marin, published in *The Work of Mourning*, Derrida notices that "In the era of psychoanalysis, *we* all of course speak, and we can always go on speaking, about the 'successful' work of mourning—or, inversely—as if it were precisely the contrary, about a 'melancholia' that would signal the failure of such work" (Derrida 2001b, 144). But, as he adds, "if *we* are to follow Louis Marin, here comes a work without force, a work that would have to work at renouncing force, its own force, a work that would have to work at failure, and thus at mourning and getting over force, a work working at its own unproductivity, absolutely, working to absolve or to absolve itself of whatever might be absolute about 'force,' and thus of something like 'force' itself" (Derrida 2001b, 144).

4. In " 'Let Others Be Ends in Themselves': The Convergence Between Foucault's Parrhesia and Derrida's Teleiopoesis," Leonard Lawlor even goes as far as stating possible ethical convergence: "The hinge between Foucault's *parrhesia* and Derrida's *teleiopoesis* . . . is Kant's categorical imperative" (Lawlor 2002b, 170).

5. I have partly done this in my monograph *Partager le visible: Repenser Foucault* (Fišerová 2013), where I have accentuated the principal methodological incompatibility between Foucault's archeology and Derrida's deconstruction. I have revised this problematic later in "There Is No Regime beyond Representation: Deconstructing Rancière's Antinomies" (Fišerová 2018b), where I have focused on their divergent understanding of the concept of representation.

6. As Bennington notices in "The Truth About Parrhēsia," Foucault adopts an aporetic double tactic in his relation to rhetoric: "rhetoric is an ambiguous *opponent* of *parrhēsia* because of its link to flattery, but an ambiguous *partner* of *parrhēsia* because *parrhēsia* cannot in fact be practiced without some possible recourse to rhetorical technique" (Bennington 2016b, 209).

7. As Crépon puts it in *Langues sans demeure*, "idiom is nothing else than a dream of an untranslatable language. The home without home itself, inappropriable home (unreducible to any community) is only in a language, which resists to any translation, which even demonstrates this resistance as the sense of its being" (Crépon 2005, 59).

8. According to Amend and Ruiz, "writing is a physical process. The brain sends an order through the nervous system to the arm, hand and fingers, where

together they manipulate the writing tool. In this way, the intent to write forms deep within the creative processes of the mind and makes writing an expressive gesture representative of the mind behind the pen. Despite the teaching of a standard letter model to form the letters and words necessary to express our ideas, no two writings are exactly alike" (Amend and Ruiz 1980, iii).

9. Amend and Ruiz believe that "beyond the conscious information contained in the written words, the handwriting also divulges information about you and how you felt unconsciously as you wrote" (Amend and Ruiz 1980, iii).

10. Amend and Ruiz write: "while we cannot read minds, we can see certain body movements. Tone of voice, gestures, posture, body structure and manner of dress can be interpreted as clues to inner psychological make-up and behavior. Often, the outer style reflects the inner one" (Amend and Ruiz 1980, iii).

11. Baggett writes that "handwriting is actually brain writing. It is an expression of small electrical impulses from the brain to the hand" (Baggett 1998, 13).

12. The psychological benefits Baggett promises to achieve, are the following: "to take the frustration out of meeting and selecting people to date and improve all your current relationships. It will also help you make better choices and be more effective at accomplishing your relationship goals" (Baggett 1998, 11).

13. For Baggett, "analyzing personality through handwriting is much the same way as viewing a Monet painting. It is easy to look at just the individual strokes of the pen and get lost in the myriad of meaning. But as you complete the picture and put all the strokes in their proper place, the entire painting of the person comes out to look as interesting as piece of classic art" (Baggett 1998, 14).

14. According to Roberts, "it is as personal to you as your fingerprint or DNA. Only fingerprints equal an autograph when considering ease and accuracy in making an identification" (Roberts 2002, 129).

15. Ronald M. Buckley, Russell W. Driver, and Dwight D. Frink claim in "Should We Write Off Graphology?" that "graphology should not be used in a selection context" (78) in human resources management because it did not demonstrate acceptable validity. The authors see this selection technique as not helping to assess personality because "interpretation is in terms of the individual graphologist, and that person's biases and perceptions" (Buckley, Driver, and Frink 1996, 83).

Chapter III

1. In *Words of Light*, Eduardo Cadava recalls that "the forgetting of the photograph's ghostly or spectral character, of its relation to death that survives itself, corresponds to what Benjamin refers to as 'the decline of photography.' This decline is at first presented as a decline that can be understood temporally, that can be traced the history of the photographic event" (Cadava 1997, 13). As he emphasizes, "photography's decline does not coincide, as one might expect, with a

decline in the technical efficiency of the camera or in its capacity to register what is photographed. Rather, it corresponds to the technical refinement of the camera's performance" (Cadava 1997, 14). In Benjamin, the technological progress itself is a decline in traditional ways of depiction, especially in manual work. A similar evolution—corresponding to "decay of the aura" (Benjamin 2007, 222)—can be seen in the contemporary shift from the authenticity of the handwritten signature to arbitrariness of the electronic signature, which is no longer a manual trace and resigns to its aura of unique occurrence.

2. As Gasché puts it in *Of Minimal Things*, "if Benjamin continues to distinguish between the aura of natural and that of historical objects, it is for other reasons. Depreciation of the here and now through reproduction affects objects of nature as well as those of art, yet 'in the case of the art object, a most sensitive nucleus—namely, its authenticity—is interfered with whereas no natural object is vulnerable on that score.'" (Gasché 1999, 86). The difference between natural and historical objects concerns indeed this "most sensitive nucleus, not a qualitative difference as regards their aura" (Gasché 1999, 87).

3. Semantic *drift* is a shift in meaning of the text caused by its interpretation. Such a drift occurs in the process of explaining the text's meaning for the purpose of comment, critique, translation, and so forth. The concept of semantic drift can be used to understand semiosis as a process of translation, where every rigorous recognition of the text's own meaning remains problematic.

4. This characteristic is proposed by Andrew Reynolds in *Peirce's Scientific Metaphysics* (Reynolds 2002, 18–22). As the author emphasizes, Peirce's scientific thinking was deeply rooted in the nineteenth-century paradigm of physics, which followed Newton's conception of physics as a mechanical explanation of natural phenomena.

5. In *On the Name*, Derrida follows Kant's conception of transcendental metaphysics as inevitable order of meanings generated by a universally conceived human mind, which establishes the supreme authority of the law not only in mathematical and physical, but also in legal and linguistic domains. Derrida finds it problematic that this conception of the law requires identical repetition: it is pervaded by semantic violence of metaphysical principles. If the metaphysical requirement of identity is enforced on living beings, it produces various fluctuations and deviations, which are suppressed, regulated, and punished as illegal. The revolutionary call for justice, which is born from resistance to legal oppression, comes from the marginal zone of Western metaphysics, from the interval between graspable and ungraspable that Derrida—following Plato—calls *Khôra* (Derrida 1995, 89–127). From this position, Derrida formulates his deconstruction of the total presence of meaning; contrary to the law, the melancholic "madness" of desire for justice will never be totally present. Moreover, according to Senatore's *Germs of Death*, Derrida's interrogation of *Khôra* allows him "to think the general condition for generation and history and, thus, the very concept of history" (Senatore 2018, 50).

6. In *Foi et savoir,* Derrida claims that all nation-states are born from and founded in the revolutionary violence of an upcoming law: "the moment of foundation, the establishing moment precedes the law or the legitimacy that it establishes. It is *outside the law*, and thus violent. . . . This founding violence is not only forgotten; it tends by essence to organize amnesia, sometimes under a celebration and sublimation of the great beginnings" (Derrida 2000, 131).

7. This characteristic is asserted by Mayorga Rosa Maria Perez-Teran in her book *From Realism to "Realicism." The Metaphysics of Charles Senders Peirce* (Perez-Teran 2009), where she demonstrates the link between the Peirce's metaphysical thinking and the scholastic realism of Duns Scotus.

8. As Sean Gaston noticed in *The Impossible Mourning of Jacques Derrida*, from 1959, Derrida has been occupied with the prefix pre-, before-. His reflections on death come as on what happens *before*-hand: "Derrida describes this 'question of the possibility of the question,' this question for the *'transcendental I* . . . of its own death *[de sa propre mort]*,' as 'opening itself, the gap *[l'ouverture elle-même, la béance]*.' Alan Bass has translated *la béance* as 'the gap,' and one could also translate it as 'gaping,' as the *gaping*, open wound. It is this gaping opening, 'opening' itself, that raises the impossible question, the question *of* the impossible, of the *precedent* that comes *and* goes first, *that gives up its place* as it takes precedence. The *precedent* always predeceases, goes on ahead" (Gaston 2006, 4).

9. As Robert Smith notices in *Derrida and Autobiography*, not only the signature, but the civic name itself is merely a given attribute that the citizen is forced to adopt: "the attachment of name to person would seem to be legalistic rather than essential, a matter of positive rather than structural law, for the structural law sees no attachment—and this entails a question of chance. For if a name does not properly belong to its bearer, not only is a signature always forged even by its rightful owner, but worse, there is nothing to distinguish it from common nouns in general" (Smith 1995, 36).

10. Peirce indicates that the Icon is a Representamen, which has the Firstness for its representative quality: "anything is fit to be a Substitute for anything that it is like" (Peirce 1955, 104).

11. Peirce mentions that the *Index* is a Representamen, whose representative quality consists in the fact that it is an individual second. "If the Secondness is an existential relation, the Index is genuine" (Peirce 1955, 108). This is the case of "authentic" handwritten signature as an existential trace.

12. Peirce writes that "A Symbol is a Representamen whose Representative character consists precisely in its being a rule that will determine its Interpretant. All words, sentences, books, and other conventional signs are Symbols" (Peirce 1955, 112).

13. According to Derrida's *Archive Fever*, "The death drive tends thus to destroy the hypomnesic archive, except if it can be disguised, made up, painted, printed, represented as the idol of its truth in painting. . . . The death drive is

not a principle. It even threatens every principality, every archontic primacy, every archival desire. It is what we will call, later on, *le mal d'archive*, 'archive fever'" (Derrida 1998, 12). The fever Derrida writes about is the archive's "silent vocation is to burn the archive and to incite amnesia, thus refuting the economic principle of the archive, aiming to ruin the archive as accumulation and capitalization of memory on some substrate and in an exterior place" (Derrida 1998, 12).

14. In his paper "A Short Genealogy of Realism: Peirce, Kevelson and Legal Semiotics," Geoffrey Sykes exposes Roberta Kevelson's interpretation of Peirce's Thirdness as a semiotic foundation of the juridical doctrine of legal realism (Sykes 2008).

Chapter IV

1. I agree with Geoffrey Bennington's paradoxical claim in "For the Sake of Argument" that "nothing is more logocentric than the presentation of the relation of Derrida's thought (or deconstruction more generally) to ('analytic') philosophy as a relation of critique, conflict or warfare" (Bennington 2001, 41).

2. Michel Foucault summarized his numerous objections to Derrida's pedagogical critique in his paper "Mon corps, ce feu, ce papier" (Foucault 2001).

3. John R. Searle published his critical confrontation of Derrida's confused critique in his paper "Reiterating the Differences. A Reply to Derrida" (Searle 1977).

4. Besides grafting, which intentionally lets a well-known concept act in another meaning, Derrida's playful strategy of textual parasitism can be realized by scratching and composing words into neographisms.

5. In this respect, I follow Geoffrey Bennington's claim in "Deconstruction and Ethics" that deconstruction cannot propose an ethics; it can only propose an "arche-ethical" warning (Bennington 2000, 64–65).

6. I do agree with Critchley's note that Derrida's deconstruction is motivated by "a profound ethical engaging" (Critchley 2011, 53). As such, "it doesn't disturb the distinction of genre between philosophy and literature, nor tries to reduce politics, society and history on an ontic level" (Critchley 2011, 53).

7. In this respect, I follow Zima's claim that Derrida's work assumes an "extreme and ahistorical position starting from the assumption that all texts are ambivalent and aporetic" (Zima 2002, 175).

8. Derrida commented on this in *Psyché*, where he writes the following: "I am trying to speak *about* metaphor, to say something proper or literal on this subject, to *treat* it as my subject, but I am obliged, by metaphor (if one can say that) to speak of it *more metaphorical*, in its own manner. I cannot *treat it* without *dealing with it* [traiter avec elle], without negotiating the loan I take out from it in order to speak about it" (Derrida 2007b, 49).

9. Derrida explains: "The metaphor, at the very least, without which the concept of metaphor could not be constructed, or, to syncopate an entire chain of

reasoning, the metaphor of metaphor. This extra metaphor, remaining outside the field that it allows to be circumscribed, extracts or abstracts itself from this field, thus subtracting itself as a metaphor less. By virtue of what we might entitle, for economical reasons, tropic supplementarity, since the extra turn of speech becomes the missing turn of speech, the taxonomy or history of philosophical metaphors will never make a profit" (Derrida 1982c, 220). Therefore, "The field is never saturated" (Derrida 1982c, 220).

10. As Bennington puts it, "Meta-force displaces metaphor, and introduces Derrida's turn to the concept of original metaphori*city*, which is neither a rhetoric, nor even a linguistic concept. As he exposes, this force or this meta-force (another name, another 'un-synonymic substitute' for différance [written with an 'a']), briefly mentioned in *White Mytology* by means of the still rhetorical concept of 'catachresis,' is what causes that deconstruction is no philosophy of language, no 'correlationism' in any case, and thus makes the so called 'new realism' impossible" (Bennington 2016a, 13).

11. In *Genèses, généalogies, genres et le génie*, Derrida mentions that the "concept of *genius* must get rid of both its current sense, and its—evident and presumable—adherence to homogenous, homogenetic, genetic, generational and generic series (genesis, genealogy, gender). To get rid of them and even to disturb their order" (Derrida 2003a, 27).

12. As Francesco Vitale writes in *Biodeconstruction*, Derrida's philosophical inquiries are triggered by his deep concern for the problem of life and its metaphysical ungrasparability. Thus, we shall consider Derrida's "investigation of *life* not only an issue of deconstruction but the latter's very matrix; we shall think *différance* as the irreducible and structural condition of the life of the living, and thus *trace* and *text* as the structures of the organization of life (from the most elementary forms to the organization of the psychological system of the human being, to the formation of the ideal objectivities that structure life and institutions in our cultural habitat)" (Vitale 2018a, 1–2).

13. As Derrida puts it in *Aporias*, "I suggested that a sort of nonpassive endurance of the aporia was the condition of responsibility and of decision" (Derrida 2006, 16).

Chapter V

1. In "The Spatial Arts," Derrida notes: "One needs to do more than write one's name to sign. On an immigration form you write your name and then you sign. Thus the signature is something other than merely writing down one's own name. It is an act, a performative by which one commits to something—that it is done, that it is I who has done it. Such a performativity is absolutely heterogenous; it is an exterior reminder to whatever in the work signifies something. There is a

work there—I affirm it, I countersign. There is a 'thereness' to the work which is more or less the set of analyzable semantic elements. An event has taken place" (Derrida 1994b, 17).

2. Austin distinguished the *illocutionary act*, which is defined as a performance of a sentence correlatively to the locutor's intentions, from the *perlocutionary act*, which means the effect on the locutor, provoked by the performed sentence. The *illocutionary force*, which produces *illocutionary forms of enunciation* (requirement, declaration, promise, baptism, etc.) acts by means of performative verbs or performatives (to require, to declare, to promise, to baptize, etc.).

3. According to Barry Smith, "Searle's achievement, now, was to give substance to Austin's idea of a general theory of speech acts by moving beyond this cataloguing stage and providing a theoretical framework within which the three dimensions of utterance, meaning, and action involved in speech acts could be seen as being unified together" (Smith 2003a, 6).

4. Henry Staten notices in *Wittgenstein and Derrida* that Derrida's iterability is a kind of transgression: "iterability of a code ruptures its authority because it makes it essentially permeable to the deformations of context and yet makes it independent of the power of any given context to determine its meaning once and for all, because the sign carries an irreducible structure that will not let itself be absorbed into a present intention that would fix it in relation to an intentionally totalizable present context" (Staten 1984, 123).

5. According to Ramond, no context "will be ever able to guarantee the *presence of sense*, or the total felicity of performative. . . . There is always an original difference, original gap, original *iterability* or *citability*, original deviation, which cannot be legitimately reduced, because no context can be perfectly mastered" (Ramond 2001, 41).

6. As Williams puts it in his preface to *Signature Derrida*, "By beginning with a single word or phrase Derrida showed us the first step in the long process of reading the inexhaustibility of a text and confronting the impossibility of explicating the whole. A common misunderstanding of Derrida's work is that he sought out opposed binaries in a word or larger text. This was not the end of reading. Derrida did not have a signature move or even a method, which is often labeled 'deconstruction.' . . . What he did do was deploy various tactics of reading specifically called for by the text at hand that would lead his own readers to often surprising and delightful revelations. He exposed what might have seemed straightforward as ambiguous. The ambiguous might become contradictory" (Williams 2013, X).

7. Therefore, I disagree with Fraenkel's claim in "La signature: du signe à l'acte" that handwritten signature can be explained by theory of speech acts. She considers handwritten signature to be an occasional sign regulated by communicational norms: "The first concerns necessary presence of the signing person. This norm indicates that signature's effectivity is partly determined by the fact that signature is done 'here' and 'now.' We sign personally, in the presence of a witness, in a certain

way. It is necessary to admit the ceremonial dimension of this act, more precisely, to become aware of the required conditions of Felicity. Thus, signature belongs to the paradigm of speech acts" (Fraenkel 2008, 21).

8. As Derrida puts it in *Poétique et politique du témoignage*, the performativity is the foundation of the testimony as a guarantee of authenticity: "Witness indicates or claims that for him is or was present something that is not or was not present for his addressees, to whom the witness is bound by a contract, an oath, a promise, a commitment. Its performativity founds the testimony and turns it into a warranty, a guarantee" (Derrida 2005a, 36).

9. Derrida explained the problem of signature as signer's supplement, which is not only an existential remainder, but also a textual addition. For example, an autograph is usually grafted to a particular dedication, which makes this particular given signature unique, personal, authentic. As Derrida puts it, the signature "by rights . . . is not reproducible. At least not technically (and yet, as you know, it is more complicated: a certain iterability, as I tried to show elsewhere, constitutes the very uniqueness of the event of the signature). In the case of the signed photograph, the event is not reproducible; in principle, it must have taken place only once, and what guarantees this singularity is neither the photograph nor the signature; it is the name of the dedicatee. This is the contract that links the two names. The same photographic portrait can be signed as many times as one likes. Only once does it bear the name of the one who receives it. The seal of the original is thus the site of this destination; and the true signature of the gift then returns to the one who does nothing but receive—or desires to receive, with a desire that sets the signature in motion, however narcissistic this desire may remain" (Derrida 2010b, 25).

Chapter VI

1. Beatrice Fraenkel mentions this problem in *La signature. Genèse d'un signe*, where she writes: "Each occurrence of the sign of signature can be declared to be the same. This means that identity of the signature depends on its ability to assimilate itself with its specimen" (Fraenkel 1992, 205).

2. Derrida mentions in *Specters of Marx* that spectrality concerns the "question of repetition: a specter is always a *revenant*. One cannot control its comings and goings because it begins by coming back. Think as well of Macbeth, and remember the specter of Caesar. After having expired, he returns" (Derrida 1994a, 11).

3. The problem of reproducibility of original works is discussed by Walter Benjamin in his theory of the aura of handmade works of art. In his opinion, if a work of art is copied manually, the copy cannot reach identity with the original. Mechanical copy eliminates the *aura* that is characteristic for the handmade original work. In the case of handwritten signature, this means that the specimen signature is auratic, but no further signing can reach identity with its shape. This can be

reached only by mechanical reproduction, which is no longer auratic—therefore, no mechanical copy of a handwritten signature is considered authentic. Not only the original specimen signature, but every signature that is sufficiently similar to it and is done by the same signer's hand, is considered to be authentic. In other words, signing is not copying. Handwritten signature is *auratic*; it is neither a mechanical nor a manual copy.

4. As Smith mentions, Deleuze finds difference not only between beings, but also in the beings themselves: "The project of *Difference and Repetition*, in other words, is to provide an immanent analysis of the ontological difference in which *the different is related to the different through difference itself*: Being must not only be able to account for the external difference between beings, but also the fact that beings themselves are marked by an 'internal difference'; and the ontological difference must not only refer to the difference between Being and beings, but also the difference of Being from itself, 'an alliance of Being and itself in difference'" (Smith 2003b, 51).

5. As Sean Bowden mentions in *The Priority of Events*, "Deleuze asserts the ontological priority of events by establishing a relation between the works of various thinkers in such a way that they can be said to collectively pose and resolve the 'problem of the event'" (Bowden 2011, 6); particularly Stoics, Leibnitz, structuralism, and psychoanalysis. All the intellectual figures Deleuze works with are helpful in his conception of philosophy as creation of concepts, which are created to grasp ontologically prior events.

6. I agree with Philippe Mengue, who claims that Deleuze's critique focuses on the representation, because Deleuze understands it as "'unable to think difference in itself,' structurally following the demands of identity" (Mengue 1994, 139).

7. In *Trace and Archive, Image and Art*, however, Derrida mentions that even words can be made as pictures; they can be motivated by the need for such iconic goals as rhythm or succession, when "iconic means structured correlatively to need and to law of the image, visual or musical" (Derrida 2014, 25).

8. This opinion is supported by Eric Alliez, who claims that "Deleuze has never ceased proposing descriptive notions that participate in a *phantastique* of the imagination" (Alliez 2004, 6).

9. While in Deleuze, graffiti tags would positively establish the tagger's territory, in Derrida, they would indicate that *Khôra* may be situated there. As he claims in *On the Name*, *Khôra* is a "place occupied by someone, country, inhabited place, marked place, rank, post, assigned position, territory or region. And in fact, *Khôra will* always already be occupied, invested, even as a general place, and even when it is distinguished from everything that takes place in it" (Derrida 1995, 109).

10. As Williams notices in *Gilles Deleuze's Difference and Repetition*, Deleuze is aware that every "recognition depends on representation" (Williams 2005, 120), which excludes true difference and repetition.

11. I follow here Bennington's comment from *Not Half No End*, where he mentions that "Derrida is prepared to say that some *failure* of this structure of 'normal' mourning, something more of the order of what Freud calls, then, 'melancholia' (broadly speaking, the state of one who does not achieve the goal of mourning, but remains attached to the lost other), is in some important, 'ethical,' sense preferable to mourning 'proper.' In fact, he thinks that only something that looks more like melancholia, as a kind of protest against mourning, a militant melancholia, then, gives any 'ethical' dimension to mourning" (Bennington 2010, 39). My claim is that this militant melancholy motivates all Derrida's work, not only his thoughts on human death and loss, but also his deconstructive shaking of the pre-judgmental expectations—or *préjugés*—generated by Western metaphysics. In this sense, Derrida's work is ethically active and militant, but always in a melancholic way: he is aware he cannot go further than to aporias, or inevitable metaphysical traps, because there is a way out of metaphysical thinking. One cannot quit Western metaphysics by using—metaphysical—tools such as critique, analysis, or methods. One can only inhabit its margins, while remaining partly inside its trap.

12. The philosophical problem of expression should be understood differently in Derrida and in Deleuze. While in Derrida, this concept is linked to the transcendental violence of meaning's origin and total presence, in Deleuze, who is inspired by Spinoza's pantheism and Bergson's vitalism, the concept of expression is linked to variations on the plane of immanence. Contrary to Deleuze, Derrida explicitly distances himself from the metaphysical concept of expression. In "The Original Discussion of Différance," he even states: "I have never said that *différance expresses* our epoch and if I do not use this concept of expression, it is not by chance" (Derrida 1988b, 86).

13. As Lambert puts it, "for Derrida, the task of philosophy is largely demonstrative, and although the creation of a new concept can serve to demonstrate a shift in or transformation of the old ground (or closure), it cannot become the highest definition of philosophical activity. In fact, this supreme act of creativity, 'this frenzy of experimentation and proliferation of schematization' as Derrida would say, is only the effect of a more primordial dislocation, which becomes the condition of any subsequent 'play' and 'creation.' Although the force of creativity is often characterized as a power (for example, as a power of imagination and affection), in fact it is the power of a fundamental passivity, weakness, impotence, disengagement—*critique and emancipation*. Consequently, deconstruction is not an act of creation, but rather the demonstration (monstration, or the bringing to manifestation) of a silent lapsus that insists in any order of signification, marking the very opening of this order to what exceeds it" (Lambert 2012, 152).

14. Peggy Kamuf tried to characterize Derrida's style of writing, his philosophical signature, in her paper "Composition Displacement." In it she makes an observation, "which any persistent reader of works signed by Derrida will have had

occasion to make . . . between texts being read, cited, paraphrased, and commented upon, on the one hand, and on the other, assertions, affirmations, propositions, declarations, arguments, and so forth, that are being made in his own name and assumed by the signatory, the seam can often almost disappear, even though when one looks for it, usually it can be traced with some assurance" (Kamuf 2016, 163).

Chapter VII

1. According to Jean, writing was invented to satisfy the need to archive commercial data that exceeded the capacity of human memory. He observes a progressive cultural evolution from conventional picture to phonetic writing: in social exchange of informations, individual depictions became increasingly formally simplified and conventionalized; they progressively became pictograms. Use of pictograms signified a turn from depiction of individual objects to representation of types of objects. As Jean puts it in *Writing*, "A significant step in the progress of writing occurred when the signs came to represent the sounds of the spoken language. The representation of sounds lies at the root of all true writing" (Jean 1992, 16).

2. In *Strategies of Deconstruction*, Evans writes that "speech, which is the medium of philosophy and of the life worth living, and which must be generated ever anew (cf. Evans n.d.), presupposes a certain form of 'writing.' Contrast the emphasis on speech in Socratic wisdom with the emphasis on writing in the Talmudic tradition. . . . This contrast, not between speech and writing, but between a certain kind of speech and a certain kind of writing, might be thought to raise serious and pressing issues in a time that in so many ways has lost its living tie with both tradition and the power of critical thought that for Kant, as for Socrates, was the very essence of enlightenment" (Evans 1991, 183).

3. In *Deconstruction and Pragmatism*, Derrida characterizes his work this way: "I absolutely refuse a discourse that would assign me a single code, a single language game, a single context, a single situation; and I claim this right not simply out of caprice or because it is to my taste, but for ethical and political reasons. When I say that quasi-transcendentality is at once ironic and serious, I am being sincere. There is evidently irony in what I do—which I hope is politically justifiable—with regard to academic tradition, the seriousness of the philosophical tradition and the personages of the great philosophers. But, although irony appears to me necessary to what I do, at the same time—and this is a question of memory—I take extremely seriously the issue of philosophical responsibility. I maintain that I am a philosopher and that I want to remain a philosopher, and this philosophical responsibility is something that commands me" (Derrida 2005b, 159).

4. In *Paper Machine*, Derrida claims that he does not propose any rigorous philosophy: "deconstruction is not a philosophy" (Derrida 2009, 117). But his work is not literature, either, as he states in *Remarks on Deconstruction and Pragmatism*:

"I have never tried to confuse literature and philosophy or to reduce philosophy to literature" (Derrida 2005b, 81).

5. As Giovanna Borradori noticed, "deconstruction seeks to disassemble any discourse standing as a 'construction.' Given that philosophy is about ideas, beliefs, and values constructed within a conceptual scheme, what is being deconstructed is the way in which they hold together in a given scheme. Unlike a general method or analytical procedure, deconstruction is a highly individualized type of intervention aimed at destabilizing the structural priorities of each particular construction" (Borradori 2003, 138).

6. In "Table ronde sur la traduction," Derrida claims that every interpretation or translation is based on desire to remain true to the original and to reproduce the original meaning by keeping its core untouched. This *taboo of virginity*, which every translator or interpreter is supposed to respect, establishes a relation of desire to "the untouched core which is pre-historical, pre-original, which is the thing any desire can be constituted from. But, although the desire or *phantasm* of the untouched core is unreducible, there is no untouched core" (Derrida 1982d, 153).

7. In *Of Grammatology*, Derrida writes: "travelling along the system of supplementarity with a blind infallibility, and the sure foot of the sleepwalker, Rousseau must at once denounce *mimesis* and art as supplements (supplements that are dangerous when they are not useless, superfluous when they are not disastrous, in truth both at the same time) and recognize in them man's good fortune, the expression of passion, the emergence from the inanimate. It is the status of the *sign* that is marked by the same ambiguity. Signifier imitates signified. Art is woven with signs" (Derrida 1997, 203–4).

8. In *Of Grammatology*, Derrida points out that Rousseau sees a threat of the perversion in this dependence on writing and its supplementarity: "The supplement will always be the moving of the tongue or acting through the hands of others. In it everything is brought together: progress as the possibility of perversion, regression toward an evil that is not natural and that adheres to the power of substitution that permits us to absent ourselves and act by proxy, through representation, through the hands of others. Through the written [par écrit]. This substitution always has the form of the sign. The scandal is that the sign, the image, or the representer, become forces and make 'the world move.' This scandal is such, and its evil effects are sometimes so irreparable, that the world seems to turn the wrong way (and we shall see later what such a catastrophe can signify for Rousseau); then Nature becomes the supplement of art and society" (Derrida 1997, 147).

9. Starobinski writes: "No exchange is possible between opposites: Jean-Jacques's transparency is static, the darkness outside him is congealed. The veil, too, has changed: no longer thin and fluttering, it has turned solid and clamped down on the world it once hid. But only the human turns world opaque. Nature remains close to Jean-Jacques, in the realm of transparency, where he looks for fluid substances for assistance" (Starobinski 1988, 257).

10. In *Derrida/Searle*, Moati shows that to deconstruct means to expose the legal logic of present meaning to a *playful destabilization*. Such a destabilization goes across an unlimited iteration of signs, being "always already grafted in advance onto the contexts that escape the attention of the speaker using them. The present context does not saturate the graphic disposition of a sequence of signs capable of being grafted onto an indefinite series of contexts latent to it, that is to say, capable of continuing to make meaning, to perform, *beyond all determined intentional mobilization*" (Moati 2014, 54).

Postscript

1. The precarious biometric idea of the recognizable identity of individual expressions is even questioned by graphologists and forensic analysts themselves. This questioning makes their work of recognition more complicated and the authority of their own scholarly effort less sure. As these experts in handwriting observe, no signer is able to repeatedly produce identical shapes; a signer can only produce shapes that are similar to her previous traces. Paradoxically, the signer who manages to reproduce exactly the same shape of writing will be suspected of forgery.

Bibliography

Alliez, Eric. 2004. *The Signature of the World*. London: Continuum.
Ambrose, Gavin, and Paul Harris. 2010. *Design Thinking*. Lausanne: AVA Publishing.
Amend, Karen, and Mary S. Ruiz. 1980. *Handwriting Analysis. The Complete Basic Book*. Franklin Lakes: The Career Press.
Appelbaum, David. 2009. *Jacques Derrida's Ghost: A Conjuration*. New York: State University of New York Press.
Athanasiou, Athena, and Judith Butler. 2013. *Dispossession: The Performative in the Political. Conversations with Athena Athanasiou*. Cambridge: Polity Press.
Austin, John L. 1962. *How to Do Things with Words*. Oxford: Oxford University Press.
Baggett, Bart A. 1998. *The Secrets to Making Love Happen! Mastering Your Relationships Using Handwriting Analysis & Neuro-Linguistic Programming*. Dallas: Empresse Publishing.
Benjamin, Walter. 2007. "The Work of Art in the Age of Mechanical Reproduction." In *Illuminations*, 217–51. New York: Schocken.
Bennington, Geoffrey. 2000. "Deconstruction and Ethics." In *Deconstructions,* edited by Nicholas Royle, 64–82. New York: Palgrave.
Bennington, Geoffrey. 2001. "For the Sake of Argument." In *Arguing with Derrida*, edited by Simon Glendinning, 34–51. Oxford: Blackwell.
Bennington, Geoffrey. 2010. *Not Half No End: Militantly Melancholic Essays in Memory of Jacques Derrida*. Edinburgh: Edinburgh University Press.
Bennington, Geoffrey. 2016a. "Métaphore, méta-force." *Rue Descartes* 89–90 (2): 13–20.
Bennington, Geoffrey. 2016b. "The Truth About *Parrhēsia*: Philosophy, Rhetoric, and Politics in Late Foucault." In *Foucault/Derrida Fifty Years Later: The Futures of Genealogy, Deconstruction, and Politics*, edited by Olivia Custer, Penelope Deutscher, and Samir Haddad, 205–20. New York: Columbia University Press.
Bennington, Geoffrey, and Jacques Derrida. 1999. *Jacques Derrida*. Chicago: University of Chicago Press.
Bergson. Henri. 2008. *Laughter: An Essay on the Meaning of the Comic*. Rockville: Wildside Press.

Bert Jean-Francois. 2004. "Y a-t-il un structuralisme chez Foucault?" In *Abécédaire de Michel Foucault*, edited by Stéphane Leclercq, 206–8. Paris: Vrin.
Borradori, Giovanna. 2003. "Deconstructing Terrorism: Derrida." In *Philosophy in Time of Terror: Dialogues with Jürgen Habermas and Jacques Derrida*, 137–72. Chicago: University of Chicago Press.
Bowden, Sean. 2011. *The Priority of Events: Deleuze's Logic of Sense*. Edinburgh: Edinburgh University Press.
Buckley, M. Ronald, Russel W. Driver, and Dwight D. Frink. 1996. "Should We Write Off Graphology?" *International Journal of Selection and Assessment* 4 (2): 78–86.
Butler, Judith. 2011. *Bodies That Matter: On the Discursive Limits of "Sex."* London: Routledge.
Cadava, Eduardo. 1997. *Words of Light*. Princeton: Princeton University Press.
Caligiuri, Michael P., and Linton A. Mohammed. 2012. *The Neuroscience of Handwriting: Applications for Forensic Document Examination*. New York: CRC Press.
Caputo, John D. 1997. *Deconstruction in a Nutshell: A Conversation with Jacques Derrida*. New York: Fordham University Press.
Cisney, Vernon W. 2018. *Deleuze and Derrida: Difference and the Power of the Negative*. Edinburgh: Edinburgh University Press.
Cixous, Hélne. 2009. "Jacques Derrida: Co-Responding Voix You." In *Derrida and the Time of the Political*, edited by Pheng Cheah and Suzanne Guerlac, 41–53. Durham: Duke University Press.
Colapietro, Vincent M. 1988. *Peirce's Approach to the Self: A Semiotic Perspective on Human Subjectivity*. New York: State University of New York Press.
Crépon, Marc. 2005. *Langues sans demeure*. Paris: Galilée.
Critchley, Simon. 2011. "Déconstruction et communication: Quelques remarques sur Derrida et Habermas." In *Derrida: La deconstruction*, edited by Charles Ramond, 53–70. Paris: PUF.
Danesi, Marcel. 2014. *Signs of Crime: Introducing Forensic Semiotics*. Berlin: Walter de Gruyter.
Daylight, Russel. 2012. *What if Derrida Was Wrong about Saussure?* Edinburgh: Edinburgh University Press.
Dekeyser, Hannelore. 2006. "Authenticity in Bits and Bytes." In *Sign Here! Handwriting in the Age of New Media*, edited by Sonja Neef and Jose van Dijck, 76–88. Amsterdam: Amsterdam University Press.
Deleuze, Gilles. 1990. *Logic of Sense*. London: The Athlone Press.
Deleuze, Gilles. 1994. *Difference and Repetition*. New York: Columbia University Press.
Deleuze, Gilles. 2000. *Proust and Signs*. London: The Athlone Press.
Deleuze, Gilles. 2006. *Foucault*. Minneapolis: University of Minnesota Press.
Deleuze, Gilles, and Félix Guattari. 1994. *What Is Philosophy?* New York: Columbia University Press.

Deleuze, Gilles, and Félix Guattari. 2005. *A Thousand Plateaus: Capitalism and Schizophrenia II*. Minneapolis: University of Minnesota Press.
Derrida, Jacques. 1977a. "Limited Inc abc. . . ." In *Limited Inc*, 29–107. Evanston: Northwestern University Press.
Derrida, Jacques. 1977b. "Signature Event Context." In *Limited Inc*, 1–24. Evanston: Northwestern University Press.
Derrida, Jacques. 1978a. "Cogito and the History of Madness." In *Writing and Difference*, 36–76. London: Routledge.
Derrida, Jacques. 1978b. "Structure, Sign and Play in the Discourse of the Human Sciences." In *Writing and Difference*, 351–70. London: Routledge.
Derrida, Jacques. 1981a. "Dissemination." In *Dissemination*, 287–366. Chicago: University of Chicago Press.
Derrida, Jacques. 1981b. "Plato's Pharmacy." In *Dissemination*, 61–171. Chicago: University of Chicago Press.
Derrida, Jacques. 1981c. "The Double Session." In *Dissemination*, 173–286. Chicago: University of Chicago Press.
Derrida, Jacques. 1981d. *Positions*. Chicago: University of Chicago Press.
Derrida, Jacques. 1982a. "The Linguistic Circle of Geneva." In *Margins of Philosophy*, 137–54. Brighton: The Harvester Press.
Derrida, Jacques. 1982b. "The Supplement of Copula: Philosophy before Linguistics." In *Margins of Philosophy*, 175–205. Brighton: The Harvester Press.
Derrida, Jacques. 1982c. "White Mythology: Metaphor in the Text of Philosophy." In *Margins of Philosophy*, 207–72. Brighton: The Harvester Press.
Derrida, Jacques. 1982d. "Table ronde sur la traduction." In *L'oreille de l'autre: otobiographies, transferts, traductions. Texts et débats avec Jacques Derrida*, edited by Claude Lévesque and Christie McDonald, 125–212. Montréal: VLB Éditeur.
Derrida, Jacques. 1984. *Signéponge/Signsponge*. New York: Columbia University Press.
Derrida, Jacques. 1986. *Glas*. Lincoln: University of Nebraska Press.
Derrida, Jacques. 1987a. *Feu la cendre*. Paris: Des femmes.
Derrida, Jacques. 1987b. *The Postcard: From Socrates to Freud and Beyond*. Chicago: University of Chicago Press.
Derrida, Jacques. 1987c. *The Truth in Painting*. Chicago: University of Chicago Press.
Derrida, Jacques. 1988a. "Letter to a Japanese Friend." In *Derrida and Différance*, edited by David Wood and R. Bernasconi, 1–6. Evanston: Northwestern University Press.
Derrida, Jacques. 1988b. "The Original Discussion of Différance." In *Derrida and Différance*, edited by David Wood and R. Bernasconi, 83–96. Evanston: Northwestern University Press.
Derrida, Jacques. 1992. "Force of Law." In *Deconstruction and the Possibility of Justice*, edited by David Gray Carlson, Drucilla Cornell, and Michael Rosenfeld, 3–87. New York: Routledge.

Derrida, Jacques. 1993. *Memories of the Blind: The Self-Portrait and Other Ruins*. Chicago: University of Chicago Press.
Derrida, Jacques. 1994a. *Specters of Marx*. New York: Routledge.
Derrida, Jacques. 1994b. "The Spatial Arts." In *Deconstruction and the Visual Arts: Art, Media, Architecture*, edited by Peter Brunette and David Wills, 9–32. Cambridge: Cambridge University Press.
Derrida, Jacques. 1995. *On the Name*. Stanford: Stanford University Press.
Derrida, Jacques. 1997. *Of Grammatology*. Baltimore: John Hopkins University Press.
Derrida, Jacques. 1998. *Archive Fever: A Freudian Impression*. Chicago: University of Chicago Press.
Derrida, Jacques. 2000. *Foi et Savoir*. Paris: Seuil.
Derrida, Jacques. 2001a. "Une certaine possibilité impossible de dire l'événement." In *Dire l'événement, est-ce possible? Séminaire de Montréal, pour Jacques Derrida*, edited by Soussana Gad and Alexis Nouss, 79–112. Paris: L'Harmattan.
Derrida, Jacques. 2001b. *The Work of Mourning*. Chicago: University of Chicago Press.
Derrida, Jacques. 2002. "Artifactualities." In Jacques Derrida and Bernard Stiegler, *Echographies of Television: Filmed Interviews*, 1–28. Cambridge: Polity Press.
Derrida, Jacques. 2003a. *Genèses, généalogies, genres et le génie: Les secrets de l'archive*. Paris: Galilée.
Derrida, Jacques. 2004. *Points . . . Interviews, 1974–1994*. Stanford: Stanford University Press.
Derrida, Jacques. 2005a. *Poétique et politique du témoignage*. Paris: L'Herne.
Derrida, Jacques. 2005b. "Remarks on Deconstruction and Pragmatism." In *Deconstruction and Pragmatism*, edited by Chantal Mouffe, 79–90. New York: Routledge.
Derrida, Jacques. 2005c. *On Touching—Jean-Luc Nancy*. Stanford: Stanford University Press.
Derrida, Jacques. 2006. *Aporias*. Stanford: Stanford University Press.
Derrida, Jacques. 2007a. *Learning to Live Finally: The Last Interview*. New York: Palgrave Macmillan.
Derrida, Jacques. 2007b. *Psyché: Inventions of the Other*. Stanford: Stanford University Press.
Derrida, Jacques. 2008a. "Heidegger's Hand (*Geschlecht* II)." In *Psyche: Inventions of the Other, Volume II*, 27–62. Stanford: Stanford University Press.
Derrida, Jacques. 2008b. *The Animal That Therefore I Am*. New York: Fordham University Press.
Derrida, Jacques. 2009. *Paper Machine*. Stanford: Stanford University Press.
Derrida, Jacques. 2010a. *Athens, Still Remains*. New York: Fordham University Press.
Derrida, Jacques. 2010b. *Copy, Archive, Signature*. Stanford: Stanford University Press.
Derrida, Jacques. 2011. *Politique et amitié*. Paris: Galilée.
Derrida, Jacques. 2012a. *Les yeux de la langue: L'abime et le volcan*. Paris: Galilée.
Derrida, Jacques. 2012b. *Histoire du monsonge*. Paris: Galilée.

Derrida, Jacques. 2014. *Trace et archive, image et art.* Paris: Ina Éditions.
Derrida, Jacques. 2016. *Surtout, pas de journalistes!* Paris: Galilée.
Derrida, Jacques. 2018. *Before the Law: The Complete Text of* Préjugés. Minneapolis: University of Minnesota Press.
Derrida, Jacques. 2020. *Life Death.* Chicago: University of Chicago Press.
Derrida, Jacques, and Giovanna Borradori. 2003. "Autoimmunity: Real and Symbolic Suicides." In Giovanna Borradori, *Philosophy in Time of Terror: Dialogues with Jürgen Habermas and Jacques Derrida,* 85–136. Chicago: University of Chicago Press.
Derrida, Jacques, and R. Kearney. 2012. "La déconstruction et l'autre: Entretien avec Richard Kearney." *Les Temps Modernes* 669/670: 7–29.
Derrida, Jacques, and Bernard Stiegler. 2002a. "Artifactuality, Homohegemony." Chap. 2 in *Echographies of Television: Filmed Interviews,* 41–55. Cambridge: Polity Press.
Derrida, Jacques, and Bernard Stiegler. 2002b. "Spectrographies." Chap. 8 in *Echographies of Television: Filmed Interviews,* 113–34. Cambridge: Polity Press.
Derrida, Jacques, and Bernard Stiegler. 2002c. "Acts of Memory: Topolitics and Teletechnology." Chap. 3 in *Echographies of Television, Filmed Interviews,* 56–67. Cambridge: Polity Press.
Dresbold, M., and J. Kwalwasser. 2006. *Sex, Lies and Handwriting: A Top Expert Reveals the Secrets Hidden in Your Handwriting.* New York: Free Press.
Eco, Umberto. 1979. *A Theory of Semiotics.* Bloomington: Indiana University Press.
Eco, Umberto. 1992. "Reply." In *Interpretation and Overinterpretation,* edited by S. Collini, 139–51. Cambridge: Cambridge University Press.
Eco, Umberto. 1994. *The Limits of Interpretation.* Bloomington: Indiana University Press.
Eco, Umberto. 2000. *Kant and the Platypus.* New York: Harcourt Brace.
Evans, Claude J. 1991. *Strategies of Deconstruction: Derrida and the Myth of the Voice.* Minneapolis: University of Minnesota Press.
Evans, Mihail. 2014. *The Singular Politics of Derrida and Baudrillard.* New York: Palgrave.
Finn, Margaret R. 1950. *A History of Latin's Pelaeography.* New York: Fordham University Press.
Fišerová, Michaela. 2013. *Partager le visible: Repenser Foucault.* Paris: L'Harmattan.
Fišerová, Michaela. 2017. "Hopes of Derrida's Reading? On Emergence of Peirce's Texts in the Poststructuralist Context." In *How to Make Our Signs Clear: C. S. Peirce and Semiotics,* edited by Vít Gvoždiak and Martin Švantner. Leiden: Brill.
Fišerová, Michaela. 2018a. "Pragmatical Paradox of Signature." *Signata* 9 (1): 485–504.
Fišerová, Michaela. 2018b. "There's No Regime beyond Representation: Deconstructing Rancière's Antinomies." *Philosophy Today* 62 (1): 215–34.
Flusser, Vilém. 2011. *Does Writing Have a Future?* Minneapolis: University of Minnesota Press.

Flusser, Vilém. 2014. *Gestures*. Minneapolis: University of Minnesota Press.
Foucault, Michel. 1989. *The Order of Things*. London: Routledge.
Foucault, Michel. 2001. "Mon corps, ce feu, ce papier." In *Dits et écrits: Tome I. 1954–1975*, 1113–65. Paris: Gallimard.
Foucault, Michel. 2011. *Le beau danger: Entretien avec Claude Bonnefoy*. Paris: Éditions EHESS.
Fraenkel, Beatrice. 1992. *La signature: Genèse d'un signe*. Paris: Gallimard.
Fraenkel, Beatrice. 2008. "La signature: du signe a l'acte." *Sociétés et représentations* 25: 15–23.
Fraenkel, Beatrice, and David Pontille. 2006. "La signature au temps de l'électronique." *Politix* 74 (2): 103–21.
Frank, Manfred. 1997. *The Subject and the Text: Essays on Literary Theory and Philosophy*. Cambridge: Cambridge University Press.
Frazer, Persifor. 1909. "Identification of Human Beings by the System of Alphonse Bertillon." *The Journal of Franklin Institute* 167 (5): 321–58.
Galton, Francis. 1909. *Essays in Eugenics*. London: The Eugenics Education Society.
Gardner, Bill, and Anne Hellman. 2014. *Logo Lounge 8*. Beverly: Rockport.
Gasché, Rodolphe. 1994. *Inventions of Difference: On Jacques Derrida*. London: Harvard University Press.
Gasché, Rodolphe. 1997. *The Tain of the Mirror*. London: Harvard University Press.
Gasché, Rodolphe. 1999. *Of Minimal Things: Studies on the Notion of Relation*. Stanford: Stanford University Press.
Gasché, Rodolphe. 2007. *Views and Interviews: On "Deconstruction" in America*. Aurora: The Davies Group.
Gasché, Rodolphe. 2016. *Deconstruction, Its Force, Its Violence*. New York: State University of New York Press.
Gaston, Sean. 2006. *The Impossible Mourning of Jacques Derrida*. London: Continuum.
Gehring, Petra. 2008. "The Jurisprudence of the 'Force of Law.'" In *Derrida and Legal Philosophy*, edited by Peter Goodrich, Florian Hoffmann, Michael Rosenfeld, and Cornelia Vismann, 55–70. New York: Palgrave Macmillan.
Gendron, Sarah. 2008. *Repetition, Difference, and Knowledge in the Work of Samuel Beckett, Jacques Derrida, and Gilles Deleuze*. New York: Peter Lang.
Glendinning, Simon. 2001. *On Being with Others: Heidegger—Derrida—Wittgenstein*. London: Routledge.
Goldschmit, Marc. 2003. *Jacques Derrida, une introduction*. Paris: Pocket.
Graff, Gerald. 1988. "Summary of Reiterating the Differences." In Jacques Derrida, *Limited Inc*, 25–29. Evanston: Northwestern University Press.
Groethuysen, Bernard. 1949. *J.-J. Rousseau*. Paris: Gallimard.
Gros, Frédéric. 2002. "La parrhesia chez Foucault." In *Foucault, le courage de la verité*, edited by Frédéric Gros, 155–66. Paris: PUF.
Harman, Graham. 2002. *Tool-Being: Heidegger and the Metaphysics of Objects*. Chicago: Open Court.

Harralson, Heidi. H. 2013. *Developments in Handwriting and Signature Identification in the Digital Age*. Oxford: Elsevier.
Heidegger, Martin. 1992. *Parmenides*. Bloomington: Indiana University Press.
Hill, Leslie. 2007. *The Cambridge Introduction to Jacques Derrida*. Cambridge: Cambridge University Press.
Hill, Leslie. 2010. *Radical Indecision: Barthes, Blanchot, Derrida, and the Future of Criticism*. Notre Dame: University of Notre Dame Press.
Huber, Roy A., and A. M. Headrick. 1999. *Handwriting Identification: Facts and Fundamentals*. New York: RCR Press.
Hylkema, Henk, Gerard P. van Galen, and Ruud G. J. Meulenbroek. 1986. "On the Simultaneous Processing of Words, Letters and Strokes in Handwriting: Evidence for a Mixed Linear and Parallel Model." In *Graphonomics: Contemporary Research in Handwriting*, edited by Henry S. R. Kao, Gerard P. van Galen, and Rumjahn Hoosain, 5–20. Amsterdam: Elsevier.
Impedovo, Sebastiano. 1994. "Frontiers in Handwriting Recognition." In *Fundamentals in Handwriting Recognition*, edited by Sebastiano Impedovo, 7–39. Berlin: Springer.
Jean, Georges. 1992. *Writing: The Story of Alphabets and Scripts*. New York: Harry N. Abrams.
Kafka, Franz. 2009. *The Trial*. Oxford: Oxford University Press.
Kamuf, Peggy. 1988. *Signature Pieces: On the Institution of Authorship*. London: Cornell University Press.
Kamuf, Peggy. 2016. "Composition Displacement." In *Derrida Now: Current Perspectives in Derrida Studies*, edited by John W. P. Phillips, 160–83. Cambridge: Polity Press.
Kant, Immanuel. 1998. *Critique of Pure Reason*. Cambridge: Cambridge University Press.
Kates, Joshua. 2005. *Essential History: Jacques Derrida and the Development of Deconstruction*. Evanston: Northwestern University Press.
Kittler, Friedrich A. 1999. *Gramophone, Film, Typewriter*. Stanford: Stanford University Press.
Klimoski, Richard J., and Aant Rafaeli. 1983. "Inferring Personal Qualities through Handwriting Analysis." *Journal of Occupational Psychology* 56: 191–202.
Krell, David Farell. 2015. "Geschlecht II: Heidegger's Singular Hand." In *Phantoms of the Other: Four Generations of Derrida's Geschlecht*. New York: State University of New York Press.
Lahey Dronsfield, Jonathan. 2013. "The Performativity of Art." In *Performatives after Deconstruction*, edited by Mauro Senatore, 169–85. London: Bloomsbury.
Lambert, Gregg. 2003. "The Philosopher and the Writer: A Question of Style." In *Between Deleuze and Derrida*, edited by Paul Patton and John Protevi, 120–34. London: Continuum.
Lambert, Gregg. 2012. *In Search of a New Image of Thought: Gilles Deleuze and Philosophical Expressionism*. Minneapolis: University of Minnesota Press.

Lawlor, Leonard. 2002a. *Derrida and Husserl*. Bloomington: Indiana University Press.
Lawlor, Leonard. 2002b. "Let Others Be Ends in Themselves: The Convergence Between Foucault's Parrhesia and Derrida's Teleiopoesis." In *Between Foucault and Derrida*, edited by Yubraj Aryal, Vernon W. Cisney, Nicolae Morar, and Christopher Penfield, 169–85. Edinburgh: Edinburgh University Press.
Legrand, Pierre. 2003. "The Same and the Different." In *Comparative Legal Studies. Traditions and Transitions,* edited by Pierre Legrand and Roderick Munday, 240–311. Cambridge: Cambridge University Press.
Legrand, Pierre. 2009. "Introduction (Of Derrida's Law)." In *Derrida and Law*, edited by Pierre Legrand, xi–xli. London: Routledge.
Lombroso, Cesare. 2006. *Criminal Man*. London: Duke University Press.
Majdanski, Delphine. 2000. *La signature et les mentions manuscrites dans les contrats*. Bordeaux: Press Universitaires de Bordeaux.
Marder, Michael. 2011. *The Event of the Thing: Derrida's Post-Deconstructive Realism*. Toronto: University of Toronto Press.
Marin, Louis. 1988. *Portrait of the King*. Minneapolis: University of Minnesota Press.
Marin, Louis. 2005. *Politiques de la représentation*. Paris: Kimé.
Martin, Jean-Clet. 1993. *Variations: La philosophie de Gilles Deleuze*. Paris: Éditions Payot.
Mason, Stephen. 2012. *Electronic Signatures in Law*. Cambridge: Cambridge University Press.
McCance, Dawne. 2019. *The Reproduction of Life Death: Derrida's La vie la mort*. New York: Fordham University Press.
McFarland, James. 2013. *Constellation: Friedrich Nietzsche and Walter Benjamin in the Now-Time of History*. New York: Fordham University Press.
McLuhan, Marshall. 1994. *Understanding Media: The Extensions of Man*. Cambridge: The MIT Press.
McLuhan, Marshall. 1997. *The Essential McLuhan*. New York: Basic Books.
McNichol, Andrea, and Jeffrey A. Nelson. 1994. *Handwriting Analysis. Putting It to Work for You*. Chicago: Contemporary Books.
Mengue, Philippe. 1994. *Gilles Deleuze ou le système du multiple*. Paris: Kimé.
Michon, Jean-Hippolyte. 1875. *Système de graphologie*. Paris: Bibliothèque graphologique.
Moati, Raoul. 2014. *Derrida/Searle. Deconstruction and Ordinary Language*. New York: Columbia University Press.
Naas, Michael. 2012. *Miracle and Machine: Jacques Derrida and the Two Sources of Religion, Science, and the Media*. New York: Fordham University Press.
Nancy, Jean-Luc. 2000. *Being Singular Plural*. Stanford: Stanford University Press.
Neef, Sonja, and Jose Van Dijck. 2006. "Sign Here! Handwritting in the Age of Technical Reproduction." In *Sign Here! Handwritting in the Age of New Media*, edited by Sonja Neef and Jose van Dijck, 7–19. Amsterdam: Amsterdam University Press.

Ormiston, Gayle. 1988. "The Economy of Duplicity: *Différance*." In *Derrida and Différance*, edited by David Wood and Robert Bernasconi, 41–50. Evanston: Northwestern University Press.

Owen, John M. 2006. "Authenticity and Objectivity in Scientific Communication: Implications of Digital Media." In: *Sign Here! Handwritting in the Age of New Media*, edited by Sonja Neef and Jose van Dijck, 60–75. Amsterdam: Amsterdam University Press.

Pearson, Keith Ansell. 1999. *Germinal Life: The Difference and Repetition of Deleuze*. London: Routledge.

Peirce, Charles Senders. 1955. *Philosophical Writings of Peirce*. New York: Dover Publications.

Perez-Teran, Mayorga Rosa Maria. 2009. *From Realism to "Realicism": The Metaphysics of Charles Senders Peirce*. New York: Lexington Books.

Pirlo, Giuseppe. 1994. "Algorithms for Signature Verification." In *Fundamentals in Handwriting Recognition*, edited by Sebastiano Impedovo, 435–54. Berlin: Springer.

Plato. 2002. *Phaedrus*. Oxford: Oxford University Press.

Plato. 2015. *Theaetetus and Sophist*. Cambridge: Cambridge University Press.

Poché, Fred. 2007. *Penser avec Jacques Derrida: Comprendre la déconstruction*. Lyon: Chronique sociale.

Poulin, Richard. 2011. *The Language of Graphic Design*. Beverly: Rockport.

Ramond, Charles. 2001. *Le vocabulaire de Derrida*. Paris: Ellipses.

Revel, Judith. 2002. "La pensée verticale: une éthique de la problématisation." In *Foucault, le courage de la vérité*, edited by Frédéric Gros, 63–86. Paris: PUF.

Reynolds, Andrew. 2002. *Peirce's Scientific Metaphysics*. Nashville: Vanderbilt University Press.

Roberts, Paula. 2002. *Love Letters: The Romantic Secrets Hidden in Our Handwriting*. Franklin Lakes: The Career Press.

Roman, Klara Goldzieher. 1962. *Handwriting: A Key to Personality*. New York: Noonday Press.

Ronell, Avital. 2005. *The Test Drive*. Chicago: University of Illinois Press.

Ronell, Avital. 2006. *Amercan Philo: Entretiens avec Avital Ronell*. Paris: Stock.

Rorty, Richard. 1979. *Philosophy and the Mirror of Nature*. Princeton: Princeton University Press.

Rorty, Richard. 1996. "Is Derrida a Transcedental Philosopher?" In *Derrida: A Critical Reader*, edited by David Wood, 235–46. Oxford: Blackwell.

Rorty, Richard. 2005. "Remarks on Deconstruction and Pragmatism." In *Deconstruction and Pragmatism*, edited by Chantal Mouffe, 13–18. New York: Routledge.

Rousseau, Jean-Jacques. 1998. *Essay on the Origin of Languages and Writings Related to Music*. Hanover: University Press of New England.

Rousseau, Jean-Jacques. 2002. *The Discourse on the Sciences and Arts and the Social Contract*. New Haven and London: Yale University Press.

Royle, Nicholas. 2000. "What is Deconstruction?" In *Deconstructions: A User's Guide*, edited by Nicholas Royle, 1–13. New York: Palgrave.
Royle, Nicholas. 2003. *Jacques Derrida*. London: Routledge.
Samara, Timothy. 2014. *Design Elements: Understanding the Rules and Knowing When to Break Them*. Beverly: Rockport.
Sassoon, Rosemary. 2007. *Handwriting of the Twentieth Century*. Chicago: Intellect Books.
de Saussure, Ferdinand. 2011. *Course in General Linguistics*. New York: Columbia University Press.
Searle, John. R. 1977. "Reiterating the Differencies. A Reply to Derrida." *Glyph* 1: 198–208.
Searle, John. R. 1979. *Expression and Meaning: Studies in the Theory of Speech Acts*. New York: Cambridge University Press.
Searle, John. R. 1980. "The Background of Meaning." In *Speech Act Theory and Pragmatics*, edited by John R. Searle, K. Ferenc, and K. Bierwisch, 221–32. Dordrecht: D. Reidel.
Senatore, Mauro. 2018. *Germs of Death. The Problem of Genesis in Jacques Derrida*. New York: State University of New York Press.
Sherwin, Richard K. 2011. *Visualizing Law in the Age of Digital Baroque. Arabesques and Entanglements*. London: Routledge.
Short, Thomas L. 2007. *Peirce's Theory of Signs*. Cambridge: Cambridge University Press.
Smith, Barry. 2003a. "John Searle: From Speech Acts to Social Reality." In *John Searle*, edited by Barry Smith, 1–33. New York: Cambridge University Press.
Smith, Daniel. W. 2003b. "Deleuze and Derrida: Immanence and Transcendence." In *Between Deleuze and Derrida*, edited by Paul Patton and John Protevi, 46–66. London: Continuum.
Smith, Robert. 1995. *Derrida and Autobiography*. Cambridge: Cambridge University Press.
Starobinski, Jean. 1988. *Jean-Jacques Rousseau, Transparency and Obstruction*. Chicago: University of Chicago Press.
Staten, Henry. 1984. *Wittgenstein and Derrida*. Lincoln: University of Nebraska Press.
Sykes, Geoffrey. 2008. "A Short Genealogy of Realism: Peirce, Kevelson and Legal Semiotics." *International Journal for the Semiotics of Law* 21: 103–16.
Teilmann-Lock, Stina. 2016. *The Object of Copyright*. London: Routledge.
Tselentis, Jason. 2011. *Type: Form and Function*. Beverly: Rockport.
Vitale, Francesco. 2018a. *Biodeconstruction: Jacques Derrida and the Life Sciences*. New York: State University of New York Press.
Vitale, Francesco. 2018b. *The Last Fortress of Metaphysics: Jacques Derrida and the Deconstruction of Architecture*. New York: State University of New York Press.
Waldenfels, Bernhard. 2015. "For Example." In *Exemplarity and Singularity: Thinking Through Particulars in Philosophy, Literature, and Law*, edited by Michele Lowrie and Susanne Lüdemann, 36–45. London: Routledge.

Walsham, Alexandra. 2010. *Remains and Relics*. Oxford: Oxford University Press.

Wetzel, Michael. 2006. "The Authority of Drawing: Hand, Authenticity, and Authorship." In *Sign Here! Handwritting in the Age of New Media*, edited by Sonja Neef and Jose van Dijck, 51–59. Amsterdam: Amsterdam University Press.

Wiener, Philip P. 1966. "Introduction." In Charles Senders Peirce, *Selected Writings: Values in a Universe of Chance*, vii–xxii. New York: Dover Publications.

Williams, James. 2005. *Gilles Deleuze's Difference and Repetition*. Edinburgh: Edinburgh University Press.

Williams, Jay. 2013. "Preface." In *Signature Derrida*, edited by Jay Williams, vii–xii. Chicago: University of Chicago Press.

Winthorp-Young, Geoffrey, and Michael Wutz. 1999. "Translator's Introduction." In Friedrich A. Kittler, *Gramophone, Film, Typewriter*, xi–xxxviii. Stanford: Stanford University Press.

Wood, David. 1988. "*Différance* and the Problem of Strategy." In *Derrida and Différance*, edited by David Wood and Robert Bernasconi, 36–70. Evanston: Northwestern University Press.

Ystehede, Per J. 2013. "Demonizing Being: Lombroso and the Ghosts of Criminology." In *The Cesare Lombroso Handbook*, edited by Paul Knepper and Per J. Ystehede, 72–97. London: Routledge.

Zehfuss, Maja. 2007. "Derrida's Memory, War and the Politics of Ethics." In *Derrida. Negotiating the Legacy*, edited by Madeleine Fagan, Ludovic Glorieux, Indira Hašimbegovic, and Marie Suetsugu, 97–111. Edinburgh: Edinburgh University Press.

Zima, Peter V. 2002. *Deconstruction and Critical Theory*. London: Continuum.

Zourabichvili, François. 2012. *Deleuze: A Philosophy of the Event*. Edinburgh: Edinburgh University Press.

Name Index

Alliez, E., 216
Ambrose, G., 205
Amend, K., 56, 208–209
Appelbaum, D., 134
Athanasiou, A., 187, 202
Austin, J. L., 116–127, 198, 214

Benjamin, W., 26, 69–71, 89, 201, 205–206, 209–210, 215
Bennington, G., 106, 109, 208, 212–213, 217
Bergson, H., 217
Bert, J.-F., 45
Borradori, G., 48, 77, 93, 219
Bowden, S., 216
Butler, J., 115, 187, 202

Cadava, E., 209–210
Caligiuri, M. P., 61–62, 116
Caputo, J. D., 90
Cixous, H., 50, 184
Colapietro, V. M., 28
CRÉPON, M., 208
Critchley, S., 212

Danesi, M., 30
Daylight, R., 75–76
Dekeyser, H., 8–9, 12, 14–16
Deleuze, G., 78, 95, 132, 135, 137–139, 142, 144–148, 150–152, 157, 198, 216–217
Derrida, J., ix–xi, 3–5, 18–24, 26, 28, 37–42, 44–53, 64, 71–84, 86–95, 97–115, 117–128, 132–137, 139–144, 147, 150–151, 153, 155–178, 180–181, 183–187, 189, 191–193, 197–204, 207–208, 210–219
Dresbold, M., 58

Eco, U., 5, 28–35, 168–169, 193, 199–200, 206–207
Evans, J. C., 160, 218
Evans, M., 139

Finn, M. R., 37–38
Flusser, V., 18, 20, 22, 204
Foucault, M., 28–29, 34, 43–49, 51–53, 117, 144, 168, 191, 199, 207–208, 212
Fraenkel, B., 9–10, 13, 214–215
Frazer, P., 203

Galton, F., 11, 204
Gardner, B., 205
GASCHÉ, R., 70, 100, 162–164, 187, 203, 210
Gendron, S., 91
Goldschmit, M., 171

Graff, G., 120
Groethuysen, B., 170
Gros, F., 46
Guattari, F., 144–146

Haedrick, A. M., 205
Harralson, H. H., 60–61, 69
Harris, P., 205
Heidegger, M., 23, 51, 163
Hellman, A., 205
Hill, L., 87, 115–116, 123, 164
Huber, R. A., 205

Impedovo, S., 62–63

Jean, G., 158

Kafka, F., 136
Kamuf, P., 181–183, 217–218
Kant, I., 31, 33–34, 99, 105–106, 111, 160, 203, 207–208, 210, 218
Kates, J., 162–163
Kittler, F. A., 51, 53–54
Klimoski, R., 55
Krell, D. F., 23
Kwalwasser, J., 58

Lahey Dronsfield, J., 158–159
Lambert, G., 145–146, 151, 161, 217
Lawlor, L., 160, 208
Legrand, P., 71–72, 125
Lombrosco, C., 10–11, 203–204

Majdanski, D., 68
Marder, M., 176
Martin, J.-C., 148
Mason, S., 14
McLuhan, M., xi, 18–20, 22–23, 53, 193
Mengue, P., 216
Moati, R., 117–118, 120–122, 220
Mohammed, L. A., 61–62, 116

Naas, M., 21
Nancy, J.-L., 83–84
Neef, S., 15, 60, 69

Ormiston, G., 186
Owen, J. M., 13

Pearson, K. A., 138
Peirce, Charles, S., x, 28–35, 50, 64, 78–81, 85, 90, 94, 141, 167–168, 180, 197–198, 200, 206–207, 210–212
Perez-Teran Mayorga, R. M., 211
Pirlo, G., 62
Plato, 39, 91, 132–133, 137, 139, 170, 174, 185, 210
POCHÉ, F., 135–136
Pontille, D., 13
Poulin, R., 204–205

Rafaeli, A., 55
Ramond, C., 106, 214
Reynolds, A., 210
Roman, K. G., 55–57
Ronell, A., 82, 187
Rorty, R., 162–164
Rousseau, J.-J., 52, 76, 117, 153, 169–178, 219
Royle, N., 108, 134, 156
Ruiz, M. S., 56, 208–209

Samara, T., 25, 204
Sassoon, R., 38, 207
Saussure, F. de, 21, 52, 74–76, 117, 141
Sherwin, R., K., 17
Short, T. L., 206
Searle, J. R., 95, 117–122, 127, 198, 212, 214
Senatore, M., 210
Smith, B., 214
Smith, D. W., 139, 216
Smith, R., 211

Starobinski, J., 174–175, 219
Staten, H., 214
Sykes, G., 212

Teilmann-Lock, S., 69–70
Tselentis, J., 205

Van Dijck, J., 15, 60, 69
Vitale, F., 107–108, 213

Waldenfels, B., 104
Walsham, A., 27, 206

Wiener, Ph. P., 80
Williams, James, 145, 216
Williams, Jay, 108, 135, 214
Winthorp-Young, G., 53
Wood, D., 160–161
Wutz, M., 53

Ystehede, P. J., 204

Zehfuss, M., 151
Zima, P., 212
Zourabichvili, F., 138

Subject Index

Abstraction, 25–26, 85
Aporia, ix–xi, 3, 8, 12, 14–15, 39–40, 42, 50, 52, 64, 68, 80, 92, 94–95, 99–102, 104, 108, 110–111, 114, 117, 122, 124–126, 128–129, 131, 135–136, 140–141, 150–152, 166–169, 171, 176, 179, 182–184, 186–187, 192–193, 197–203, 213, 217
Authenticity, 3, 7–9, 12–16, 22, 26, 29–30, 34–36, 58–60, 62–64, 67, 69–71, 81, 85, 89–90, 114, 116, 124–128, 131, 133, 146, 149–150, 168, 175–176, 179, 181, 189, 192–198, 200–201, 205–206, 210, 215

Becoming, 94, 137–139, 144, 148, 150

Citizen, x, 9–10, 22, 27, 29, 36, 67–68, 88, 90–91, 113, 135, 136, 146–147, 150–151, 166, 172, 183, 185, 188, 194, 201, 211
Continuity, 93, 138, 141, 148, 200
Critique, 4, 46, 48–49, 72, 76–77, 88, 97–99, 101, 103, 105–106, 110, 122, 137, 160, 163, 178, 192, 207, 210, 212, 216–217

Difference, 3, 9–10, 16, 18, 20–21, 26–28, 30–31, 34–35, 42–43, 45, 51, 56, 63–64, 76, 83, 91, 100, 103–104, 108, 118, 124–127, 137–140, 142, 144, 146, 149–150, 152–153, 157, 159, 179, 181, 186, 193–194, 196, 198, 210, 212, 214, 216
Différance, 82–83, 99, 106, 124, 135, 159–161, 186, 213, 217
Discourse, ix–xi, 3, 13, 16, 22–24, 29–31, 33–36, 41–44, 47, 49–56, 58–59, 61, 63–64, 67, 72, 81, 101, 104, 106–107, 124, 127, 131, 140, 159, 161, 165, 166–168, 170, 173, 175, 178, 180–181, 188–189, 191–197, 199–200, 204, 218–219
Discursive expectation, ix–xi, 3, 16, 19, 21–22, 24, 27–28, 30–31, 33–37, 39, 41–43, 45, 47, 49–51, 53–55, 57–59, 61, 63–65, 167–169, 188–191, 193, 195, 197, 199
Dissemination, 73, 95, 98–99, 107, 119–120, 122–123, 128, 132–133, 143, 155, 164, 173, 176, 183, 185
Double bind, ix, 14, 20, 52, 68, 71, 92, 111, 114, 117–118, 123, 131

Event, ix, xi, 8, 25, 42, 45, 48,
50–51, 53, 68, 82, 84, 87, 92, 94,
95, 106, 109–111, 119, 124, 127,
129, 131, 135, 137–139, 142, 145,
147–148, 150–153, 158–159, 161,
169, 173, 175, 178–179, 183–185,
187, 189, 193, 200–202, 209,
214–216

Evidence, 8–9, 61, 74–75, 174, 185

Expertise, 9, 33, 36, 54, 58–59,
67–68, 116, 167, 189

Expression, 1, 9–11, 13, 17–18, 22,
24–26, 32, 34, 37, 54–56, 58, 60,
63–64, 73, 76, 82, 91, 95, 107,
110, 113, 116, 120, 127, 133, 135,
138–139, 146–149, 151–152, 157,
166, 173, 178, 188–189, 193–198,
200–202, 206, 217, 219, 220

Firstness, 28–29, 33, 64, 81, 197, 206,
211

Force, 8, 33, 38–39, 41–42, 44, 52,
64, 67–69, 71, 74, 78, 80–84, 87,
93, 95, 106, 108, 110–111, 118,
121, 124–125, 135–136, 141, 151,
159, 161–162, 165, 167, 169,
183–186, 188–189, 192, 200, 208,
211, 213–214, 217–219

Forgery, 25, 69–70, 87, 116, 126,
131, 150, 166, 182, 192, 196, 198

Forensic analysis, x, xi, 3–4, 9–10,
12–13, 16–18, 21–22, 24, 27–31,
33–36, 38, 43, 50–51, 54, 59–61,
63–65, 67–69, 80–81, 116, 127,
131, 141, 143, 166–168, 173,
188–189, 191–199, 201, 206

Graphology, 3–4, 9–11, 16–17, 26–31,
33–36, 43, 51, 54–56, 58–59,
63–65, 67–69, 80–81, 116, 127,
131, 166–168, 189, 191–197, 199,
201, 209

Handwriting, ix, 1, 4, 7, 9–12, 15–21,
23, 26–28, 30–31, 33–38, 42–43,
53–64, 68–69, 71, 82–83, 85, 94,
109, 116, 125, 127–128, 131–132,
141, 143–144, 146, 149–150, 152,
155, 157, 164, 167–169, 173,
176, 179, 182–183, 192, 194–202,
204–205, 207, 209, 220

Handwritten signature, ix–xi, 1, 3–5,
7–9, 11–19, 21–31, 33–39, 41,
43, 45, 47, 49–51, 53–55, 57–65,
67–71, 81–95, 104, 107, 109–117,
123–125, 127–129, 131–135, 141–
150, 152–153, 155–156, 158–159,
161, 165–169, 172–173, 176, 179,
182–183, 185, 188–189, 191–202,
205–206, 210–211, 214–216

Identity, ix–xi, 3, 7–9, 13–15, 24–27,
29, 33–36, 39, 42, 54, 57, 64,
67–68, 71, 77, 79, 81, 87–88,
90–92, 94–95, 98–99, 102–104,
107, 109–110, 114–116, 122, 124,
126–129, 131–132, 135, 138–145,
147, 149–150, 152, 155, 157–159,
167–169, 173, 175, 179–180, 185–
186, 188–189, 192–198, 200–203,
210, 215–216, 220

Image, 4, 17, 23, 26, 29, 41, 74–75,
82, 86, 93, 104, 137, 141–142, 148,
157, 164, 174, 205, 207, 216, 219

Imitation, 24, 27, 34, 59, 63, 69, 82,
89, 94, 95, 125, 131, 152, 155,
179, 182–183, 196–197

Interpretation, x–xi, 3–4, 7, 13,
16–19, 28–31, 34, 41, 43, 50–51,
53–55, 63, 71, 73, 77–78, 80,
92–93, 98, 100, 108, 110–111,
118–119, 121, 126, 133–135, 157,
159–161, 163–167, 170, 174, 184,
188, 193–194, 199, 204, 206–207,
209–210, 212, 219

Interval, 8, 34, 54, 64, 83, 86–87, 95, 112, 124–125, 128–129, 140, 155, 176, 183, 196, 210
Iteration, 8, 24, 92, 95, 106, 109, 114–115, 118, 121–122, 128–129, 131, 135, 142–143, 151–152, 176, 178–180, 197, 202, 220

Law, 8, 10, 29, 52, 70, 72, 76, 79, 80, 85, 90, 94–95, 97–98, 102, 110–111, 124–126, 128, 131, 135–136, 141–143, 153, 155, 158–160, 162, 167, 169–170, 181, 183–185, 187–189, 202, 206, 210–211, 216
Life, 8, 70, 85–86, 89–90, 92, 94–95, 104, 110–111, 135–136, 141–142, 145, 152–153, 156, 158–159, 167, 170, 181, 187–200, 202, 213, 218

Materiality, 7, 39, 84, 150, 178, 183, 186–187, 198, 201
Mediation, xi, 3–4, 11, 15–16, 18–23, 35–36, 43, 52–53, 67–68, 71, 109, 125, 133, 149, 158, 168, 170, 174, 178, 181, 191, 193, 195, 198–200, 202
Medium, 3, 5, 8, 11, 13–24, 27–28, 33, 35, 53, 64–65, 67, 84, 86, 89, 114, 157–158, 175, 189, 193–195, 197, 199, 201, 218
Melancholy, 5, 99, 147, 161, 168, 192, 200–201, 217
Metaphysical expectation, x, 3, 14, 21–24, 28, 30–31, 33–36, 42–43, 39, 42–43, 49–53, 55, 63–65, 67–69, 71, 73, 75, 81, 85, 89, 91, 94, 109–110, 126, 134–136, 156, 167–170, 173, 176, 188–189, 191–195, 197, 199–201, 217
Metaphysics, xi, 15, 24, 33, 36–37, 39, 48–49, 51, 72–74, 78–80, 89, 97–102, 104–106, 108–112, 115, 124–126, 131–135, 139–140, 146–147, 155, 161–165, 167, 171–173, 175–176, 178, 180, 186, 188–189, 192, 197, 200, 202, 207–208, 210–211, 217

Name, ix, 1, 7–8, 13–14, 17–18, 24–26, 29, 32, 42, 48, 55, 58, 64, 67, 71, 76, 81, 83–85, 88, 91, 94, 109, 111, 113, 116, 124–126, 135, 138, 141, 143–144, 146–150, 158–161, 164–165, 167, 171–172, 180–183, 185–186, 194, 197–198, 210–211, 213, 215, 218

Originality, 26, 88, 90, 109, 129, 149, 152, 175, 192

Pattern, 24, 37–38, 55, 61–62, 75, 128, 143, 148–149, 152, 196
Performative, 78, 90–91, 95, 107–108, 113, 115–119, 121–128, 133–135, 139, 142–143, 147–148, 151–152, 160, 179–182, 184–185, 187–188, 200, 202, 213–214
Picture, 7–9, 13, 17–18, 24–26, 29, 39, 41, 55–56, 64, 67–69, 71, 81, 83–85, 89, 91, 100, 108, 141–142, 144, 146, 148, 157–159, 167, 193–194, 196, 204, 209, 216, 218
Plasticity, 24–26, 85, 144, 146–147, 183
Power, 1, 16, 20, 29, 40–41, 88, 115, 124, 133, 137, 140, 176, 186, 201, 204, 214, 217–219, 222
Presence, 1, 8–9, 12, 16–17, 20–21, 27, 36, 39–41, 45, 59, 67, 69–74, 77, 80–82, 86–90, 93, 95, 98–99, 101, 103, 106–110, 113–116, 119, 121, 124, 126, 129, 132, 134, 141, 151, 155, 162, 164–165, 167, 170–173, 175–177, 185–186, 189,

Presence *(continued)*
193, 196–198, 201, 205, 208, 210, 214, 217
Promise, 57, 80, 82–84, 97, 116, 118, 126, 136, 150–152, 184, 209, 214–215
Proof, 8–9, 13, 36, 60, 67–69, 87, 90, 110, 116, 124, 149
Psychology, xi, 1, 3–4, 7, 9–11, 13, 17, 28–29, 31, 33, 35–36, 43, 45, 54, 56–659, 63–64, 67–69, 82, 85, 90, 128, 173, 188–189, 192–193, 196–198, 201, 209, 213

Repetition, 8, 17, 26–27, 33, 81, 88–91, 94–95, 114–116, 118, 120–123, 125, 128, 132, 135, 137–139, 141, 144–148, 150–152, 155, 159, 167, 176, 179, 185–186, 188, 198, 202, 210, 215–216
Representation, 3–4, 20, 22–24, 27, 39–50, 56, 71–74, 77, 79, 82, 84, 87, 99–100, 107–108, 111, 133–137, 139, 141, 151–153, 158, 161–162, 165, 169, 171–172, 174–175, 177–178, 180, 191, 201, 207–208, 216, 218–219
Reproduction, 15, 24, 26–27, 69–71, 82, 88–89, 94, 137, 147, 149–150, 176, 197, 205, 210, 216
Resemblance, 1–2, 12, 43, 58, 81, 85, 94–95, 131, 145, 155, 177, 193, 195–198, 200
Revenant, 80, 82, 84, 109, 123, 134–135, 141–142, 151, 164, 176, 215

Sample, 1, 24, 30, 54, 65–57, 59, 61–62, 112–113, 196–198, 207
Secondness, 28–29, 33, 64, 81, 197–198, 206, 211
Self–portrait, xi, 24, 57, 94, 144–145, 147–149, 200, 224
Shape, ix, 8–11, 17, 19, 23, 26, 31, 34, 36, 54, 58, 64, 67, 91–92, 124, 128, 131, 144, 149, 152, 155, 159, 166–167, 179, 185, 188, 194–196, 198, 200, 205, 215, 220
Similarity, 9, 12–13, 15, 26, 34, 36, 54, 60, 64, 81, 85, 102, 106–107, 110, 116, 124–127, 129, 131, 141, 150, 152, 168, 178, 180, 188–189, 198
Soul, 3, 9–13, 21, 26, 28–31, 33–35, 54–56, 58–59, 63–64, 81, 83, 85, 87, 90, 108, 110, 116, 124, 127, 150–151, 155, 167–168, 173, 179, 188–189, 193–194, 196–197, 200, 202
Specimen, 1–2, 9, 12, 14, 17, 24–26, 38, 60, 62, 67–69, 80, 85, 90–92, 94–95, 124, 131–132, 134–135, 147, 149–150, 152, 155, 159, 166–167, 172, 176, 179, 185, 188, 194, 198, 199–202, 205, 215–216
Specter, 80–82, 86–87, 89–90, 99, 109, 123, 134–135, 142, 151, 176, 179, 215
Speech act, 112, 116–123, 126–128, 133, 187, 193, 198, 214–215
Style, 1, 3, 11–12, 16–17, 24–27, 30–31, 33, 35, 38, 52, 56, 59–60, 63–64, 68, 71, 81–83, 85–87, 92, 95, 107–108, 113, 116, 125, 127–129, 131–133, 138–139, 141–152, 164, 168, 173, 176, 179–180, 182–183, 189, 193–200, 202, 205, 209, 217
Supplement, 3–4, 39, 55, 61, 71–74, 77, 80, 83, 99–103, 106–107, 113, 119–120, 133–136, 139–140, 164, 169–180, 186, 201–202, 213, 215, 219

Thirdness, 28–29, 33, 64, 81, 197–198, 206

Totality, 41, 48, 75, 77, 87, 108, 145, 156, 180

Trace, ix–xi, 8–9, 12–17, 21–22, 24, 27, 29–30, 33–36, 53, 55, 59–64, 67–68, 70–73, 76–77, 81–83, 85–87, 89–90, 93–95, 98–100, 107, 109–116, 124–129, 131–134, 141–142, 144, 146, 149–153, 155–160, 169, 172–173, 176, 179–180, 183, 185–186, 188–189, 193–202, 209–211, 213, 216, 218, 220

Transformation, 11–12, 15, 23, 35, 53, 59, 73, 77, 81, 87, 99, 128, 138, 156, 160, 187, 189, 217

Variation, 26, 32, 36, 59–61, 82, 91, 95, 114–115, 125, 132, 134, 138, 142, 145–146, 148–149, 159, 166, 169, 199, 217

Word, 4, 7, 17–18, 23, 25, 37, 39, 43–44, 48, 55, 74, 76, 85, 102, 119–121, 133, 143–145, 157, 167, 174, 177, 183, 193, 205, 207, 209, 211–212, 214, 216

www.ingramcontent.com/pod-product-compliance
Ingram Content Group UK Ltd.
Pitfield, Milton Keynes, MK11 3LW, UK
UKHW041917140426
5217IPUK00013B/201